Discover *Your*
Authentic Self

About the Author

Psychic since childhood, Sherrie Dillard has been a professional intuitive, medium, medical intuitive, and teacher for over thirty years. Among her international clientele are spiritual leaders, celebrities, and business executives. Sherrie's love of service combined with her intuitive ability have catapulted her intuitive practice around the globe. She has given over 50,000 readings worldwide.

Sherrie has taught intuition and medium development classes at such diverse places as Duke University and Miraval Resort and across the United States, Europe, Costa Rica, and Mexico. Her passion for the fusion of intuition, spirituality, and conscious self-growth has made her a popular speaker and teacher at retreats and conferences. She has been featured on radio and television for her innovative books and her work as a psychic detective, medical intuitive, and medium. Sherrie is the award-winning host of the weekly radio program *Intuit YOUniversity* on transformationtalkradio.com.

With a lifelong devotion and dedication to be of service, Sherrie has worked with diverse populations in unique settings. Along with her work as a professional intuitive, she has helped to house and feed people who are poor and homeless in New York City, San Jose, and San Francisco. She has built simple water systems in Indian villages in the mountains of southern Mexico and Guatemala and created art therapy programs in treatment centers for troubled youth in North Carolina and Georgia.

Sherrie holds a BS in Psychology and a MDiv in New Thought pastoral counseling. Originally from Massachusetts, Sherrie has made Durham, North Carolina, her home for the past eighteen years and can often be found walking along the river with her dogs.

Author photo by Abigail Blosser.

Other Books by Sherrie Dillard

Discover Your Psychic Type
(Llewellyn, 2008)

Love and Intuition
(Llewellyn, 2010)

You Are a Medium
(Llewellyn, 2013)

Develop Your Medical Intuition
(Llewellyn, 2015)

Acknowledgments

I am so grateful to the hardworking and dedicated people at Llewellyn for their wisdom and encouragement. Without their never-ceasing efforts to bring a unique and enlightened voice to the marketplace, this book would have not been possible.

I would especially like to thank editor extraordinaire, Angela Wix, who suggested this topic. Through her support and acceptance, I have been able to find a comfortable and creative space to be me. Thank you, Andrea Neff, for your editing voice of reason and for your support and encouragement. I am very grateful. Thank you to Alisha Bjorklund, for your concise and accurate descriptions, and much gratitude to Kat Sanborn, for tirelessly raising the Llewellyn flag each and every day and promoting these words, visions, and ideas.

I would also like to extend appreciation to my many teachers and guides, both in the physical and the spiritual realms, who have helped me to perceive and accept the gifts and blessings that have come my way on this sometimes rugged but always interesting journey to the authentic self.

Dedication

This book is dedicated to my sister Sandee Washington, who taught me at a young age that it is all right to defy authority and be yourself. Through her example, I also learned that at times it may be necessary to run like hell.

Discover *Your* Authentic Self

Be You, Be Free, Be Happy

SHERRIE DILLARD

Llewellyn Publications
Woodbury, Minnesota

FIRST EDITION
First Printing, 2016

Cover art: iStockphoto.com/43014680/©karandaev
          iStockphoto.com/50074314/©karandaev
Cover design: Ellen Lawson

Llewellyn Publications is a registered trademark of Llewellyn Worldwide Ltd.

Library of Congress Cataloging-in-Publication Data
Names: Dillard, Sherrie, 1958- author.
Title: Discover your authentic self : be you, be free, be happy / by Sherrie Dillard.
Description: First Edition. | Woodbury : Llewellyn Worldwide, Ltd, 2016. |
   Includes bibliographical references.
Identifiers: LCCN 2016002865 (print) | LCCN 2016012246 (ebook) | ISBN
   9780738746401 | ISBN 9780738748696 ()
Subjects: LCSH: Self--Miscellanea. | Self-knowledge, Theory of--Miscellanea.
   | Authenticity (Philosophy)--Miscellanea. | Spiritual life. | Occultism.
Classification: LCC BF697 .D585 2016 (print) | LCC BF697 (ebook) | DDC
   158.1--dc23
LC record available at http://lccn.loc.gov/201600286

Llewellyn Worldwide Ltd. does not participate in, endorse, or have any authority or responsibility concerning private business transactions between our authors and the public.
   All mail addressed to the author is forwarded but the publisher cannot, unless specifically instructed by the author, give out an address or phone number.
   Any Internet references contained in this work are current at publication time, but the publisher cannot guarantee that a specific location will continue to be maintained. Please refer to the publisher's website for links to authors' websites and other sources.

Llewellyn Publications
A Division of Llewellyn Worldwide Ltd.
2143 Wooddale Drive
Woodbury, MN 55125-2989
www.llewellyn.com

Printed in the United States of America

Contents

Chapter 6: Relationships: Mirror of Self   171

Chapter 7: Spirit Mentors, Power Animals, and Guides   203

Chapter 10: Your Archetypal Gifts: Living Your Purpose   **291**

Final Thoughts: You Are the One   **343**

Introduction

YOU ARE WHO YOU ARE LOOKING FOR

The journey to discovering your authentic self promises to be the most rewarding adventure of your life. When you know yourself, you are free. You have a power and presence that radiates from deep within and shines out confidently into the world. You did not come into this life to suffer, to be manipulated and denied. Whatever binds you and keeps you from living your truth is false and can be shed. It takes courage to embrace your authentic self and live life on your own terms. Yet to be uniquely you, to listen within and love yourself for all of your vulnerabilities and missteps, is what your soul longs for.

Not being true to who we are is like living with a tight cord wrapped around our heart. No matter how hard we try to squeeze the love and joy out of life, an inner pressure stifles our attempts. We have all, at one time or another, stuffed away and denied our truth, smiled with complacency, and protectively guarded our dreams and hopes from the criticism and judgment of others. When we continually do this, we live in the world as a stranger, adrift, with no anchor. Yet as detrimental as it can be to deny and hide our truth from others, it is even more dangerous when we hide it from ourselves. Without awareness of our truth, we live without true power and presence. We are empty, and a resounding hollowness that can never be filled echoes through our soul. Yet our truth can never really leave us. Although it unhappily rumbles around within when it is denied, once recognized and acknowledged, it enthusiastically springs forward. Despite attempts from the world and from ourselves to quiet and ignore its existence, our truth is our compass. It is always present, humming away and broadcasting its presence.

My Journey

When my publisher asked me to write this book, I was thrilled and grateful. My previous books have been focused primarily on developing intuition and psychic and medium abilities. Although I have been a professional psychic and medium for many years, my journey to accepting my abilities and expressing them in the world has not always been an easy one. I grew up in an academic and religious family. Psychic phenomena, life after death, and even listening to our intuition were never discussed. Although for the most part I was comfortable with the psychic experiences that occurred spontaneously throughout my early years, I never shared or spoke of them to anyone. This went on until I was in my late teens. I kept what I intuitively saw, felt, and heard a secret. It was only when I experienced an overwhelming surge of psychic episodes that I began to share this part of myself with others.

I kept this part of myself hidden away because I had a fear of being labeled and judged by others. Psychics and mediums seemed to be a bit kooky, easy targets of ridicule, and quite possibly fake charlatans. I both identified with being a psychic and harbored a low opinion of them at the same time. It was not only the opinions of others that I feared, but my own as well. My journey to living authentically was motivated by my inner confusion about who I was and who I wanted to be. I knew that I had to discover a truth within me that went deeper than labeling and judging myself and accommodating what others, primarily my family, expected of me. I couldn't live in secret anymore. My inner truth was breaking down the false walls, and I had to find peace with being me.

Even though experiencing psychic and mediumistic phenomena pushed me to dive deep into myself and discover my truth, we all are called to this journey. Authentic living begins with being able to discern and acknowledge our personal truth, however perplexing or unsettling we may judge it to be. This is the fundamental building block of all our successes. In our relationship and career choices and all of the many decisions we make on a daily basis, it is essential to know who we are. Otherwise we create and experience only discontent and emptiness.

How to Work with This Book

I wrote this book as a way to take your hand and walk with you into the magnificent truth of who you are. You are who you are looking for. Everything you need to learn, know, and experience and all the love, strength, and courage you desire is wrapped up inside of you. We will seek out those times when you have run away from yourself and reclaim the truth that you may have left behind. The layers of false masks and the emotions, beliefs, and perceptions that darken your inner light will be shed. Then, in the shining glow of your truth, the loving, wild, and perfectly imperfect creature that you are will reappear.

The light of your true self illuminates a wide path and is the jumping-off point into deeper mysteries. Within you there are greater truths to encounter. I have attempted to make a cozy spot for you to further investigate and identify your less tangible but still essential truths. We will explore your intuition, your connection to your power spirit animals, your subtle energy body, and the archetypal gifts that you are here to give and share with the world. Your authentic self works in alliance with an awe-inspiring force. Spirit has branded you and left its stamp on your soul. You are spirit and energy, and when you know yourself in this way, you activate your most powerful and authentic self. I hope to inspire you to better connect with this greater part of who you are and allow it to shine forth.

This book is written as a collection of essays covering a wide range of topics. Some essays are meant to inspire and motivate, while others include meditations and exercises. As you read these pages and practice the exercises, adopt the curious perspective of an explorer and adventurer. Although I wrote this book to be a process that will guide you through the many different phases of self-discovery, you do not have to read it cover to cover. Discovering the authentic self can be a crazy, nonlogical business, so jump ahead if you feel moved to do so, or go slow, or read fast. Whatever you want to do is fine. After each essay, there is a one-sentence affirmation that will reinforce and help you to further integrate its message. When you repeat, focus on, and meditate on affirmations, they sink deep into the unconscious and become the thoughts that create your reality. Essay 62 further explores affirmations and how to work with them.

I hope to inspire you to embrace all of who you are and allow your light to shine forth. Not only do you need the authentic you, the world needs you too.

Chapter 1

THE INVITATION

Every moment whispers to you to explore the depth of who you are. I encourage you to accept this timeless invitation. On the journey to knowing your authentic self, you may have expectations and hopes of what you wish to experience and accomplish. Yet I encourage you to let go of your preconceived ideas. Abandon the known self and be curious, vulnerable, open, and accepting of the you that unfolds. This is the highest form of loving self.

1. Within the Mandala

Your life is a mandala, a circle of wholeness, with your authentic self in the center. We tend to view ourselves with tunnel vision. We weigh and judge our decisions and choices, rate our physical attractiveness, and view our thoughts and emotions as concrete and solid evidence of who we are. At any given time, one aspect of our being or one area of our life consumes us in its totality. We define ourselves by the current problem or issue and judge ourselves by our ability to solve or overcome it.

When you perceive your life as a mandala, all of this changes. Everything in your life—the people, the conditions, and your thoughts, emotions, desires, dreams, and soul—is part of the wider expanse of who you are. You are the smile that spreads across your face when you see someone you love. You are also the joy you feel when you look at the sun setting over the ocean and the anger that simmers when you feel as if you have been wronged. Your original and inspirational ideas and the brooding thoughts of grumpiness are a part of you. The beliefs about yourself and life that lie unnoticed in your subconscious mind, creating and attracting challenging situations, are a part of you, as is the intuitive awareness that you are here for a specific purpose. You are the kindness in your heart and the jealousy that you may feel when a loved one turns their attention to another. You are love in all its degrees and varieties. You are the soul that has come to this earth and will one day, once again, become pure spirit and essence. There is no end to you. You are finite and you are infinite. You are powerless and at the same time the source of all true power flows through you. You are life and you are death. Every day you are reborn and every day a bit of you dies. Within your mandala, you are at the center of the universe.

Your authentic self does not have an endpoint. You are an evolving and ever-changing mix of emotions, thoughts, beliefs, soul, and spirit. The work of self-awareness is to know and be true to all of who you are, even the conflicting and opposing aspects. Embrace the totality of your being and all the challenges, conditions, and circumstances that you experience. Your authentic self weaves in and out of the many layers of this mandala. Flow with the changes that come your way and accept all of who you are.

I am whole and complete within the rich mandala of my life.

2. The Call to Know Self

The journey to the authentic self often begins with the nagging, uncomfortable feeling that you are not being true to yourself. Do you ever feel that you are going about the daily motions of living but you are not truly alive? You yearn to feel passion for something, but you are not sure what it is that you long for.

For some, inner discontent haunts their relationships. You may desire to be truly known and loved by another, but you have difficulty expressing yourself and being truly intimate with another. Perhaps you do not feel valued in your career or work. You get a regular paycheck and have security, but you do not derive any purpose or meaning from your job. At one time life may have seemed simpler. The future you envisioned, what you believed would make you happy, now feels distant and unattainable.

Unfortunately, we do not always know how to dig deep into the depth of who we are. Living in our more superficial aspects, we may know our favorite restaurants, television shows, actors, sport teams, or vacation spots. We may love our partners, family members, and lovers and have fun with our friends and be active in our community. Yet until we know the inner truth of who we are, we experience a constant, undefinable inner craving and feeling of emptiness.

Feelings of discontent, frustration, or dissatisfaction may slowly creep in or they may come suddenly, with a piercing jolt. Either way, when these emotions sink deep into our heart and gut, we begin to search for something better—a more loving partner, a more satisfying job, or more interesting and exciting friends. Yet what we are really searching for can only be found within.

Resist the temptation to repress or deny feelings of dissatisfaction. Welcome and listen to them. Divine discontent is a calling card from spirit motivating you to ask deeper questions of yourself and life. Your soul is not here to waste time and go through the motions of living. There is a sacred presence within that is part of the greater mystery of self. Become comfortable with the ever-changing and evolving being that you are. Be brave and be determined to know the true you.

I make the decision to know who I am.

3. The Relief of Being Seen

Every day I work with people who desire connection, help, and guidance from the spirit realm. Some wholeheartedly believe that a psychic-medium such as myself can offer them essential guidance and direction. Others schedule a session with me out of desperation. Having sought advice and help from other sources, they may still be confused or in pain and are willing to try anything. Some are simply curious. A friend or family member may have had a session with me and they are excited, a bit fearful, but adventurous enough to come in for a reading. Whatever the initial reason may be for seeking my services, their experience is rarely what they expected.

The world that I perceive as a psychic is a bit bigger, broader, and more inclusive than the world we live in with our five senses. When the layers of falsities and superficiality are peeled away through intuitive insight, the heart opens in welcome gratitude, relieved to be seen and acknowledged. Even though we live behind our safe masks, according to what is accepted and external, we yearn to be truly known.

When another sees us, we know that we exist. It is a welcome relief when our soul and spirit, our passions and potential, our beauty and boundless self, are reflected back to us. Even our struggles, challenges, and the angst and suffering we feel seem more worthy when another acknowledges them.

The journey to knowing your authentic self offers this kind of relief. Since childhood, most of us have been indoctrinated to seek security and safety. Over time, our adherence to external expectations and compliance with accepted norms blind us to our authentic self. We become superficial and numb and do what is expected. When our inner self cries out in stifled yearning, we seek external gratification in an attempt to quiet our discontent. We turn to things like eating, alcohol, sex, shopping, or improving our social status. All the while, the unsettling sense that there is something more continues to reverberate from the depths of our heart and soul.

If you acknowledge and listen to this inner longing, your path separates from the pack. A restlessness and desire to know, feel, and experience something that cannot be fully grasped calls to you. Once you begin to question who you are and what life is, something alive in your soul and in the soul of the world comes and grabs you by the hand.

Be the fool and the adventurer that seeks your truth. Take hold of the elusive wisp of your soul when it extends itself to you and let yourself loose. There will be challenges, risks, and tests on your way to laying claim to your authentic self, all of which will awaken, strengthen, and enlighten you. Unfurl your glorious banner.

I am ready for the adventure of knowing me.

4. Go Easy

When we begin the journey of self-awareness, we often approach it in the same way that we tackle other areas of our lives. We are so accustomed to pushing ourselves to finish all that we need to get done. We may take the same unrelenting approach to knowing self. We may want to follow a plan, ask the right questions, and achieve clear and understandable results. Yet, to truly know yourself is a nonlogical process. From moment to moment, our moods, opinions, thoughts, and feelings change. As much as we may want to take charge of this journey, it is more important to listen, be patient and nonjudgmental, and allow for surprises.

To better connect with your own pure essence, you may need to shift gears, slow down, and take your time. If you find yourself constantly busy, rushing and trying to get everything done, give yourself permission to take a break. You do not need to be a perfectionist on this journey of self-discovery. There are no standards that you need to live up to. Do what feels right to you. Let your preferences, inclinations, and feelings guide you. Think for yourself and notice when you unconsciously go along with what others expect or want from you.

For instance, if your parents kept their home in a pristine state, it does not mean that you need to. If your neighbors buy a hot tub or keep their lawn green and well mowed and win the yard of the year award, it does not mean that you have to compete. Discover what feels right for you—what gives you a sense of satisfaction and peace. Aim to live your life in a way that supports your inner serenity.

The world is not going to give you permission to get off the merry-go-round of constant busyness and activity. You need to do this for yourself. Your authentic self will not be found on a to-do list. Knowing the rich inner depth of who you are requires an attentive but gentle awareness. When you listen within and follow your inner direction, it may sometimes feel as if you are walking in circles. Compared to the strategy of getting as much accomplished as possible, knowing self may seem to move you backward and away from your goal. It does not always feel productive.

Redefine what it means to get *a lot* done. You will discover that there is magic and a sense of wholeness in this process.

I slow down and take it easy.

5. Begin the Journey with Intent

The juncture between you and the divine is your most powerful spot in the universe. This meeting place is your authentic self. When you are flowing in this current, you are unstoppable. Even in the midst of problems, challenges, and uncertainty, your strength and stability come from the powerful presence within. Yet for all of its positive benefits, embracing your authentic truth often takes courage and devotion. Although the payoffs are high, we all experience some inner resistance when we seek to change. There will be times when you will want to turn away and instead live in the haze of comfortable inertia.

To keep yourself motivated on the long and sometimes arduous journey to discovering your true self, state an intent. An intent is a concise, positive statement of what you want to create and experience. It focuses your energy toward a specific goal. It is a proclamation to yourself and the universe of what you want to devote your time, attention, and energy to.

Create an intention that will support the aspects of your true self that you would most like to experience. This can be a simple statement, such as *I allow my truth and goodness to emerge. I am living my truth.* Or *I experience, manifest, and express my truth.* Make your intention worthy of the most loving and wise part of you.

Write down your intent and continually repeat it to yourself. The more attention you give it, the sooner you will experience it manifesting in your life. Take action on your intent whenever possible. In this way, you align yourself with the universal flow of vital life force energy. Be aware of any doubt, fear, or frustration that surfaces, and reaffirm your intent through writing and speaking it and through positive thought and action.

I create a positive intent.

6. Accept It All

It is not always easy to know what is true and right for us and what is not. Those things, attitudes, beliefs, and opportunities that will ultimately not bring us joy or speak to our soul can at times be difficult to spot. These false temptations do not always come marching up to us and look us in the eye. They are much too clever and insidious. Instead, the false often hides behind feelings of desire, excitement, and hopes of fulfillment and comes our way in a lovely package all neatly tied up with a big bow. Yet, despite our past disappointments, we all too often fall into the same trap and allow ourselves to be led by appearances and false hopes.

Sometimes we blame ourselves and our inadequacies when what comes our way does not bring us the happiness that we thought it would. Sometimes we blame others or life. Yet we have to know the false and what does not work for us in order to recognize the real and true.

The journey to knowing and embracing your true and authentic self begins by recognizing what feels right for you and what does not. Accept all that you experience as valuable information. Resist the inclination to become a victim and take on feelings of low self-esteem and shame when you encounter challenges and disappointments. Allow your experiences to be a guide that can lead you to better know who you are. Be present to the moment. Don't turn away; listen to and learn from all that comes your way.

I learn from all that I experience.

7. The World Needs Your Genius

Since the beginning of time, self-sacrifice has been ingrained within our consciousness. Like herd animals, we have huddled together throughout the centuries to keep safe, claim our territory, and ensure our longevity. Conforming and adhering to what was best for the group, the leaders, and those with power was expected and enforced. Suppressing our individuality and being overly compliant is an ingrained pattern that can be traced back through history. Sometimes it can feel as if we do not have a choice. We unconsciously give away our pure authenticity without knowing it.

In varying degrees, we have all experienced an inner resentment when we feel we cannot be who we are meant to be. We work at jobs that we do not necessarily like or enjoy. We stay in unsatisfying relationships that do not speak to our heartfelt needs. Meanwhile, debt piles up to pay for the home, cars, clothing, and other gadgets that we hope will help us feel accepted and good about ourselves. The resentment builds and our truth sinks deeper and deeper into a silent inner prison.

Conformity and compromising your authentic self is a dead end. The world no longer needs complacency and the safe and predictable. It needs your ideas and your genius. We have lost our individuality and uniqueness, and we suffer, individually and culturally. Nothing in this world will be solved through conformity. In the all-important and crucial areas of medicine, the environment, our energy needs, world hunger, politics, poverty, war, and conflict, we need new ideas, inventions, risk takers, out-of-the-box thinkers, and those who are willing to tell the truth.

Be the most that you can be. Find what makes you unique and shout it out to the world. Every day there is the opportunity to approach the traditional and accepted with curiosity and clear vision.

Begin with yourself. Challenge your thoughts and your patterned way of relating to life. See the original within yourself and in others and express it in everything you do. You are your security. There is no outside corporation, government, or cultural support that is more reliable than you. Keep one hand in the heavens, always feeling around for the pure and magical. Plant your feet firmly on the earth and do what you came here to do.

I value my uniqueness.

8. The Beginning

Every day we are offered renewal and a new start. The dawn heralds a reawakening for all of life to begin anew. The first faint bird song and rustle in the leaves of the morning breeze invites you to begin again.

There is no better time than right now to let go of the past. You are not what you have experienced. You are not what you have said, thought, felt, heard, or done. Within the truth of who you are, there is constant renewal and purity.

Breathe and let go. Close your eyes and greet the sunrise of your soul. Let it awaken within you an awareness of the new journey awaiting you. Breathe and let go and imagine a beautiful place in nature. It may be in the mountains, near the sea, or in a lush valley. Smell the fragrant breeze and feel the touch of sunlight or dew on your face. This is your place of safety, love, and comfort. This is where you can go, at any time, to begin again. The slate is clean. Breathe and let go of anything that you no longer need. Let go of the worries and concerns that keep you in a hyper state of anxiety. Breathe and let go. Forgive yourself and forgive all others for any conscious or inadvertent acts, words, and thoughts that did not honor who you really are.

Breathe and settle into your safe place. Imagine a clean and pure stream, river, or fountain in this special spot where you can relax and rest. Feel the energy of this place within. Breathe in the invigorating energy of love. Open your heart and let go of any sadness or pain that may still linger. Release any negativity and past hurts into the water's flow, where they will be transformed into positive energy.

Breathe, relax, and hear the true you calling. Make the intent to be the person that you know you are. In your mind's eye, see yourself living authentically and joyously.

I breathe, let go, and begin anew.

Chapter 2

Reclaiming
What Was Lost

Sometimes, to go forward we have to look back. This chapter empowers you to discover characteristics and aspects of your true self that may have been discarded and left behind. Before we are able to fully appreciate our unique gifts and sensitivities and embrace our potential, we may unknowingly discard and suppress our innate true self. Yet it is never too late. Your truth is always within, waiting to be rediscovered.

9. You Came from the Stars

You have come here from the stars and the light with a to-do list taped to your soul. Previous to coming to planet Earth, you may have been enjoying yourself on the love planet Venus, sharpening your mind energy on Mercury, or absorbing the wisdom of the masters. Your memory of where you were before you came here has faded. Your awareness of your innate soul knowledge and power has also likely dimmed.

All that we need to learn and know to make it in this world takes priority over the faint memories of the sublime and spiritual. Yet in moments of illumination, we sometimes remember. Something within stirs with familiarity. There is a peace and sense of connectedness that moves us into an intangible but very real knowing of who we are. A thought, a whisper, or a sensation lures us back into a state of awareness.

Early one morning several years ago, I took a car ferry from an island to the coast. It was empty except for myself and one or two other people. It was a misty morning, and as I watched the sun rise, I could feel the joy of my spirit spreading throughout my entire being. In this moment of transcendent awareness, the ferry stopped to pick up more passengers. Within a few minutes, it was full of cars and people talking, smoking, eating, and crowding in all around me. Although I could still feel the essence of my spirit, its unfettered emergence retreated with the busy commuter traffic.

When we are young, we are all on the crowded ferry together. We take on the characteristics, behaviors, and beliefs of those around us and of the world and we cannot simply get off the boat. Remembering the warm center of self becomes more difficult. Yet the soul never forgets. Stirring within is a rich soul elixir that can transform whoever and whatever you believe yourself to be. The authentic you is a timeless being. Give yourself the space and time you need to remember, to retrace your steps and lift off the layers of what you were taught and told. Reconnect with your truth.

I review what I have learned from my past.

10. Re-parent Yourself

Your authentic self is held precious and safe within your soul. The circumstances and conditions of your childhood are a determining factor in how the true essence of who you are emerges in the world. Although your personality, beliefs, and judgments were shaped and formed in large part by your early childhood experiences, within you there is an individualized spirit that is uniquely you. If you were loved and encouraged to be yourself as a child, the true you was reinforced and likely naturally surfaced. If your childhood lacked unconditional love or if you were molded into someone who is not the true you, you may still struggle with understanding and accepting your authentic self. Yet it is never too late to heal, encourage, and support the true you.

Do you feel as if you had a happy childhood? Are there things about it that you would change? Maybe you grew up in a home that was fraught with tension and stress or you had a parent or sibling who struggled with an addiction. Perhaps your parents went through an ugly divorce and you were caught in the middle. Economic problems, job loss, illness, or a home life that was unstable and unpredictable are a few of the conditions that some young children have to confront. For others who may have had a more conventional two-parent family, economic stability, and what looked like an idyllic life, there may have been difficult issues that were less obvious. Emotionally distant parents and the pressure to perform and live up to high standards of perfection create their own stress and anxiety.

While you cannot go back in time and relive your childhood, you can heal and create a different and more nurturing present. Pick one area that you would like to focus on. For instance, maybe you did not receive the kind of love and support you needed or you had a home life that was chaotic and unpredictable. Decide what you need in present time and make a commitment to give this to yourself. Perhaps you want to feel loved and supported. Begin by making a commitment to love and care for yourself. Practice loving and supportive self-talk. Notice when you are critical or judgmental of yourself and cancel these thoughts with positive, supportive statements. Choose loving and supportive friends who encourage and understand you. Express love to others and be kind and forgiving. Allow yourself to receive love and kindness from others. Imagine the innocent and vulnerable child within you. Send him or her love and support.

I give to myself what I wish to receive.

11. Recapture Your Innocence

The authentic you is not static and rigid. It flows with imaginative and creative energy. As the journey to discovering the true you unfolds, you will constantly change and evolve. What you perceive as true for you today may not be true tomorrow. The more you know and express your truth, the more your perception changes. As your self-awareness increases, so does your ability to perceive life fresh and new. There is an innocence within you that can see clearly, without bias and judgment. When you perceive life in this way, it comes alive with possibilities.

In the presence of my three-year-old granddaughter, life is magic. This charming quality was clearly evident when we walked by an old playground near her home one afternoon. The small park had seen better days and had only two outdated pieces of equipment. One was a slide and the other was a set of long metal monkey bars. As we stood in the playground's weed-infested lot, we each saw something quite different. While I stared at the dilapidated state of the slide, my granddaughter ran off laughing and climbed to the top of it. I joined her, and before you knew it, the slide became a train, with my granddaughter the conductor. As she shouted orders and maneuvered around all kinds of obstacles, I held on tight and marveled at her imaginative skill.

My granddaughter did not know or care that this was an old, abandoned park that had not seen any children in a long time. Through her clear vision of possibilities, she transformed it into exactly what she wanted it to be.

There was a time when we saw everything through the eyes of wonder. As we grew older, we unconsciously absorbed and accepted judgments and limitations as reality. Imagine what would happen if we as adults could perceive potential and possibilities in all that we see and experience. The old slide in the playground was not a magical train, but its essence and my granddaughter's experience of it was. Our lives are lived through what we perceive. This then becomes what we experience. Recapture your childlike innocence and your world will transform.

I see the world through innocent eyes.

12. You Chose Your Family

The family environment that you were born into was perfect for you. Before you made the journey from the light into this life, your soul was aware of the important lessons, purpose, and gifts that you came here to share and experience. You picked your parents, your environment, and the challenges that you are experiencing.

If you are anything like me, you may wonder why you picked such a challenging childhood. More than once I have questioned the idea that I had full knowledge and agreed to the circumstances of my early life. Yet I am also aware that despite conditions not always being to my liking, my childhood motivated me to develop compassion, inner strength, and independence. It also activated an early awareness of the spirit realm and my connection to it. My family was not a haven of acceptance and love in the way that I would have liked it to be, yet it did provide me with the drive and desire to become aware of and tune into a deeper source of wisdom and love.

Your family has contributed to your growth and evolution in ways that you may not fully realize. If you were not loved and cared for in the way that you needed to be, or if your true self was suppressed and denied expression as a child, know that something in you was and is strong enough to overcome this. Although you were not able to change or control the circumstances of your early life, you are not a victim. Be angry, disappointed, and upset and feel whatever feelings you may still harbor about your early family environment. Then let go of them, forgive yourself and others, and heal.

Your past challenges and difficulties have refined and purified your soul. When you accept and forgive your past, you discover the gifts inherent within the struggles. Whatever you have been through, whatever love and care has been denied, open the door to your heart, mind, body, and soul and know that you can receive it right now.

I recognize the gifts that my early family environment has given to me.

13. Finding Your Tribe

We all want to belong. It is a biological, emotional, and spiritual need. In primitive times, survival was dependent on being a part of a group. To reproduce and ensure that we were safe from predators and had food and shelter, community was essential. As our basic needs were met, the feeling of being part of something bigger than one individual provided group members with emotional, mental, physical, and spiritual support and connection. Adherence to the group's norms, beliefs, and customs created harmony and reinforced expectations and continued functioning. The belief that a god, goddesses, and deities watched over, protected, and cared for the human realm reinforced group solidarity.

We instinctually want and need to be part of a tribe. We seek our identity and fulfill our desire for community by bonding with others. Connecting with others of like mind and heart is healthy. However, it is important to bond with others through your most loving and positive aspects. When we form close ties with others through negative and fear-based commonalities, this only reinforces and exaggerates these qualities within ourselves. It is tempting to align with others through our prejudices, judgments, superficial likes and dislikes, fears, wounds, and other constrictive similarities and sentiments. Yet you will find that a minor dislike can become a prison of hate and limitations when it is reinforced by group consciousness.

Seek others who uplift, inspire, and motivate you to be the best you can be. When you desire to be part of a group of friends or co-workers, a political party, a spiritual or religious community, or any other type of gathering, ask yourself if your authentic self will be supported. Will you feel as if you can be who you are, or will you have to take on beliefs and opinions that do not feel right for you? Feeling accepted for who you are, feeling heartfelt warmth, and finding support for personal growth and continued learning are trust-worthy signs that a group may be a good fit. It can be a leap of faith to open up and share who you are with others. Be careful to be with those who reinforce your highest aspirations and support your efforts to be your most honest and true self.

We all need a tribe who can see our truth and support it.

I pay attention to how I feel when I am in the company of others.

14. Being Nice

It is not always easy to be yourself. It can be especially difficult if you were brought up to be nice and please others. When we want another to like and respect us, it is tempting to align with their likes, opinions, and expectations. Even though you may want to share your opinions and feelings with another, you may hold back and stifle your truth if you feel it is counter to what they think or feel. You may have been brought up to believe that disagreement or a difference in opinion my cause waves or problems. Sometimes it may feel as if you have to make a choice between being true to yourself or failing to live up to what and who another expects you to be. While appreciating another's perspective and point of view is a positive way to get to know the person and become closer, be careful not to stuff away your authentic thoughts and feelings. All too often in our desire to be nice, we compromise and silence our truth.

When we are young, we are taught the value of playing nice, sharing our toys, and not being demanding and mean to others. As we get older, we continue to be taught in overt and subtle ways to silence our emotions and wait our turn. While these lessons can be valuable and help us to respect others and refine our ego, they can also give us the unconscious message that the raw truth of who we are cannot be trusted. One false move in saying something that another does not agree with or sharing a feeling that may be too intense could doom us to a life of loneliness.

The tendency to hide our true self is made easier when we know what another wants and expects. A friend, family member, coworker, or acquaintance may be blatant or subtle in expressing their desires and expectations, and it can be tempting to simply submit. Being able to make another happy, keep the peace, or sympathize and support another's beliefs and opinions seems innocent enough. Yet attempting to influence and connect to another with behavior, emotions, or beliefs that are not genuine only creates a false connection.

Being nice can be a trap that eventually leads to a loss of self. If you expect others to always be nice or if someone expects this from you, real intimacy and deep sharing may be compromised. There is a difference between being nice and being kind. When you are kind, you can speak with truth and compassion. Being nice often means smiling when you do not agree or like something. Be kind and give your true self to others.

If you are finding it difficult to be yourself when confronted with another's expectations, take small steps. Sometimes it is enough to simply say nothing. You can be quiet and detach from the pressure to join in and act in ways that do not feel authentic. You can be polite and kind and still be you. Being yourself does not mean that you have to be outspoken and confrontative. If you do not feel comfortable speaking your truth, breathe deeply and know that this will not always be the case. Take some time away from those who pressure you to align with their vision of who they want you to be. Recognize your true thoughts, feelings, and beliefs. Focus on what you need to do to take care of yourself. Be kind to you.

I practice kindness in my relationships.

15. Alone in the Playground

The pressure to conform, be part of a group, and choose sides is felt at an early age. On the journey to developing autonomy and a sense of who we are, we are often challenged by more dominant and assertive personalities. One of my first lessons in peer pressure occurred in the playground of my elementary school when I was in third grade. My school had a large outdoor area where all of the students went after lunch. Like many other seemingly innocent playgrounds, mine was a hotbed for budding alphas to test their ability to exert control over the more timid and vulnerable.

One of the most popular games among my classmates was the girl chase. I don't remember being given a choice to play or not play. It was what we did. Participation was mandatory. Through some unknown criteria, the girls separated into different groups. The alpha girl leader of the group would run and the other girls would follow her like a swarm of birds. One group would then chase the other groups. I can't recall what we did once we caught them or when we were caught, but it had a sinister and almost desperate feel to it. I was frankly scared of the whole breathless running and chasing of one another, but I felt too intimidated not to continue the charade. I didn't want to be on my own, alone in the big playground. Reluctantly, I ran with the rest of the girls, screaming and chasing others as if my life depended on it. Even at that young age, I felt foolish. But I kept it up.

That was not the only time I went along with what others were doing. When I got older, I drank beer at parties and I kissed boys and had sexual experiences, mostly out of curiosity and because others were doing it. Somewhere in me I knew I could say no, but I did not have the confidence and self-awareness yet to go against the norm.

It wasn't until I was in college that I began to make choices based on what I wanted to do and what felt right to me. I discovered that listening within and acting on what was true for me offered me an exhilarating freedom that I didn't want to give up. I finally found my "no" voice, and I used it as often as I wanted to. I would like to say that I am completely free now of compromise and conformity, and for the most part I am. But I also recognize that this is a lifelong process. Sometimes I still find myself going along with another's plan or not taking care of myself in order to fulfill another's desire or expectation. I still can fall into the trap of feeling that my choice is to go along with another's program or to be alone in the big playground of life. Fortunately, I come to my senses a bit more quickly now and kindly opt out, knowing that individuality does not mean loneliness.

Give yourself this gift. Choose what you want to do and with whom you want to do it. Inner happiness and peace are the result.

I choose what I want to participate in.

16. Let Go of the False

From a young age, you have been led to believe many things about yourself and the world that are not necessarily true. You most likely have been labeled, characterized, categorized and given attributes, interests, talents, and abilities that are not in alignment with who you are and what you have come into this life to experience. Some of what you assumed to be right and true for you has come from the opinions and feedback of well-meaning family and friends. Some of your perceptions and beliefs have come from observing others in the world and accepting traditional norms. Over time, these falsities become your reality.

For instance, from a young age, it was assumed that Jed, a client of mine, would go to college, grad school, and maybe medical or law school. Even though he felt an undeniable passion for music and writing, Jed felt that at best this would only be a pastime and hobby. He, too, felt that college and grad school were his only real option. While in college and then grad school, he did his best to deny and dismiss his musical interests, as they did not "fit in" with his self-perception. Still, he felt most alive when playing and writing music. Upon graduating from law school, Jed was fortunate to be hired by a busy law firm. It was at this time that he put music completely aside to focus on his career, yet his love for writing, playing, and performing music never subsided. A few years into his career as an attorney, he started to struggle with depression and anxiety. It took a few more years of soul-searching and help from a therapist for Jed to accept what he had always known. Music had to be a part of his life. He eventually left the law firm to focus on a career as a musician. Although it was not as lucrative as law, Jed has never regretted his decision.

On the journey to knowing self, it is necessary to first accept all of who you are, even those characteristics and attributes that don't seem to make sense or fit in with the life you envision for yourself. Be honest about your likes and dislikes, your feelings, emotions, thoughts, and beliefs. Practice full acceptance and embrace all of who you are. Be honest and listen to your feelings and beliefs as well as your dreams, passions, and longings. As you do this, you make way for new insights and awareness. Take all of who you are and evaluate what feels right for you. What is true and what is not true for you will become clear. You will begin to naturally shed the illusions of what and who you imagined yourself to be and allow your truth to shine through.

It can feel vulnerable and scary to become aware of and question whether you are involved in and doing what is right and true for you. Yet when you know and live from the truest part of yourself, you experience an inner synergy that expands into every area of your life. A constant supply of inspiration, passion, positive energy, love, and wisdom flows through you from the depths of your being.

I accept all of who I am.

17. The Price of Popularity

From a young age, we are pressured to conform and fit in with the accepted norms. Instead of encouraging self-acceptance, some parents knowingly and unknowingly teach the opposite. Out of concern that their children may be teased or bullied for being different, some parents teach their children to be like the other kids, fit in, and sacrifice their individuality. Starting from a young age, well-meaning parents may buy their children the most popular toys, games, clothing, sneakers, and various accessories in the hope that this will help their child to be liked. Many inadvertently motivate their children to ignore what they desire in favor of what they believe will help them to be like the other kids. Although they have the best of intentions, there is a potentially soul-robbing message in guiding a child to adopt outer norms in favor of discovering what feels right and best for him or her.

If being like others and fitting in is emphasized from an early age, the authentic inner voice is ignored and suppressed. As we grow older, if we continue on the path of looking outside of ourselves for reassurance and security, we may miss out on the important process of inner self-growth and development. The authentic self is a wise, innate compass that keeps us in touch with our true talents, desires, and needs. When we lose connection with this inner self, we search for who we are in the world and in others.

As adults, children who have denied their ability to trust and listen to their inner self are set adrift in a confusing world, not knowing their purpose and reason for being. We may try new things, buy the latest gadgets and comfort items, or go to the most popular places in a misguided attempt to feel a connection and find ourselves. Or we may play it safe, fear change of any kind, and judge and criticize those who are different.

To some degree, we have all repressed and ignored our inner impulses in order to fit in and please others. The way back to self takes concentrated effort. Think of something you wanted to try or experience as a child but never did. Actively explore, learn, and participate in this hobby, interest, or desire. Even if it seems to be a childish activity, find some way to rekindle an old curiosity or passion. Indulge yourself a bit. You likely have been denied too long.

I actively pursue an old interest.

18. Soulful Memories

There are times in our childhood when we get a transcendent peek into our true nature. We touch and feel something within us that is deep and true. Although we can rarely understand and put into words what we are experiencing, we want to hold on to that inner spark and absorb whatever magic it holds. Do you have a soul-glimpsing memory from long ago tucked away within you that still whispers to you?

When I was young, my family rented a cottage on a lake for a few weeks in the summer. Although I do not have many memories of this particular place, the few that I have stand out in their vividness. One still has a visceral effect on me.

The lake was in a mountainous area of winding and narrow dirt roads. Driving through the forest, you could barely see through the heavy trees and foliage. There was a spot at the top of a peak where, looking into the distance, you could see the lake. The translucent blue sunlit water shone and sparkled through the trees like soft, fluid clouds. I remember sitting in the back seat of our station wagon feeling hypnotized by the green and blue shimmering forest and distant lake. One sunny morning on the way to the lake, I experienced a moment of lucid awareness. The light of the sparkling blue sunlit water, the forest greenery, and the golden rays of the sun all wove together through the dark woods in mystical harmony. My body tingled and a calming, surreal, and almost magnetic sensation moved through me. This simple scene affected me to the depths of my being. It was an invitation into a magical world that spoke to me in a compelling and mystifying language. I felt I could dissolve into it.

Try to remember what moved you when you were young. What bypassed your thinking and touched your heart and a deeper part of you? In moments of heightened awareness, the world and the true authentic you cross paths. Something in you lights up and awakens.

Over time as we get older, this inner connection gets quieted and dulled. Yet the authentic you still rises in recognition when you encounter something in the world that touches your heart and soul. Pay attention to these kinds of impulses and sensations, however slight they may be. As you listen and feel for them, they will grow stronger and inspire your heart to leap with joy and wonder.

I listen and feel with pure innocence.

19. Conforming: The Early Years

When we are young, our parents are like gods. They are the final and infallible judges of who we are and what we need. Like little sponges, we absorb their thoughts and feelings and their beliefs and biases. These thoughts and feelings sink deep into our unconscious and become the norm. As we get older, we begin to form our own preferences and likes and dislikes separate from our family. Quite often, this more authentic self conflicts with our early childhood conditioning, especially in our early teen years, when our individuality may surface in confusing and tumultuous ways. For many of us, it is when our true self begins to emerge that the stress of being different surfaces.

In overt and subtle ways, we are taught that love equals loyalty and devotion. To love our family, our country, and God means to submit to and adopt values, norms, opinions, and beliefs that may not necessarily ring true to our inner sense of self. Conformity provides the illusion of safety and protection from life's inevitable problems and unexpected surprises. For many, the price of individuality comes with feelings of isolation and separation from those we love. The choice of being oneself or being alienated from family members is too difficult for some to bear. To fit in, those interests, talents, beliefs, opinions, and desires that go against the grain of the family system are further denied or repressed.

If you have experienced or are currently experiencing what feels like a choice between being yourself and being accepted by family members or close friends, choose yourself. You will never regret this empowering step into who you are. Love is freedom, individuality, and acceptance of our truth.

Most likely, the family members and friends who require your conformity and adherence to their values and choices were once in a similar situation. Their parents and their parents before them likely demanded the same. As you claim your freedom, you allow others to make a radical departure from a restricting form of love. Your courage inspires and motivates family, friends, and those who are fearful of who and what is different to choose another way.

Be the one who is strong enough to go it alone. There is an invisible ray of magnetism that will draw to you those who share your passion and strength.

I am strong enough to be me.

20. Young Extroverts and Introverts

There is considerable psychological evidence suggesting that we are born with specific preferences in relating to others and the world. These predetermined inclinations are a cornerstone of our authentic self. As much as we or others would like to change these preferences, we are hard-wired with specific tendencies. One of the most significant contributions that famed psychologist Carl Jung made was his insight into and understanding of these innate preferences.

Extroversion and introversion describe the way that individuals relate to the world and receive energy. Extroverts are energized by people and the outer world. They tend to be gregarious, action-oriented, and enthusiastic. Introverts are energized through solitude and reflection. They often find excessive outer stimulation exhausting. Neither preference is better or worse than the other. While most people lie somewhere along the continuum of extroversion or introversion, not being in sync with our family's predominant preference can cause misunderstandings and feelings of shame.

The Extroverted Child

While parents and their children often share common traits and characteristics, there may be inherent differences that can be challenging. No amount of positive or negative feedback and coercion can change a child's inner wiring. A child that is highly extroverted needs active social time with friends, can become bored when alone, can be talkative, and may want a lot of interaction with their parents. If a parent is equally extroverted, there is likely to be harmony and mutual understanding. However, if the parent is an introvert, they can quickly become exhausted and overwhelmed with a high-energy, socially interactive child.

When an extroverted child is not appreciated for their outgoing nature and their need for external stimulation is not met, a parent can give the child the unintended message that there is something inherently wrong with them. An extroverted child who is constantly told to settle down, go to their room, and be quiet and is pushed to play alone can become tired, depressed, and lonely.

If you were an outgoing, active, and enthusiastic extroverted child who grew up in an environment that did not support your natural way of relating to the world, you may still feel that you can be overwhelming and simply too much for others. Recognize that your introverted parent, teacher, grandparent, or whoever it was that gave you this message did the best they could do. They likely felt overwhelmed and inadequate in meeting your needs.

Find others who share your outgoing nature and live it up. Participate in activities that promote interaction, activity, stimulation, and the opportunity to meet new people. Know that your charming extroverted self is a wonderful gift.

The Introverted Child

Although being an extroverted child can have its challenges, an introverted child is more likely to be misunderstood. Extroverts make up roughly 75 percent of the population and introverts a mere 25 percent. To be outgoing, interactive, and social is the expected cultural norm, especially for children. While adults may be able to have alone time, avoid overstimulation, and enjoy introspection and reflection, children with these same qualities are often viewed as a bit odd, shy, or moody. Unless a child has a parent who either is an introvert themselves or understands introversion, life can be particularly difficult.

I grew up with extroverted parents and three extroverted siblings. As an introvert, I was often overstimulated and exhausted by the constant noise and level of activity in my home. I would often escape alone to the basement to just sit and quietly play. Even then, my mother, an off-the-chart extrovert, would send my sister or one of my brothers or a neighbor child to play with me. As I got older, my mother did her best to encourage me to invite more friends home, join groups, and generally be more like my other siblings. Although I had friends and was active in sports and other activities, I needed alone time and this was a cause of concern for her. I grew up believing that I should be more outgoing and social. Although I did my best to curb my introversion and be more like the rest of my family, I only became cranky and tired. As much as I tried to join in, all the activity and constant noise overwhelmed me. It wasn't until I took a psychology class in college that I came across the theory of extroversion and introversion and began to better understand myself and others. Reading over the research and findings, I felt that I had found the Holy Grail. My perception of myself began to change. I was able to shed some of the judgment and shame that I had acquired over the years. As I better understood my own introverted nature, my self-esteem and confidence improved.

Schools and after-school and weekend activities keep children constantly busy and active. Introverted children are naturally reserved and need time alone to recharge their batteries, yet they are often expected to be as interactive as extroverts. They can feel the differences between themselves and others and know they are not like other kids. Pushing themselves to be more outgoing and social can feel awkward and stressful. This can create a feeling of angst and even shame. Introverted children can be as bright, cheerful, and friendly as extroverted children, but they need time alone to daydream, ponder, and reflect.

If you were a misunderstood introverted child, you may still be uncomfortable with your need and desire for solitude and time away from activity and interaction. There is nothing wrong with you. It is essential that you trust and listen to your needs. Your authentic self will emerge and blossom in the quiet and solitude. You will be healthier, happier, and a better, friend, parent, coworker, and partner when you listen to and give yourself the quiet and alone time that you need.

I accept and honor both my need for alone time
and my need for interaction with others.

21. Little Thinkers and Feelers

In addition to extroversion and introversion, Carl Jung theorized that we come into the world with a predetermined preference for decision making. This is the thinking and feeling continuum.

Feeling Children

A child with a predominant feeling function tends to be sensitive, empathic, and naturally emotionally intelligent and attuned to the emotional climate of their home. If there is an extreme amount of stress, anxiety, tension, or worry in the home, the child will feel it but not necessarily understand it. Because children have not yet developed psychological maturity, they are egocentric. They believe that everything that happens and everything they feel has a direct link to them. They mistakenly assume that they are the source and cause of all that they feel and experience. Not able to comprehend and put a name to the emotions and feelings that they absorb, they often act out and react to the emotional climate of their environment. Easily overwhelmed by the emotions and feelings that they unknowingly absorb, emotionally sensitive children can get labeled as difficult, rebellious, anxious, or unruly. They may have nightmares, crying fits, an upset stomach, or headaches. Children who respond to the world through the feeling preference are often vulnerable and easily hurt.

If your feeling nature was understood and nurtured as a child, you are likely empathetic, emotionally intelligent, and caring. You may be a source of love and comfort for your friends and family and the one whom others go to when they need help, nurturing, and understanding. If you did not have the benefit of an emotionally loving and nurturing environment as a child, you may feel that your emotional sensitivity is more of a curse than a blessing. You may need to be especially kind and compassionate toward yourself and heal old emotional wounds. You can begin the process by making the intent to open your heart and feel and release any emotional pain and judgments about your emotional sensitivity.

It is never too late to experience the gift of your emotional and sensitive nature. Your emotions empower you to tune into a higher form of love and healing. Your authentic self is naturally attuned to and can absorb the lofty vibrations of healing love energy. You will find that when you stay connected to your inner self, you are strengthened and comforted by a higher form of love.

Thinking Children

On the opposite end of the continuum is the thinking preference. Children with a dominant thinking function in some ways have an easier time being understood and making sense of the world, yet they can also experience some unique challenges. Thinking children want to understand and make sense of everything. They are inquisitive, curious, and often intelligent and natural problem solvers. They can also be blunt and honest about what they perceive, often to the shock and embarrassment of their parents.

For instance, a friend of mine, Janet, told me a classic story of an encounter she had with a thinking child. While waiting for the dance class of her four-year-old granddaughter, Beth, to end, she was approached by another four-year-old. This little girl looked up at Janet and asked her who she was.

"I am Beth's grandmother," Janet said.

With a quizzical look on her face, the little girl stared at her for an uncomfortable few minutes. Finally she walked back to her mother, who was a few feet away. She pointed to Janet and asked her mother, "Why does *my* grandmother have lines on her face?" Then she added, "My grandmother looks old."

For children with a strong thinking preference, there is usually no judgment involved in their observations. They simply want to know why things are the way they are and seek to understand.

Thinking children can be shamed and punished for their perceptions and their honesty in sharing them. Instead of teaching children how to communicate effectively in ways that will empower them to understand other people's feelings and not alienate them from others, children often get the message to be quiet and keep their thoughts to themselves. Unfortunately, in a child's egocentric mind, this message can get further translated as *my thoughts are bad and I cannot express them*. They may even hear a more dangerous judgment, such as *I am bad*. Over time, if this message is reinforced, it gets buried deep within the mind and becomes their truth.

If you were given the message not to express your thoughts as a child, you may have an unconscious resistance to sharing your true thoughts with others as an adult. You may fear that you will be rejected or misunderstood. Often we are not aware of why we withhold our true self with those we care about. Explore your thoughts, and do not judge or criticize what you think. Once you are aware of what you are thinking, you can choose if and how to express it.

I accept both my thinking and my feeling preferences.

22. Sensing and Intuition

Let your senses come alive. Close your eyes for a moment and listen. What do you hear? Open your eyes and look all around you. Notice the colors and patterns in your environment or go outside and look up at the sky. Take it all in. Breathe in. What do you smell? Hold something smooth, then something with texture. How does this feel? Taste your food. What spices and herbs pop out at you? You are a part of the rich tapestry of life.

Young Sensors

Our innate preference for gathering information lies somewhere along the sensing and intuiting continuum. Those with a high sensing function perceive the world through their five senses. What they can see, touch, taste, hear, and smell is real. Sensing children are very much at home in the practical and material world. They tend to do well with routine, focus on detail, and are comfortable in predictable situations and experiences. As they grow older, they often continue in this uncomplicated and matter-of-fact way. They may excel at athletics and academics and be comfortable in social situations.

As they mature, those with a strong sensing function may experience a nagging feeling that something is missing. Because they are not always comfortable using their imagination and intuition, possibilities and potential may elude them. Although sensors tend to do well in the here and now, they have less of an aptitude for the nonphysical realm of essence.

The authentic self lives in both the physical and the nonphysical realms. Sensors may have a strong and positive appreciation of themselves as physical beings in a material world, yet the authentic self can also be elusive, ever changing, evolving, and difficult to grasp. If you approach and understand the world through your senses, take some time to explore your inner self. You may not know what you are looking for and you may wonder if you will recognize it when you find it. But there is a rich inner world that will respond to this invitation.

Young Intuitives

Do you sometimes know something without knowing how you know it? Do you ever feel others' feelings as your own or know their thoughts? Intuition is on the opposite end of the spectrum from sensing. In the general population, only 25 percent of people use intuition as their primary means of interaction and perception, while 75 percent have a sensing preference.

I believe that all children are intuitive. However, not all children use their intuition as their main tool for understanding themselves, others, and their environment. Intuitive children feel, know, sense, and sometimes see what others do not. However, what they easily and intuitively know and perceive is often met with disbelief or denial by others.

It is normal and natural for intuitive children to spontaneously announce that Uncle Bob, who died a few years earlier, is in the house or that Dad is not really working late like he said he was. However, family and friends might not welcome and be especially pleased about these insights. Intuitive children often know how others feel and are confused when their insights are rejected or met with a blank stare. They may know when others are not being honest and when events are not going to go as planned. When a child has little or no support for what they perceive and when what people say and do conflicts with what their gut tells them is true, confusion and self-doubt can spin out of control. Many intuitive children learn to keep their insights to themselves. In some cases, they repress and deny their intuitive abilities and do their best to disregard their inner knowing.

If you were an intuitive child, you may still be uncomfortable or fearful of your intuition. It may even be so repressed that you are no longer able to use it in positive and helpful ways. If so, it is time to claim, reactivate, and ignite your intuition. Take the time to listen within. Trust your gut feelings and inner knowing and act on what you receive. Do not wait for someone else to verify what you know is right to you. Reconnect with this natural part of who you are.

I value both my sensing and my intuitive natures.

23. Celebrate Individuality

We all need to feel like we belong. Being part of something—a group or a religious or political belief system—gives us a sense of security and identity. The drive to belong is particularly strong when we are young, especially when we are teenagers. It is also in the teenage years that we become more aware of our individuality. The differences between ourselves and our family members and popular culture are magnified. We go in search of what appeals to us and reject what does not. We can develop strong opinions, interests, and judgments about others, types of entertainment, hobbies, school, and society in general.

For some young people, the process of discovering their individuality and identifying with a group is relatively easy. Allegiance to a certain sport or team or an interest in a specific type of music or band provides a sense of belonging and a safe haven. However, many young people fake interest in what is popular and repress their natural tendencies in order to feel as if they belong. Others struggle with feelings of loneliness and isolation when they do not experience the kind of connection or affinity with others that they would like.

Overcompromising, denying, and not listening to our inner voice in order to be like others and fit in comes with a hefty price. Squashing our natural impulses leads to feeling empty and estranged from self. This inner void can be a crippling and soul-crushing suffering. In our society, these feelings among young people are epidemic. Drug use, addictions, crime, suicide, and violent rampages have their roots in those individuals who feel they have no place in mainstream society or feel as if they must compromise their true self to be seen and accepted. Being shut out, ostracized, shunned, or rejected by others and by ourselves leads to depression, isolation, and anger.

If you are strong enough to be yourself, flaunt it. Be unusual, different, and creative and wave your flag of individuality high. There are many who need to see it and know that they are not alone. We owe it to others, particularly young people, to be free and audacious enough to be ourselves. Be a happy and secure role model for those who need to know that they, too, can be who they are and make it in this world. Let them be part of your pack. Wave and smile at and compliment those who are bizarre and unusual. Let them know they belong.

I support others in being who they are.

24. Remember Who You Are

You are meant to be here at this time. There is no one quite like you. You have come here to create, love, forgive, and express the special magic of you. Unfortunately, not everyone is always going to understand and appreciate you. We all get beat up somewhat in this life. Be resilient and do not expect too much from the world. Your strength, love, and life force come from the light of the beyond.

Trust what comes your way. You came into this life with everything you need to experience joy and meaning. There are certain people you are meant to meet who will love, bless, and support you. There are relationships that you came here to explore, heal, and work through. There are friends, family members, partners, and lovers you are here to love, help, forgive, and bless on their journey. Remember that not everything that comes your way is meant to last a lifetime. Those challenging situations, conditions, and unexpected changes that seem to come and go at random are in keeping with the lessons that you have come here to experience.

Notice when you get stuck in emotions such as anger, confusion, or pain, and remember that you have a powerful heart. You are sustained from within. No matter what this world throws your way, know that you are a powerful being. Even if you cannot recall the brilliant light that shines from within, the spirit of the most holy resides within you. Physical life is temporary and provides you with the opportunity to experience the joy of being human. With the light of the stars guiding you and anchoring you to the heavens, open your heart and remember who you are. Be gentle in your love for yourself and others.

I remember that the strength and love
within my heart sustain me.

25. Challenging Childhood Messages

Is there a belief about yourself or about life that you received as a child that you are ready to let go of or change? Maybe you grew up believing that you were not very smart and that you lacked the intelligence to make it in this world. Did your family emphasize education and good grades? Did you feel that you measured up to their expectations? Perhaps you excelled in other interests and hobbies, but you grew up believing that they had little or no value. Maybe you believe that you are unattractive or that you are destined to be overweight. Perhaps, like many others, you grew up believing that you are meant to work in a certain field. Your abilities, education, and skills have been focused in an area that you do not enjoy. As hard as you try to make it work, you have no passion for what you are doing.

It takes time to know who you are and what works for you. Like many, you have derived a sense of self from your childhood environment. Well-meaning parents, teachers, and friends have guided you in forming your identity. Your beliefs about who you are and what is possible in your life may keep you confined and limited. Some of these messages feel true and right for you, but maybe not all of them. Because much of our sense of self was developed at such a young age, it may feel like there are certain qualities, characteristics, and personality attributes that we cannot change.

You can redefine who you are. Begin by examining areas in your life that you would like to change. Ask yourself what early childhood experiences may have helped to form your current beliefs and experiences. Feel in your heart what is true for you. Be honest with yourself. If there is a belief or an area of your life that does not ring true for you, make the decision to change it. Ask yourself what does feel right for you. Brainstorm new ideas and beliefs, try them on, and ask yourself how they feel. Can you see and feel yourself doing things differently or adopting a new belief? How does it feel in your heart and gut? What actions can you take to support what feels right for you? Take your time with this process. Be kind and encouraging in your efforts to do things differently. Reinforce your truth, and eventually it will integrate itself into your life and feel more natural.

I challenge childhood messages that are no longer true for me.

26. Early Spiritual Awareness

I was baptized at a young age in a Baptist church and went to Sunday school every week. We sang songs about Jesus and the Bible and watched with rapt attention as our Sunday school teacher moved felt figures of Jesus and Moses across a whiteboard in the front of the class.

Although I was well schooled in the Bible, I didn't have a sense of God in a spiritual way. Instead, it was in the woods near my house where I felt the undeniable presence of a greater power. Among the trees and streams and shining down from the clouds in the sky, I felt a presence and a warmth in my heart. Unlike church and Sunday school, which required a lot of sitting still, listening, and repeating words that I did not understand, nature does not require conformity. It took me many years to fully understand that what I was experiencing was spiritual, holy, and good and that everyone has access to it. It took me even longer to accept that this was what those in church called God.

When we are young, we have a natural and authentic connection to spirituality that has nothing to do with judgment, sin, and salvation. Before we have a name for it, many of us feel and experience a spiritual presence. Over time, we discount or forget this heartfelt knowing and connection or believe it to be just in our imagination. For many people, it becomes the avenue through which they experience a transcendent connection with a higher love and presence.

What are your early memories of religion or spirituality? Reignite the innocence and spiritual awareness of your early years. What in your heart do you know is true for you? Let your imagination take flight and trust your spiritual awareness.

I explore my spirituality.

27. You Are Not a Label

If you were labeled with an emotional or mental disorder as a child, know that you were born perfect and you are still a perfect being. Some of the most common developmental and learning disabilities diagnosed in children and young adults are autism, attachment disorder, conduct disorder, and oppositional defiant disorder. In addition to personality disorders, eating and social anxiety disorders are being more frequently diagnosed in younger children.

For many reasons, it is advantageous to receive an accurate diagnosis for a child who is struggling and in need of support. Getting treatment and medication and receiving tutoring and therapy can make the difference between suffering and healing for many young people. Unfortunately, it can also instill a sense of shame and embarrassment or a feeling of being faulty, defective, bad, or broken. Despite our belief that there are "normal" children and there are those who lie outside the parameters of the typical and average, all children are unique and come into this life with both challenges and special gifts and talents. It is our responsibility to discover what they are.

If you felt defective in some way as a child because of a medical label or disability, you may still consciously or unconsciously feel deficient and different. Imagine that you can peel off this artificial layer of who and what you were labeled. Perhaps a disability or disorder has in the past served or is currently serving a spiritual, mental, physical, or emotional purpose. But remember that your disability or disorder is not you. You are not your brain, your physical body, your emotions, your thoughts, your nervous system, or your physiology. You are the beautiful spark of light that shines through all of these and is present in all that you experience. Have compassion for your young self, who had to endure a system, culture, and way of being that was not fully able to understand and accommodate the truth of who you are. Honor your path. There are many ways to be in this world. Break the mold and just be you.

I let go of any labels that were given to me as a child.

28. Allow Your Past to Bless You

All of the struggles, pressures, challenges, and pain that you have been through have been divinely orchestrated for your highest good. All of the joy, love, compassion, and comfort that you have thus far experienced in your life is here to bless you. Your soul is a master builder carving out the unique masterpiece of you.

Allow all that you have experienced in the past to be a source of positivity. The family you are born into, the early school and social environment you did your best to get through, and your struggles to be yourself may not have been easy. Yet nothing that you have experienced is more powerful than what is within you. Challenges can activate our inner power and push the strength within to flow powerfully into every area of our lives.

Celebrate all that has led you to where you are right now. The tears and laughter, happiness and sorrow, gain and loss and pain and healing that you have experienced can be sources of strength. Celebrate your desire to learn, grow, and be you. Listen to the persistent call from within that motivates and inspires you to continue the adventure of self-discovery. All of this forms the roots from which the authentic you blossoms.

My past is a blessing.

Chapter 3

THE CALL TO TRANSFORMATION

Life is a mirror that reveals more than just our surface image. We unknowingly create experiences and conditions through which we can better perceive and know our innermost self. It is often through the unexpected and what appears to be random and unforeseen that we discover new aspects of who we are. This chapter encourages you to explore the transformative experiences that have the power to change your life.

29. Letting Go of Control

We go along in our day-to-day lives believing that we have some sense of control. With all of the many decisions and choices that we need to make, being cautious, careful, and exacting seems so necessary. Yet despite our careful planning, the facade that we are in control eventually cracks. Something more powerful and unexpected emerges and invites us into a new reality. This is the tipping point. The old is gone, and as hard as we try, we cannot be who we used to be. It is as the old nursery rhyme says:

Humpty Dumpty sat on a wall,
Humpty Dumpty had a great fall.
All the king's horses and all the king's men
Couldn't put Humpty together again.

Before the fall, your soul has been secretly preparing to turn your life upside down. You may not be expecting or even desiring change, yet it is inevitable. Another you seeks to rise from the depths as the known and false fall away.

We often have to let go of who we believe ourselves to be to allow our most authentic voice and self to surface. Your soul plan and reason for being here on the earth at this time may be in conflict with your personality or ego self's plans and desires. When you accept the invitation into the true adventure of life, there is a crack in the ego's empty aspirations and yearnings and they begin to fall away. The glorious, deep, complex, and multidimensional creature that you are rears its proud head and cannot be contained.

I allow my soul to lead me.

30. A Thousand Deaths

There are a thousands deaths you will undergo in your lifetime. You will crumble, break apart, collapse, and fragment. Each death will be different from every other one. Some will surprise you by creeping in and creating slow change. Others will pull the rug out from under you and sweep away all that you have relied on.

Like a snake shedding its skin, you will shed who you believe yourself to be many times over. All the false qualities and traits that the world has told you are you, the illusions that you have believed to be true, and the empty desires and wishes that will never bring you joy and happiness will fall away.

This is transformation. It is the process of being you.

You can go with this process or you can fight against it. Either way, it will happen. When you surrender and allow the illusions to turn to dust, you become more comfortable with change and the unexpected. You align with a greater force within and come to recognize your true power. Otherwise, you rage a constant battle against what is. Change comes unexpectedly, bringing with it a sense of powerlessness and shock.

Your life force energy will not support anything but the core true you. It can be a hard truth to accept, but it can also give you a sense of peace. All you can be is who you are. Life is inevitable growth, evolution, and the shedding of illusion. You are an ever-changing mystery.

I surrender to change.

31. Soul-Directed Events

There are some things you want and desire that your soul will work overtime to create and bring into your life. It will expertly weave together events, people, and situations with a masterful stroke of genius to manifest the job, relationship, or opportunity through which your beauty, love, and personal truth will emerge. Your soul will work tirelessly behind the scenes in the activities and experiences that inspire and motivate you to draw deep within, discover your core strength and love, and activate the individual wonder that you have been created to be.

However, your soul will erect detours for some of your desires in an attempt to stop you in your tracks or guide you in another direction. Your soul will not align with activities and relationships that keep the best of who you are locked away.

Soul-directed events come our way to realign us with our true self and path. These are the detours that shake us up, shatter our illusions, and push us to try new things and know ourselves in a new way.

This is what happened to Emily, a young woman I know who wanted to go to dental school. After completing the prerequisite classes and courses, she poured herself wholeheartedly into studying for the dental admission test and applying to dental schools. Yet, despite her efforts, her scores were mediocre and one application rejection letter after another filled her mailbox. The following year, she took the tests again and reapplied. Unfortunately, the results were the same. Depressed and confused as to what to do and where to go now that her dream of being a dentist had proved to be elusive and unattainable, Emily did nothing. She was getting by with a job in the library at the local college, and her future seemed on hold. However, not getting into dental school was simply a soul-directed detour.

Early one morning while walking down the hall of the college where she worked, she passed a studio art class. When she glanced in the room, something got her attention. It may have been the way the light hit the easels or the vast array of paint colors splattered across the floor. Whatever it was, her heart flushed with warmth and she sat down in the empty class and picked up a paintbrush. This was all it took. Fast-forward a few years and many art classes later, and Emily is now a successful artist, living her passion and grateful that dental school did not work out.

The soul will use any means possible to wake you to your truth. Sometimes this comes in the form of disruption of your current plans and dreams, but not always. Soul-directed events can also provide opportunities that inspire, motivate, and empower us to feel more alive and joyful. Let yourself be guided. Notice subtle signs and listen to your heart and intuition. Recognize the power that your soul yields in influencing the course of your life.

I trust that my soul is leading me to my highest good.

32. Self-Honesty

Be honest with yourself. Growth and awareness begin with allowing our truth to surface. Pick an area of your life, such as work, school, family, relationships, finances, or health. Assess where you are and your satisfaction with the current state of things. Then take a deep breath and listen within. Ask yourself what you may be denying, suppressing, or ignoring about the situation or your feelings. Give yourself some time to listen and feel what surfaces. Accept whatever you receive and feel without criticizing or becoming judgmental.

You may want to ask yourself the following questions. Breathe, relax, and take your time with each one.

- *What is my biggest challenge in this area?*
- *What is the lesson that I am learning about myself or others?*
- *Is there a repeating pattern?*
- *Do I continually get stuck or experience the same feeling or outcomes?*

Allow whatever you are suppressing—emotions, thoughts, new revelations or insights—to surface.

In the same area that you just explored, ask yourself what you truly desire to be experiencing. Listen within and allow your true wishes and desires to surface. Feel positive energy begin to flow. Create a mental picture in your mind's eye of what this looks like. Open your heart and imagine yourself experiencing the highest outcome. This is your truth.

I am honest about where I am and where I want to be.

33. Synchronicities: Dance with the Cosmic Flow

You are being led. There is a presence moving through your heart, mind, and soul that is directing and guiding you. Have you ever experienced a meaningful coincidence, or synchronicity, that opened you to a new understanding of yourself or a situation? Has something unexpected ever shown up in your life and motivated you to change the course you were on or take advantage of a new opportunity? Has unexpected good fortune ever come to you in a surprising way?

As you probably suspect, synchronicities are no accident. The universe has carefully orchestrated the seemingly impossible convergence of things, people, events, and conditions. It does not matter how great or small the coincidence may be. We immediately recognize when we intersect with the cosmic. Although others may not always be able to feel and see it, when we are touched by the transcendent, we know it. The heart smiles, the mind opens, and like an Olympian gymnast, the soul joyously flips and leaps.

Synchronicities provide us with a glimpse into a reality that we have forgotten. They speak to the authentic self that is comfortable and at home in the realm of cosmic truth. Yet despite the powerful effect that a synchronicity can have on us, we all too soon want to dumb it down by rationalizing. We want to creep back into the logical and rational, as if the cosmic doors had not flung open. The thinking mind wants to take charge and explain away the magic and unexplainable. Don't let it. Live with the mystery and allow it to wash through you like a healing balm. You have been given an invitation to experience life through the cosmic portal. Soak in the deep rays of the universal life force current that is promoting and supporting a part of you that you might not have the courage to know.

The following suggestions can move you deeper into the flow of synchronicities.

Ask for Synchronicities

It's simple but true that if you ask for synchronicities, you will experience them. Let go of your expectations of how they will come to you and in what area of your life. Just make the intent and allow the universe to manifest it.

Notice Synchronicities

No matter how big, small, or insignificant the synchronicities may be, listen to your heart and soul. You will become aware of when the divine is sending you guidance through synchronicities.

Be Positive

If you knew that your best friends were planning a surprise party for you, imagine how excited and honored you would feel. This is the attitude to adopt with synchronicities. A wonderful, personally crafted surprise is on its way.

Have Gratitude

Say thank you and blow a big kiss to the cosmic flow of all that is. Enjoy and have fun. All of creation is having a blast.

Act On Synchronicities

If you experience a synchronicity that seems to be pointing you in a certain direction, act on what you receive. Cosmic direction is a blessing that wraps you in the folds of a higher wisdom. Trust it and take action. Acting on higher wisdom and direction strengthens your soul energy and guides you into the positive.

I notice synchronicities.

34. Not Getting Your Way

Your authentic self is a powerful and positive force. It is the part of you that can act with love, wisdom, and power. When you feel like you are a victim of circumstances or when you are caught off guard and are surprised by upheaval, you may feel powerless and at the mercy of unseen and random forces. When you yearn for change but do not know how to make it happen or where to start, or when you carefully plan and follow through step by step with a well-thought-out initiative but nothing seems to go as expected, you may feel confused, frustrated, and lost.

Sometimes what we want and desire seems to elude us. Instead of pushing and forcing your will and trying to make something happen or blaming yourself or others for what you are experiencing, know that there is within you a silent force that is directing and guiding you into and through all that happens in your life. When things do not go your way, take a step back. Take time to contemplate what is happening. Listen to your core truth and come into alignment with the greater inner force of who you are. Whatever you are trying to make happen, whatever change you want, and whatever you desire may not necessarily be in your highest good. Your authentic self always guides you toward the good within yourself and in life. It is always consistent and you can trust it.

Accept the roadblocks, the disappointments and frustrations, however difficult they may be. Have compassion for and patience with yourself and life. Be grateful and know that you are being prepared for something even better.

> *I know that there is something greater that I am*
> *being led to when things do not go my way.*

35. The Best Comes When You Are Being You

We expect a lot from ourselves. For instance, we may believe that we should be able to get the job we want, make more money, find our soulmate, and lose weight, all within the time frame and in the way that we desire. We may expect ourselves to say the "right" thing to others, have enough energy to accomplish all that we want to do, or always be in a good mood and cheerful. Yet not all of our expectations are fulfilled in the way that we want them to be.

Life is an adventure. We do not always know where we are going, and at times we are not even sure of the next step. Expectations can be a way of trying to control outcomes. Allow space for the mystery of who you are and the path that you are on to unfold. Accomplishing goals can provide us with a sense of power and worthiness. It can be important to focus our attention in certain areas, be single-minded, and accomplish what we set out to do. However, it is not the goal itself that is the prize. When we allow what we do to define us and we look outside of ourselves for our value, we create a false sense of self. This will bring only temporary satisfaction.

Your expectations and goals cannot replace the satisfaction and gratification that come with an openhearted and open-minded approach to being fully present to whatever you are experiencing right now. Your authentic self does not need to be pushed and prodded and made to chase an elusive goal. It just is. Let yourself be. Instead of being motivated by outer standards and expectations, accept and love yourself exactly for who you are right now.

Flowers need both the sun and the rain to bloom. At the end of the day, tell yourself that you did your best. Even if you did not do everything that you wanted to do, you tried. You hoped and dreamed and trusted in yourself, and that is what is important. It is not simply through your experiences that you learn and evolve.

More importantly, it is through your reactions and responses to what you experience that you can better know your true self. Choosing to be compassionate and live without judgment in the present moment allows you to become more fully aware of your inner goodness. Delight in the simple you that can look up at the stars at night and know that you are a part of this wonderful creation—exactly the way that you are. Expect the best. It will come to you when you are being you.

I let go of expectations and allow life to unfold.

36. Surrender

Have you ever been in a difficult situation or confronted an issue, and as hard as you try and as much as you want to effect a positive outcome, you get nowhere? It is not always easy to know when we have done all that we can in any given situation. When we are frustrated, discouraged, or disappointed, we tend to blame ourselves or others when things do not go the way we want them to. An obstacle, relationship, skill, or problem may seem to be stronger than we are. We may want to give up and walk away or we may obsessively keep trying to control the situation and create change.

When you feel that you are banging your head against the wall or you are driving yourself crazy trying to control outcomes and conditions, consider surrendering instead of struggling. Surrendering is not the same as giving up. Surrender brings relief. It is the awareness that you are being redirected by a powerful and benevolent force of good. Surrender is the acceptance that what you desire, the problem that you want to solve, the relationship that you want to make work, or the goal that you have set is not in keeping with your highest good. With surrender, you become empowered to release your worries, stress, and anxiety and flow with the inner assurance that everything will work out.

There are times when you need to try harder, learn a new way, or give it your all. But when you get that uncomfortable feeling in the pit of your stomach that what you desire is not meant for you, listen to it.

Surrender aligns you with your authentic self. It is not a battling against circumstances or a judgment of your inadequacies or another's faults or problems. It allows you to see beyond the veil of your personal will and call forward your deeper truth and soul path. Surrender is a powerful statement to the universe that you accept its terms.

Conditions and circumstances that you have been battling against and trying to control then transform. When you allow yourself to be led in what might appear to be the opposite direction, you often get what you want or something better. Surprising changes transpire as you accept others and conditions as they are.

Here are some suggestions to try when you find yourself struggling and trying to control outcomes.

Realize that there is another way. Take a step back and become aware of the struggle that you are engaged in. How does it feel? Are you getting what you want or are you becoming frustrated and discouraged?

Make a decision to detach. It is not always easy to let go. Even when you do, you will likely want to jump back in. Make the intent to try another way. Pry your fingers off of your desires, breathe, and let go.

Become comfortable with uncertainty and change. Once you let go, you will likely experience stress and anxiety. This is normal. These are the feelings that motivated you to try to control outcomes. Lean into the feelings and allow them to surface. As difficult as this process may be, as you allow yourself to feel your feelings, they too will let go and dissipate.

Notice when opportunities come your way. Take some time away from focusing on your issues and problems. Do something fun and relaxing. Become aware of when you feel led and guided to pursue something new. Feel the flow of new energy. Open your heart, mind, and spirit and pay attention to signs, dreams, and synchronicities.

Follow through on new ideas and opportunities as they present themselves, even if you are not entirely sure of what you want. Stay positive and keep listening within and allowing yourself to be led.

Trust what comes your way and take action when you feel as if you are being led.

There is a pervasive and all-knowing power of wisdom and love at work in your life. Steer into this current. Let go of trying to control the outer events in your life and trust what comes your way. When the unexpected happens, support and reassure yourself that this too shall pass. Surrender to what is. Conditions will right themselves, bringing clarity and renewed vision.

I surrender to what is.

37. Freedom from Addiction

You cannot hear, feel, express, or be aware of your authentic self if you are actively involved in an addiction of any kind. An addiction to alcohol, shopping, eating, television, gaming, sex, drugs, or any other activity or thought that you feel a compulsive and overwhelming need to use or participate in dulls your ability to connect with the true you. Addictions such as overdependency on others or overcaretaking others can also keep you from feeling and listening to the true you.

Addiction keeps us from the raw truth of who we are. Life can be messy, difficult, and painful, and it's not always kind to and supportive of our vulnerabilities and sensitivities. Substances and activities that provide an altered state and escape hatch from our present state of being keep us preoccupied with a false sense of self. No one wants to feel powerless and unable to cope with their challenges and difficulties. Whatever the addiction may be, it is an attempt to break free from a reality that we may no longer want to be a part of and to avoid our feelings and fears. At its core, addiction is a soul-numbing void. It is fueled by the belief that you are a finite human at the mercy of what the world throws your way. When it all becomes too much to bear, addiction invites you to cower in the corner, wrapped within the cocoon of an illusory safety.

The paradox of addictions is that they do not provide any real solace or escape. They are a false road away from suffering that only circles back deeper into the depths of pain and the feelings that you want to avoid. The way out of an active addiction is rarely easy. To simply admit that you have a problem takes a level of courage that few of us know we possess. Yet the paradox of addiction is that when you freely admit that you are powerless over an addictive substance or activity, a greater power emerges to lead you to your deeper truth.

Your true self can never be dulled, manipulated, or destroyed by an addiction. You can lose your conscious connection with your authentic self and it can appear to be invisible and distant, but your truth is always with you. To transform and break the hold that addiction has on your heart, soul, and body, you cannot play small. While you may only know yourself through your fears, anxieties, problems, and past traumas, there is more to you. If you become easily overwhelmed and possess an addictive nature or have a genetic family history of addictions, this is not all of who you are.

You have to claim the total you. Begin by listening within to the voice that is telling you that you have a problem. Speak from this truth. There is power in words. Tell yourself, a friend, a counselor, or a family member. Your authentic self is the door through which your spirit emerges and is guiding you. Free and vibrant, your spirit calls to you to be honest with yourself. When you cease shielding yourself from what you feel, fear, and are experiencing, a sublime spiritual reality that does not hurt and cause pain begins to reveal itself. It unravels confusion and is a balm for and an oasis from the challenging and stressful world. To become familiar with this part of you, let go of the false barriers of addiction that offer no relief. Your authentic self offers a way out. Allow its voice to emerge. Delve into your anger, pain, suffering, and fears. Underneath this, your authentic self is present and waiting to lead the way to true freedom.

I am free of addictions.

38. You Are Not Your Problems

Many of us were raised to believe that having problems is a sign of weakness or inadequacy. We were encouraged to show others how successful, happy, and together we are. Instead of learning the tools to work through the inevitable issues and challenges that life brings our way, many learned that feeling confused or at a loss of what to do is a sign of incompetence or failure.

When you push your problems into the dark and do not talk or discuss them, feelings of isolation surface, causing you even more inner suffering. Shame is the belief that there is something inherently flawed about you. Hiding your problems and not sharing what you are experiencing with those you trust and care about encourages feelings of shame.

You may believe that others will think less of you or judge you as being deficient in some way if you expose your less-than-perfect self and life. Remember, those who judge what you are going through as a deficiency believe this to be true for themselves. They are unable to separate what they experience from who they really are. Don't buy into this kind of thinking. It is dangerous and will never inspire the best in you to emerge.

You are not alone. Everyone has problems and difficulties that often feel overwhelming. Challenges come to us to empower us to learn more about ourselves, others, and life. They prompt us to grow and move beyond a shallow perspective of who we are and what we are capable of. New aspects of the authentic self come forward. We are often not aware of our own inner strength, courage, and creative thinking until we need them. More often than not, when we confront our issues head on, we discover that there is nothing to fear. New ideas, solutions, and possibilities come to the forefront.

When you share your stress and confusion with those you trust, you allow and inspire them to be more honest and forthright about their own issues. This promotes open and honest communication and increases intimacy and warm feelings of true heartfelt connection.

I am not my problems.

39. Transform Through Joy

Although transformation often comes to us through upheaval and unexpected change, its purpose is to open us to the experience of true and authentic joy. We humans don't always like change, even when it brings new opportunities and possibilities into our lives. Yet despite our best attempts, we cannot keep change at bay. We are here to create, grow, and evolve.

We can, however, choose how change comes into our lives. When we become aware of opportunities and possibilities that promote growth, we can transform in positive and gentle ways. Taking action on new ideas and possibilities keeps us in the flow of positive life force energy. It is when we do not listen to the subtle promptings of our authentic self and dismiss the small sparks of joy that speak to our heart that we get into trouble. When we don't keep pace with our soul's journey, a cosmic brick often comes along to push us out of our complacency. Unexpected loss and a falling away of what is familiar moves us forward.

Trust joy when you feel it. It is a signal from your authentic self that you are on the right path. Joy springs from the heart and soul. It is the feeling of rightness and knowing that emanates from deep within. Despite what is happening in your outer life, joy informs you that there is inherent meaning and purpose in what you are experiencing. Joy elevates you to a higher current of positivity.

Unexpected good comes my way.

40. When Things Fall Apart

Things fall apart. No matter how hard we try, not everything goes the way we hoped and planned. Even when we know that disaster is looming, we cannot always prevent it. People disappoint us and do things that we do not like. We may be comfortable and feel safe and secure in the day-to-day ups and downs that come our way and still a surprising and unexpected event can occur and turn everything upside down. Sometimes it is not a personal problem or issue of our own that causes us distress. A friend, partner, son, daughter, parent, coworker, neighbor, or your community confronts a misfortune or challenge, yet we find ourselves as stressed and worried as if this problem were our own. Not being able to control or effectively change a situation for another can generate feelings of powerlessness.

Try not to blame yourself or others or become bitter when things fall apart. This is a part of life that we will never escape. No matter what you do, how safe you play it and how intelligent and competent you are, you will at one time or another experience unexpected change. Problems get solved, but only temporarily. Other or similar ones will crop up.

When misfortune knocks on our door and rattles us to the core, there may be little left of the life that we have known. Loss of a job, a devastating health condition, divorce, financial bankruptcy, or the death of a loved one not only changes our circumstances but can also change the way we perceive ourselves. If we recoil in fear, we feel defenseless and at the mercy of a cruel fate. However, if we make space in our lives to accommodate the inevitable, we can gain a sense of mastery and strength from our challenges.

When change comes your way, you can close down in fear or you can feel the depths of your emotions and allow them to soften you. A feeling of safety and serenity does not come about by avoiding and controlling the flow of life. Instead, you can discover calmness in the midst of the storm by accepting what is happening and embracing your feelings.

Be in present time. When you find yourself stressing over and troubled by problems and challenges, breathe and acknowledge the good that is present and be open to perceiving what is happening with a new awareness and perspective. Don't let your concerns for the future and pain from the past cause you to imagine the worst. Take it one step at a time, being ever mindful that challenges call forward hidden but potent aspects of your authentic self. Even though problems may initially seem overwhelming, you can discover a strength and compassion that you did not know you had. Distressing turns of events are often a calling card from your authentic self letting you know that you are capable of so much more than you may think.

I acknowledge that in this moment all is well.

41. The Invisible Presence

Before we perceive the light within ourselves and experience the dynamic love and joy that is our birthright, we often go through a period of confusion and darkness. Challenges often motivate us to journey into the deeper recesses of who we are. When we feel empty or thirst for something more, we go beyond the known. Sometimes we search in the outer world for things like a new job, or hobby, a better relationship, or new diversions and entertainment. Sometimes these changes work. They move us forward into new aspects of who we are and satisfy our needs. However, sometimes it is not outer remedies that we most need. Instead, it is something less definable and more obscure and mysterious that is calling to us.

When I was in college, I experienced this kind of inner calling. To pay tuition and my living expenses, I worked two jobs. One was at the college cleaning offices and the other was at a restaurant washing dishes. I was keeping everything together, but just barely. If I was not studying, I was either attending classes or working.

In my job as a dishwasher, I was usually the last one to leave the restaurant at night. One night on my way home from work, while climbing a steep hill my car sputtered a few times and died. I tried over and over to start it, but it was useless. It was not going to start, so I got out and began to walk home. This was in the days before cell phones, when you were just out of luck. The mountain roads were dark, with no traffic and no homes or businesses alongside them. It began to rain and I had many miles to go. I had an exam and a paper due the next day and I knew it would take me most of the night to walk home.

Exhausted, I stopped for a moment in the dark and quiet rain to rest. In this moment I felt a piercing and penetrating aloneness. I knew that without my car, I could not work. In the struggling economy of this small town, it had taken me months to find this job. Without it, I would not be able to pay my rent and tuition. I felt that I had no one and nothing to fall back on. As hard as I tried, I could not think of a way through this.

As I continued to walk in the dark, I began to cry. I ached with exhaustion and loneliness. To my surprise, in the midst of my despair I suddenly felt an unexpected presence of warmth both beside and within me. It was so powerful that I stopped walking and looked all around. As a shiver of warmth went thorough me, I experienced a transcendent moment of awareness. I was pulled into a depth within me that was more real than the cold, dark night and empty road. It was a moment when the undefinable and undeniable truth left no room for any other thoughts or feelings. I knew that I was connected to a source of love and kindness that was both within me and watching over me. There was no problem or issue that was more powerful or real than this awareness.

I continued to walk under the spell of this presence, only now I realized that I was not alone. Everything was going to work out. I did not know how. I just knew that it would. Sometimes when it seems the darkest and it appears that there is no help in sight, we are broken open. Desperation, hopelessness, and distress can clear the way for deeper truth to surface. Our will, thoughts, and solutions can only get us so far. Beyond these things, a door opens and reveals a vast network of love and intelligence that is more powerful than we have thought ourselves to be.

I am grateful for the presence of love
and wisdom that comes to my aid.

42. The Power of Mistakes

You may make mistakes, but you are not a mistake. Other people make mistakes too. They are not their mistakes, either. At times, our best efforts do not produce the desired results. We give something our best and we fail. We do not get what we want or we get what we want and it is not what we thought it would be. We all make decisions that do not work out the way we thought they would.

Sometimes we are taken by surprise. We trust people who let us down. We lose money on something that we thought was a sure thing. The job that we believed would bring us happiness and financial abundance disappoints and brings neither. The relationship that seemed to be heaven-sent ends in lies and infidelity.

I have made plenty of mistakes and bad decisions. At times I have even had a sense that the person I was trusting, the outcome I was hoping for, or the money I was spending was not going to give me what I needed. Yet more often than I would like to admit, I went forward anyway. I trusted someone who betrayed me. I spent money carelessly. I hoped and desired for an outcome that never came to pass.

Sometimes our mistakes feel devastating. We withdraw emotionally and close off our hearts. We may stop trusting others and live in dread and fear, doing our best to avoid possible failure or disappointment. We may beat ourselves up, allow our self-esteem to plummet, and generally feel bad about ourselves or believe that we are deficient in some way. We may even stop trusting ourselves altogether.

Loss, disappointment, grief, and failure are all a part of life. They are some of the ways through which you can learn more about who you are. Instead of not trusting yourself or closing yourself off from others, use your mistakes as a way to better know yourself and others and accept life as it is.

For instance, those who disappoint us can teach us about self-reliance and inspire us to appreciate our integrity and value. Mistakes can ignite our creativity. Loss of a job can motivate us to discover latent abilities and talents that lead to new career and moneymaking opportunities. When things do not go our way, we often find new doors opening and new aspects of ourselves coming to life. Our mistakes do not define us. How we go forward after we make one is what is important.

I am not my mistakes.

43. Awakening

The depth and breadth of your authentic self is vast and limitless. To know the whole of who you are is no small matter. We can know our thoughts, emotions, and beliefs and become more conscious of our choices and actions. Yet behind all of this, our core self pulsates with raw power and life force energy. When our everyday ego-based self is lifted into the awareness of a greater love and oneness with all of life, we perceive ourselves through the center of wholeness. We can know this aspect of self only through direct experience. While logic, reasoning, and knowledge can provide intellectual understanding, our consciousness must awaken to its true authentic self.

Awakening is deep and lasting transformation. It is more than changing our understanding of ourselves and others or setting new goals and beginning new activities. True awakening comes to us through grace. We have reached a collective tipping point. New energy is streaming into the planet and many are accepting and receiving it. We are moving from a state of spiritual sleep to that of being fully awakened. During awakening, we move out of the false belief and experience of being separate from all of life. The sense that we have to go it alone and use our personal will and power to carve out an existence that will keep us safe and protected begins to fade away. Feelings of fear, anxiousness, and stress transform into the awareness of an ever-present guiding force of love. We become more aware that what we do to others we do to ourselves.

The experience of awakening is different for everyone. It can feel like an all-encompassing, warm embrace from the universe, a sense of being aligned with a higher force of power and wisdom, or a simple, quiet inner knowing and feeling of peace. Awakening is the awareness that you are eternal spirit connected to all of life.

Awakening occurs as you become more aware of your truth and authentically live it. Take quiet time every day to listen within, feel your feelings, and open your heart. Acknowledge your basic and inherent goodness and know that there is nothing that can tarnish or diminish your authentic self. Be kind to others and to yourself. Let go of anger and do not buy into your fears. Forgive yourself and forgive all others.

I invoke an awakening through small acts of love and kindness.

44. The Signs of Awakening

Awakening is a profound shift in awareness and a renewed perception of self and of life. There is a deep alchemy in awakening. Not only does it heighten your spiritual senses and empower you to feel the inherent oneness, joy, and goodness within yourself and others, but it can also trigger confusing and physiological changes. For instance, in the awakening process you may experience an increased sensitivity to noise, light, violence, and negativity. Many experience an increase in dreams and a heightened intuitive awareness with spontaneous new insights. You may experience increased levels of higher-vibrational energy that produces dizziness and inner trembling, and you may feel exhausted but unable to sleep. Some people lose their appetite or begin to have food cravings, and many develop sensitivities to certain foods or medications and are unable to drink alcohol. You may also have an increase in mystical experiences, an inspired awareness of your purpose, and a desire to completely walk away from your current life to be of service to others.

Some are awakened suddenly and in a direct way. This was true for thirty-nine-year-old Debra, who worked for many years in pharmaceutical development. Her life was on track and predictable in most ways. She had two daughters and her husband worked for the city. Except for the debilitating headaches that she suffered, her life seemed ideal. After going to a few doctors, trying different prescription medicines, and changing her diet with no results, she made an appointment with an energy healer recommended by a friend.

During the session, the healer told Debra that she had energy blocks all through her aura. She did not know what that meant, but she felt a warm, tingling sensation move through her body when the healer removed them. During this relaxing process, Debra saw bright flashes of light in her mind's eye. This light was strangely familiar and she knew in her heart that her resistance to it was causing her headaches. Debra didn't understand all that was happening, but she felt ready to allow this light to move through her. As she did so, her heart opened and love and warmth moved through her body. Taking a deep breath, she relaxed and let go of her resistance. Immediately flooded with energy from head to toe, she felt as if she was lying on the table, but above it. While waves of blissful energy moved through her, she knew that she was being transformed. Who she was becoming and what she was leaving behind did not matter.

For some, the awakening is slower and not as obvious. This was true for Eric, who for several years felt like he was out of sync with his higher purpose. His job as a recruiter for a tech company allowed him to help others, but this was not enough. He felt a love and passion in his heart that he wanted to share and give to others. Motivated through an increasing desire to be of service and to help others to heal, he took night classes for several years to become a social worker. After graduation, he began to work in a treatment center for disadvantaged adolescents. Despite the emotional and mental toll of working with angry and challenged teenagers, Eric experienced an inner transformation. The love and compassion that moved through him to others seemed to come from a force much greater and more powerful than himself. Supported by an invisible presence of wisdom and love, he felt his connection within the oneness of all of life.

Awakening lifts our awareness and perception of who we are. Through this enlightened lens, we can come to know our true and authentic self.

I pay attention to the signs of an awakening.

45. Accidents

Sometimes transformation comes to us in unexpected, challenging, and even painful ways. Accidents often catapult us into change faster than we may be ready for. They often leave us feeling like we are the victim of cruel fate or of the recklessness or carelessness of another or ourselves. Yet accidents are not as random and without meaning and purpose as they may appear to be. When we ignore the gut feeling or inner voice that tells us that it is time for a change, or when we move in a direction counter to our life plan, an accident may come to wake us up. Your spirit uses any available means to motivate you to come into alignment with what you have come into this life to learn, experience, and participate in.

This is what happened to my client Karen, an engineer at a consulting company. Having worked on an international engineering project for over a year, she was scheduled to go to Asia with her team to present their ideas. However, while riding her bike the weekend before the trip, she collided with another bike and broke her ankle. Although Karen was disappointed by the turn of events, she accepted her fate, took a few days off, and looked for another project to devote herself to. With more leisure time available to her than usual, Karen became aware of the emptiness of her life. With her busy and demanding work schedule, she had lost touch with friends and had not been on a date in almost two years. Her apartment did not feel like a home, as she spent little time there. It became increasingly apparent to Karen that her life was out of balance. She did not know what would make her happy, and without a work project, she felt lost. For the next several months, she devoted herself to finding out more about her wants and needs. It was surprisingly difficult, but slowly she began to tune in to her authentic self. In time, Karen was grateful for the accident, as it forced her to wake up to her deeper desires for companionship, fun, and a healthier life.

Accidents are a call for deep and transformative change. If you are in an accident, try not to expend time and energy blaming yourself and others. Take care of yourself and have compassion for your situation. Accidents can be frightening, confusing, disorienting, and painful, both emotionally and physically. Take time to heal and rest. Discharge any anger, resentment, fear, or residual shock in healthy ways.

When you are feeling stronger and ready to explore the meaning behind the accident, listen within. Ask yourself what you are meant to be learning. Do you allow others to help and care for you? Have you been resisting change in any aspect of your life? Do you need to eliminate a behavior, accept a need or desire, develop patience or compassion, or focus on yourself?

Accidents may strengthen you and activate new levels of awareness about yourself and life. They can provide you with a renewed perspective and insight. Although you may want to jump back into familiar routines, take your time. Allow new ways of being to emerge. Be kind to yourself and honor the transformative process as it unfolds. Allow it to move you into new, positive forms and ways of being.

I pay attention to the lessons behind any accidents that I am involved in, even those that appear to be insignificant.

46. Death: Opening to New Life

Death is the master transformer and the bearer of deeper truth. It reminds us of the impermanence of life and the brief time we have here on earth. When we pass over into the spirit realm, the illusions of the physical world fall away. We discover that we are still very much alive and we no longer experience fear and suffering.

You can never truly predict how you will react and what you will feel when a loved one dies. Every death is unique and activates new responses and reactions. Some feel flooded with feelings of grief and sadness. Others become depressed and need alone and quiet time. Some find solace in immersing themselves in work or other projects. After the initial shock of death begins to recede, you may begin to question your own life. You may wonder if you are living your purpose or if there are past mistakes that need to be remedied. You may become aware that some of your relationships need more attention or that there are people you need to forgive. Whatever you experience after the passing of a loved one is right for you. It is an individual transformative process. There is no correct length of time or way to grieve. If you feel yourself resisting or shutting down and not allowing yourself to feel or move through the process, consider talking to a supportive friend or a counselor or go to a support group.

You may feel like you are a different person after the death of a loved one. When someone you love and care for passes over, new energy streams into your life. Despite the grief and loss that you are experiencing, you may have moments of clear awareness about the meaning and purpose of your life. You may know where you need to make changes and what is truly important to you. Some people begin anew after the death of a loved one. They may start a new career, end or begin a relationship, move to a new location, or go back to school.

One of the most profound transformations that can occur after death is the realization that your loved one who has passed over is still alive in the spirit realm. You may sense their presence or receive a sign from them. A loved one may come to you in a dream where you are able to touch, feel, and talk to them. You may find coins or feathers and feel a deep knowing that your loved one is sending them to you. You may sense a loved one's presence in the butterflies or birds that come to your window. A glimpse or flash of light may let you know that a loved one is in your home or yard. You may feel the sensation of a familiar hand on your shoulder, or the smell of a loved one's perfume may drift by you. Your loved one may send messages through songs on the radio or through feelings of love or ideas that suddenly pop up in your head. However a loved one may make their presence known, trust that they are with you, reaching out over time and space to let you know that they are alive, well, and at peace.

The sadness that you feel after a death will in time transform into unconditional love and compassion and feelings of connectedness with your loved one. The transcendent authentic self that survives death is eternal.

My authentic self survives physical death.

Chapter 4

LIFTING OFF
THE LAYERS

At some point during the journey of knowing self, you will feel as if you have had enough. You will encounter an inner resistance to letting go of who and what you have thought yourself to be. You likely will want to transform and at the same time hold on to the familiar and comfortable ways that you have been living your life. This chapter challenges you to go deeper into the thoughts, feelings, and beliefs that keep you stuck and to embrace new possibilities.

47. Cultivating the Seed of Self

The authentic self is like a seed. Until it blossoms, its potential and power can never be truly understood and known. Your everyday thoughts, emotions, choices, and actions either nurture or repress the true you. To bring the authentic self to full blossom, it is necessary to pull and dig out the false, the habitual, and the mind-numbing choices and ignorance that are not you. Dig deep and root out what is not true for you. Allow the weeds of the false to become the fertilizer that nurtures your goodness and joy.

The work of cultivating and nurturing the true self is not always easy, yet the victory is not in the final destination. Each time you listen to and express who you are, you become stronger and filled with joy. Like a mighty oak that shelters and shades, the authentic self becomes the wise, steadfast inner assurance that everything is in order and happening for a reason. Love surges through your heart and soul when you become aware that your life has purpose and meaning. Like an out-of-control bed of daisies in the sunlight, the warmth of truth spreads through you and into every aspect of your life.

I till the authentic inner garden.

48. Calm in the Midst of an Emotional Storm

Our feelings and emotions are messengers that guide us into a greater awareness of ourselves and of life. When you delve deep into your truth and live authentically, your feelings can become the stepping stones that lead you through the winding maze of self. Instead of being driven and controlled by your emotions, you can see your emotions as guideposts that, when listened to, help you to know more about who you are.

We often feel overwhelmed by our feelings and emotions. When they are powerful, they can take hold of us and control our moods, thoughts, and actions. In an attempt to feel like we have control, we often suppress or stuff away our distressing and difficult emotions or act on them in unhealthy ways. Unfortunately, this may only push our emotions deep within, where they churn and fester, unhealed and unacknowledged. We might also act out our emotions in ways that affect our self-esteem and confidence. We may eat, drink, shop, or have sex in excess. We may rage and take our anger or frustration out on others.

Instead of denying your feelings or trying to manage them in ways that can have detrimental effects, welcome your emotions as wise messengers. Listen to them and invite them to be a part of your journey to authentic living. Accept all of them—especially those that are dark, difficult, and unruly—into your awareness. Don't stuff them away, deny them, or judge them. Give your most difficult thoughts and feelings the best seats in the house. Allow them to have center stage and listen to them. Encourage your fears, anger, jealousy, and anxiety to express their woes to you. Don't turn back. Once you make the decision to allow your emotions and feelings to be known and felt, all of who you are floods in.

There are aspects of you that may have been in hiding for a long time. Behind the defensiveness, sadness, confusion, and pain, there is an open expansiveness and freedom. As you listen to your feelings with gentle compassion and accept all of them, the confusion dissipates. Despite the ferocity of your emotions, there is a calm and balanced place of peace within you.

Be present to your feelings and emotions without judgment or criticism. Wait patiently and stay in the gentle process of being fully present to yourself. Your goodness will eventually come forward. You came into this world as a magnificent being with the stuff of the heavens locked up in your heart and soul; give it the opportunity to surface.

I wait for the inner calm.

49. Free from Stereotypes

Most of us identify who we are primarily through our physical self. Our gender, age, race, hair color, eye color, and weight all define us. Cultural norms and our personal judgments of these characteristics often limit and control how we perceive ourselves.

For instance, if you are a female and possess certain physical attributes, like a slim waist and large breasts, then society reflects back to you desirability, attractiveness, and worth. If you are overweight, small-breasted, or even an average weight and average-looking, you are viewed as less desirable and often lazy and lacking. Generally speaking, young women have power and older women do not. Tall men with an athletic build are viewed as stronger, more assertive, and more capable than shorter and heavier men. Your socioeconomic status and your race also contribute to the way you are viewed by others. Young African-American or Hispanic men are judged as less reliable and responsible than older white men. If you are a young, slim woman, you are likely given preference over older women in social settings and many career and job opportunities.

Although you may not personally agree with these and other collective stereotypes, you are still in some ways affected by them. These kinds of common and broad-based biases and preferences have a subtle and often profound effect on how we perceive ourselves. If there is a prevailing view of who you are that is based on your physical self, you may unconsciously take on some of those traits and characteristics.

It is a challenge not to be affected by the prevailing stereotypes. Take a look at how you may be judging yourself. If you are not slim or skinny, do you feel less attractive and appealing? Do you harbor feelings of being less worthy when you are a few pounds heavier than you believe you should be? If you are a male, do you feel that there are certain jobs that are acceptable for you and others that are not? For instance, should you be a doctor and not a nurse? Do you feel that you need to make a lot of money to prove your value?

These judgments and others like them do not define you and have nothing to do with your authentic self. They are stereotypes, opinions, and criticisms that crowd out the truth of who you are. Do not settle for this kind of falsity and distortion. You are the being who lives inside of the physical shell. You have a heart, mind, and body that are fully equipped to serve your higher purpose in this life and experience happiness and joy no matter what your physical appearance may be.

Live from the inside out. Look beyond appearances and accept yourself for who you are. When you do this, you become beautiful. Your authentic self is powerful. Allow it to be the strongest determiner of who you are.

I look beyond appearances to see who I truly am.

50. Authentic Thinking

Your thoughts are powerful and some of them are more influential than others. Our everyday conscious thoughts usually evolve around day-to-day issues and details. They may include thoughts about current events, our job or schoolwork, friends and family, what to eat, and whatever else surfaces throughout the day. There are also random mind-chatter thoughts that continually bounce in and out of consciousness. These thoughts are a stream of consciousness where one thought leads to another and another without regard to importance or practicality. These thoughts can be entertaining or distracting. However, they do not have the potential damaging effects that judgmental and negative thoughts can have. Negative thoughts can spiral downward into a dark hole, taking us with them. They are not based on truth, but on subjective criticism, beliefs, and perceptions. Focused on ourselves, others, or events and situations, these thoughts are self-defeating. The more we think and believe them, the stronger they become and the more likely they are to manifest as self-defeating and negative experiences.

Few of our moment-to-moment thoughts are generated from our deepest truth. Instead, most of them surface from the layers and layers of accumulated beliefs, feelings, and judgments that we have collected and accepted over the years. An authentic soulful thought is one that emanates from our truest self. These thoughts are positive, wise, and intuitive and bring with them insight and peace. Unfortunately, our more superficial thoughts often cloud our ability to become aware of them.

To better tune in to the thoughts that spring from your soul, it is necessary to first become aware of and pay attention to what you are thinking. This is called *identification*. It is the process of noticing your thoughts without attachment and judgment. Once you become more aware of your thoughts, you can begin to notice their random nature and let go of them. This is called *dis-identification*. It is the ability to detach from the thoughts that do not support your highest good.

This process is often best accomplished during meditation or contemplation. Relax in a quiet place and allow your thoughts to surface one by one. Take your time and listen. Unlike our random and judgmental thoughts, which can be loud and produce feelings of stress and anxiousness, thoughts from the depths of our soul are often experienced as the still, small voice within. They are wise and insightful and create inner harmony and a feeling of freedom and expansiveness.

As you allow your true thoughts to surface, you attract the conditions, people, and situations that speak to your most authentic self. There is increased harmony in your life as you flow into alignment with your soul path.

I listen in quiet contemplation to my thoughts.

51. Will the Real You Please Stand Up

In the late 1950s, the game show *To Tell the Truth* began to air on television. It later made a short comeback in early 2001. On this show, the contestants would win money by correctly identifying, from a panel of three people, the person being portrayed. The contestants would ask each member of the panel questions to discern who was telling the truth. After the contestants cast their votes, the show would end with the announcer asking the real person being described to please stand up. If you ever watched this show, you may recall that quite often the contestants were fooled. The imposters were able to take on the personality, characteristics, and talents of the person being profiled.

The success of this show may in part be attributed to the ability that we each possess to be who others want us to be. We can hide behind a false mask and fool not only others but ourselves as well, so much so that we do not always know when we are not acting in our truth. If we take on false characteristics and do not act with integrity for an extended amount of time, we cannot always recognize our authentic feelings and thoughts. Very rarely do we do this to be deceitful or to have power or influence over others. Instead, we act this way because we want to be who others want us to be, we fear being hurt or criticized, or we are not always sure who we are.

Expressing and being true to ourselves can feel risky and cause us to feel vulnerable and insecure. Yet not being who we are rarely gives us the positive payoff that we expect. We can be left feeling empty and misunderstood, or like an imposter. Being yourself allows others to be who they are. Take the risk and stand up as the real you. When you identify and acknowledge what is true for you, the inner pressure releases. Just listening to and acting on your truth allows healing and compassion to emerge. Being you is a soothing balm that calms the inner storm. Claim your ground. It is the holy space where the authentic work of knowing self is taking place.

I tell my truth.

52. Choose the Positive

Choose to feel the positive vibe of your authentic self. When confronted with unexpected problems and stressful conditions, we often feel a combination of worry, sadness, fear, stress, and anxiety. It is important to give yourself permission to feel what you feel. Do not judge or be critical of your automatic responses. All feelings and emotions are normal and natural. They come and they go. They do not define or limit who we are and what we are capable of.

It is when we habitually cling to specific emotions and allow them to be the lens through which we perceive and judge all that we encounter that we get into trouble. There are some emotions that we are comfortable with and others that seem foreign and less appealing. We all have default emotions. Some people quickly feel anger, others confusion, and some fear or anxiety. Become aware of your default emotions and pay attention to when they surface. Whatever emotion you commonly feel is coloring your world. What you experience in your day-to-day life is being created, in part, by the energy of the emotions.

Replace your distressing default emotions with more positive ones. For instance, if you feel fear, imagine instead that you can feel the inner assurance that everything is working out exactly as it is meant to. If you feel worry, shift this into trust and confidence. Sadness can be transformed into compassion. Anxiety can be transformed into positivity, and confusion into awareness. Don't wait to naturally and automatically feel these more positive feelings. You can activate the emotion's energy. First, recognize what you feel and listen to the feeling. Then imagine a more positive, loving, and compassionate emotion right alongside it. Allow them both to coexist simultaneously within you. In time, the more positive emotion will expand and the distressing one will subside. Continuously focus for longer periods of time on the positive emotion. Eventually your nervous system, your heart, mind, and spirit, will welcome and accept these new emotional responses and they will become the norm. Be the master of your emotions. Move yourself into the life stream of positivity.

I choose to feel positive emotions.

53. On the Way to Clarity

It's okay to be confused. Maybe you were given the message when you were young that in all situations and circumstances you should know what you want, how you feel, and what will make you happy. Perhaps you give yourself this message. However, self-awareness is a never-ending process in which we are often first led away from ourselves in order to find ourselves. Knowing the depth and breadth of who we are does not happen instantaneously and on demand.

Sometimes we are confused as to what we feel and which choice and decision will produce the most positive outcome. When you are not sure what you are feeling, it is okay. Not knowing and being confused is valid and sometimes quite useful. In the process of becoming more self-aware, respect the chasm between being unconscious of your thoughts and feelings and being able to feel, know, and clearly identify them. The space in between is not always comfortable. You can feel out of touch and unable to connect with your authentic self.

You don't have to understand everything about yourself all at once. It is enough to feel your feelings and allow your thoughts to surface without judgment and criticism. Let them come and then let them go. Be a free and open, flowing channel. Resist the temptation to believe that you "should" be feeling certain feelings or feeling what others expect or want you to feel.

Give yourself permission to be honest and not know what you think or how you feel. Although it may seem like you are going in the opposite direction of what you may want, not knowing clears the path for your authentic thoughts and feelings to come to the surface.

I accept my feelings, even when I do not understand them.

54. Being Rerouted

Sometimes we arrive at a dead end. What we want does not happen or what we want does happen but it does not give us the kind of happiness and joy we thought it would. It is easy to take failure and endings personally. Our self-talk can be negative and damaging. We may tell ourselves that we have not tried hard enough, our effort was unsatisfactory, or we were just not smart, attractive, or talented enough. Although it is always wise to be honest with ourselves and learn from our mistakes, being overly self-critical and hard on ourselves can be crippling and can keep us from experiencing the true power of the moment.

We have all been grateful, at one time or another, for not getting what we thought we wanted. I had a client, Brenda, who was trying to buy a house with her boyfriend. They had been dating for over a year and she was very much in love. Over a period of six months they put offers down on three houses, and each offer was accepted. Yet for various reasons, one at a time they fell through. Discouraged and disappointed, Brenda felt as if either she had bad luck or someone had put a hex on her. That was until she unexpectedly found out some disturbing news about the man of her dreams. Soon after the contract on the third house was canceled, she discovered that her boyfriend was still married and had children he had never told her about. When she confronted him, he confessed. He was still legally married and was the father of three children. This revelation shook Brenda to the core. With immense gratitude, she now viewed her failure to buy a house as a blessing.

Life has a way of guiding us into the experiences and opportunities that we can benefit and learn from the most. Trust what happens, even when it does not look anything like your vision for happiness and success. Trust the flow, shifts, and sudden changes that come your way. Release yourself into the powerful hands of the silent and mysterious. Surrendering to the unknown is an act of mastery. This is where the magic happens. Instead of using your will to knock down walls and get your way, use your will to stay steady. Not knowing where you are going and feeling a lack of control over your environment can provoke fear and stress. Allow your authentic self to take the reins and lead you into new territory. Listen for new direction and new life. Feel the inner assurance that all is well.

> *I release my disappointments and trust that*
> *there is unexpected good coming my way.*

55. Load the Joy Truck

At some time or another, we all want something more and something better. Yet we do not always know what will make us truly happy. We often live in constant hopeful expectation that something better is on its way. Yet time passes and we may seem no closer to having the something more that we desire. It would be so much easier if the joy truck simply showed up in our driveway and dropped off our specially tailored happiness neatly packaged to our specifications.

Instead of waiting for the good to come to you, take charge and create it. If you are not sure what will make you happy, visualize the possibilities. Creative visualization is a way to use your imagination to create more of what you want. There is nothing new or unusual about using your imagination in this way. You already do it every day. Whenever you continually think, feel, or see an image, you are programming your mind to create this reality. Many athletes use creative visualization to improve their athletic performance.

Try this creative visualization exercise to attract more joy into your life.

Get into a comfortable position in a quiet place. Close your eyes and begin to breathe long, relaxing inhales and exhales.

Imagine a large, shiny new truck with the word "joy" written in bold letters on both sides. You can fill this truck with everything and anything that brings you joy and happiness, no matter how big, small, elusive, or nonphysical it may be. Now load the truck. As you do so, imagine a lift device that is able to easily put everything in the truck, no matter how ethereal or abstract it may be. Imagine what you want and let it appear.

For instance, I loaded my truck with beautiful fresh flowers, a long and empty seashore, my dogs, angels, my favorite foods, good friends, a few professional comedians, a path through the forest, a snowy day at dusk, my favorite clothes and shoes, books I enjoy, and the people I truly love.

You get the idea. Whatever makes you happy, put it in the truck. There is no space limit and you can always add new things. When you are finished, get in the driver's seat. The truck is comfortable and easy to drive. Drive your truck home. Home may be where you currently live or it may be a new home, the one you have always dreamed of living in. It can be anywhere you want it to be—in the mountains, along the seashore, in the city, or on a quiet country road.

Once you arrive at your destination, unload the truck and fill your home and yard with happiness and joy. If you prefer, you can keep some things in the truck and take them out when you most want to experience them. Just know your joy is in the truck parked at your home. You have the keys and you are in control.

Take a few minutes to breathe, relax, and soak in the joy. Feel it move through your body and circulate through your heart, mind, and soul and emerge through your authentic self.

Use this visualization often. The more you use it, the more joy you will create.

I fill my joy truck.

56. Acting with Courage

Does fear ever hold you back from going forward, trying something new, or changing an aspect of your life? If so, you are not alone. At one time or another, we have all allowed fear to control and limit what we want and what we do.

The biological function of fear is to keep us safe. It is a primal, spontaneous emotion that is meant to warn us when we are in danger. It is neither long-lasting nor an emotion that we are meant to cling to or mentally and emotionally generate at will.

The kind of fear that we live with on a day-to-day basis is habitual and destructive. It does not warn us of real and potential danger or keep us safe from predators. Instead, it distorts our perception of who we are, drains our energy, and affects our health and well-being. Fear is a pretend voice that shouts from a dark corner. When we listen to it and allow it entry into our lives, it suffocates our heart and mind.

Fear holds us back from the natural flow of growth, change, and transformation. We all too often allow it to influence our perception of the future and the outcome of our choices. In the clutch of fear, we imagine all kinds of scenarios of what lies ahead. Fear tells us that we will be hurt, embarrassed, and shamed and suffer some form of loss. Most of the time, what we fear will happen never does. But still we allow it to have power in our everyday decisions and choices. Fear hijacks our imagination and our ability to move forward. It keeps us stuck in a confused and worrisome state. Yet even though it is twisting and manipulating our perception, we believe that we are being smart by listening to it and making choices that keep us safe and secure.

All around you and within you there is an open field of potentiality. It is yours to fill with love and beauty. Don't plant the seeds of fear here. Instead, listen to the quiet voice of your authentic self. You have dreams to live and possibilities to explore. Don't wait for fear to dissipate.

Courage is the ability to do something that frightens you. To feel the dread and anxiety that fear produces and yet go forward, despite your hesitation, is powerful. It strengthens your self-esteem and confidence. When you choose courageous action, fear loses its grip on you.

I do not let fear control me. I act with courage.

57. Fall in Love

Fall in love. Get out of your way and allow powerful waves of love to move through your heart. When we fall in love, we forget ourselves and make room for the "other." When the other whom we fall in love with is someone who loves us in equal measure, our hearts open and meld as one. But the other does not have to be a person. For instance, we can fall in love with a sunset or sunrise, the mist lifting from a mountain lake, a smiling child, a creative project, music, a friend's laughter, a book, or a beloved pet.

When we fall in love with another, the relationship may last a lifetime and grant us the opportunity to grow and mature through the full spectrum and many phases of love and a shared life. But sometimes love lasts just a few months or a few years and ends with disappointment or pain. This kind of love can come into our lives with a surprising ferocity and leave the same way. Even though its purpose in our life is not always clear, the joy and pain of love and loss often stretch our heart open beyond what we thought possible.

When the other is not a person, but an experience of beauty, an awakening, or a mysterious lifting up of our heart in unexpected awareness, the initial surge of love can fade and dissolve as quickly as it arrived. Falling in love is a transitory state and an invitation to more fully experience soulful bliss and joy. Yet the true gift of falling in love should not be measured by its duration. Ultimately it is not how long we are in the initial stage of falling in love but our increased ability to open our heart and give and receive love that is most valuable.

Under the spell of love, we go running into the unknown and unexplored aspects of ourselves. In truth, it does not matter what we fall in love with. It is always ourselves, the depth of our soul, that comes churning to the surface, that captivates us. Our inner true self leaps in recognition and relief at discovering itself in the world, connected to something or someone. The object of our desire is a mirror that reflects our soul's beauty and love. It takes us deeper into who we are and at the same time moves us beyond our limitations.

Fall in love with that which inspires and lifts you out of your self-confinement. Let your heart rise like the tide of the sea. Allow it to surge forward, greet you, and unveil the depth of your being, unguarded and vulnerable. Allow love to transform you and give birth to the little sprouting seeds of your authentic self that have gone unnoticed. Release yourself to love and it will take you by surprise. Look expectantly at the world, as it is going to grace you with your true love.

I allow myself to love.

58. Overcome Doubt

Behind every genius idea, new project, work of art, budding love relationship, and step into the unknown, doubt lurks. Following an aha moment, where the clouds of confusion part and we see with clear awareness, there often comes a time of questioning. Self-doubt can make you feel as if you are inwardly divided and at odds with what you know to be your truth. Your creative, inspired, and intuitively insightful spirit and your cautious, fear-based ego mind seem to be at war with each other.

Doubt traps the authentic self in a small, dark corner. A form of judgment, doubt arises when we expect certain outcomes. For years I wanted to write a book. I had a lot of ideas, but whenever I started to write them down, I doubted my abilities. I would torture myself with questions like *What if I fail? What if I spend months and maybe years writing a book and I cannot get it published? What if no one reads it or likes what I write?*

My expectations were high. If I wrote a book, I wanted it to be published, read, and successful. Doubts plagued me. Lacking the conviction that I could be a successful writer, I turned my attention to other areas. I devoted myself to becoming a better and more accurate intuitive and medium and increasing my clientele. I also worked part-time as an art therapist at a treatment center for troubled youth. It was in this unlikely environment that my fears and anxiety about writing were transformed.

A large part of my work as an art therapist involved creating stories to engage and motivate the students. When they expressed enthusiasm with one of the stories, usually an outrageous and ridiculous one, I quickly wrote it down, hopeful that the next class would also find it as interesting. The more I wrote, the more I relaxed and enjoyed it. My relationship to writing changed, as I no longer felt pressure. Writing, I realized, helped me to feel alive, vibrant, and full of energy. It was a transcendent experience where all of me came together with passion and purpose. The dread of publishers' and others' opinions and my own perfectionist self-judgment began to fade and be less important. Writing no longer felt like a choice. I wrote for my soul. It was the elixir that helped me to feel fully alive.

If doubt immobilizes you, here are a few suggestions.

Take a break and get away from the project or issue that you feel doubtful about. Do something that helps you to feel confident and happy. It doesn't matter what it is. Go for a walk, play your favorite sport, listen to music, watch a good movie, or go to a museum.

Be honest about your expectations. Ask yourself the following questions: *What are my expectations? Are they realistic? Am I expecting too much of myself?*

Be with others who love and encourage you.

Share your feelings with someone you can trust and who is supportive. Be careful not to confide in those who allow their own doubts and a negative perspective to limit them. Learn how to take care of yourself and share your dreams with those who have followed theirs.

Be with those who uplift you and love you for who you are.

Listen within for what is right for you, and trust your intuition.

Spend some time alone. Listen to your heart and your gut. Ask yourself, *If I knew that I would succeed and that everything is possible, what would I do? What is my truth?*

Write down a plan for what you would like to accomplish and experience. Break it down into manageable steps. Give yourself small daily and weekly goals. Celebrate your progress. If you begin to feel doubt, take a time-out. Refocus on what you have accomplished and what your next steps will be.

Give it your all and remember that choosing the safe, sure thing does not necessarily mean that you will be happy, successful, or better off. You cannot control outcomes, but you can choose to participate in what brings you joy and what feels right for you.

I do not let doubt limit me.

59. Take Off the Mask

To know and express your authentic self, it is necessary to take off the false masks. To survive a difficult childhood, fit in with our peers, hide our emotional wounds and vulnerabilities, or be part of a group, we become who and what others want us to be. Over time, we begin to identify with these false masks and we forget who we are. Eventually, these masks begin to feel more like a prison than a coping strategy. When they no longer provide us with the safety and security we seek, we feel trapped by the false.

The feeling of not being true to yourself, the sense that there is something else you are meant to be doing, and feeling an inner void and emptiness are some of the signs that you have lost touch with your authentic self. When you continue to ignore these warning signs and persist in denying your true self, you suffer.

What masks are you hiding behind? Are you ready to let them go? Begin by committing to speaking your truth. Say no when you mean no and yes when you mean yes. Before you accept an invitation or agree to take on a task or responsibility, ask yourself if this is what you really want to be doing. Discover what you enjoy. Take time to investigate dormant talents and abilities by taking classes or trying new activities. Have fun, laugh, and boldly express who you are. Love yourself for the qualities that make you unique and you will find that others will love you to.

When you strip away the false, true intimacy with yourself and others becomes possible. You increase the flow of vital life force energy through your body, mind, and spirit and begin to feel more alive. Masks suppress spontaneity and our capacity to enjoy new opportunities and possibilities. When the mask is off, we can attract and magnetize to us that which speaks to and supports our true nature.

Even though your authentic self may be clouded over or hidden, it will guide you in this process. Take time to listen within. Trust that there is a healthy, wise, and loving inner self that is guiding you into pure joy.

I am complete and whole.

60. Emotional Sensitivity

Have you ever been called oversensitive or hypersensitive? Do you feel deeply and wonder why others are not as affected by negative people or events and upsetting situations as you are? Do you feel others' pain and stress?

If you are an emotionally sensitive person, life can be an emotional obstacle course. Like a strong wind blowing through an open field, the emotional energy of others and your environment can seem to come out of nowhere. You likely feel the emotions of others, even those of people who may not be physically close. It is also likely that you are affected by the emotional energy of traumatic situations or events, both near and at a distance. At times it may seem as if there is little you can do to shield yourself from the onslaught of others' feelings and emotions. You soak them in like a sponge.

Emotionally sensitive people often unknowingly absorb others' emotional energy into their physical body in an unconscious attempt to resolve or heal it. This can lead to physical pain and illness and emotional problems such as anxiety, insomnia, exhaustion, and stress-related afflictions. An emotionally sensitive person is also at risk of becoming so overwhelmed by the energy of others, especially those with whom they are in an intimate relationship, that they lose touch with their own authentic self.

Here are a few more signs of emotional sensitivity:

+ You feel drained, anxious, or exhausted when in crowds.
+ You desire to help and heal others.
+ You know what others need and do your best to try to give it to them, often before they ask.
+ You know what others are feeling, sometimes better than they know themselves.

+ You need time alone to recharge your batteries.
+ Violence in the news, movies, or video games adversely affects you.
+ People come to you with their problems. You are a good listener.
+ You are easily hurt by criticism.
+ You find yourself giving in to others' demands to avoid an argument.
+ You enjoy peaceful and serene environments.
+ You love nature and animals and often volunteer to help in these areas.
+ You require a fair amount of solitude.
+ You seek to know and understand others deeply.
+ You have a difficult time faking emotions.
+ You are always ready to help those who are suffering.

These are just some of the attributes of an emotionally sensitive person. If you believe that they may describe you, it is important to take care of your sensitive and vulnerable nature. Quite often, emotionally sensitive people are misunderstood. We live in a busy, competitive, noisy, and often aggressive and insensitive world. At times you may feel alone in your sensitivities and overwhelmed by your environment. The voice of your true self may seem small and barely audible. Yet you are stronger and have more inner resources than you may realize. Emotional sensitivity can sometimes seem like a curse, but in truth it is a blessing. Your emotional sensitivity is a core aspect of your authentic self and a beneficial strength. But to get the most out of your innate sensitivity, it is essential to take care of yourself.

Self-Care for the Emotionally Sensitive

Your emotional sensitivity may not be a choice, but you can make a choice as to what and whose emotions and feelings you absorb. Instead of feeling the vast array of others' tumultuous emotions and those of your environment, it is possible to shift your emotional receptors to receive the lofty vibrations of pure love. Emotionally sensitive people have direct access to this higher aspect of love. Wherever you are, you can tune in to and absorb positive energy.

Try these steps.

Begin by making a commitment to yourself and informing the universe that you are no longer willing to be an emotional sponge for negative and detrimental emotional energy. As much as you may want to help others to heal or resolve their difficulties, know that feeling their pain does not dissolve it. In fact, it just makes it stronger. Know that you do not have to be an emotional sponge for the free-floating emotional pain, negativity, stress, fear, and anxiety that you may encounter in crowds, while shopping in a store, or even while simply sitting in your home and watching or reading the news.

Become aware of the people in your life whose feelings you are the most susceptible to absorbing. Ask yourself if you take in their emotions in the hope of being closer to them or because you feel that this is the natural way to be in a relationship. Realize that you do not have to be emotionally enmeshed with another to maintain a positive connection. This is not the same as shutting down or not being available to those you love and care for. Instead, you are taking charge of your sensitivity and using it in a more beneficial way.

You likely absorb certain feelings and emotions more than others. For instance, some people are more likely to feel another's emotional pain, while others are more likely to absorb another's fear. We do this because like attracts like. If unresolved fear, sadness, or grief resides within you, you are more likely to feel it in others. Discover your emotional wounds and heal and release them. This will prevent you from unconsciously attracting and absorbing these emotions and feelings in others.

Spend time alone. Listen within to the inner voice of your authentic self. When a feeling or emotion surfaces, ask yourself if this emotion is your own or someone else's. If this is not your emotion, ask yourself what the source of it is and let go of it. Once you identify that the origin of a feeling or emotion is another, it is easy to release it.

If you feel overwhelmed by feelings but you are not able to name them and you feel confused, give yourself time and don't push yourself. Be compassionate and patient. You have likely been emotionally sensitive since childhood, and it may take some time to sort through your emotions and get to the core of your genuine personal feelings.

Have a source of positive energy in your life. Many people find love, peace, and solace in a spiritual practice. Meditation, rituals, and quiet time in nature can provide you with the opportunity to connect with the pure energy of unconditional love. Create a safe place in your home where you can relax, unwind, and come into balance.

Do not feel shame or embarrassment if you need more alone time than others. Be honest about your needs. If you do not want to socialize in large groups or in an environment that feels overwhelming, graciously decline and take care of yourself. Others may not understand you, so it is especially critical for your well-being that you understand and have compassion for yourself. As you do this, you will be able to be more present and available to the people and activities that are most important to you.

I honor and care for my emotional sensitivity.

61. The Inner Mind: Doorway to Change

To delve deep into the authentic self, go beyond your everyday thoughts and understand the power of the unconscious and the subconscious mind. The unconscious and the subconscious mind are closely related and are what I refer to as the inner mind. Our primal instincts, beliefs, buried memories, subjective perceptions, and reality map are stored here. Although we are not normally aware of our unconscious material, it has a powerful effect on our everyday choices, decisions, and experiences. For instance, a long-forgotten childhood trauma can affect our ability to trust others and feel at ease in new situations. A fear of flying may stem from an unconscious fear of not having control.

Psychologists and scientists have theorized that as much as 95 percent of our behavior and decisions stem from what is buried deep in the inner mind. Despite our desire and efforts to change, we will continue to experience the same defeating patterns over and over again until we become aware of these forgotten influences and heal and reprogram them.

There are a few different ways to become more aware of what is contained within the inner mind. One of the most common is through our dreams. A window into what is hidden and unknown, dreams never waste our time. There is always a message for us within them. Although it may be difficult at times to decipher the puzzling symbols in our dreams, there are many good books that can help us interpret and gain insight into their deeper meaning.

Hypnotherapy is another useful tool for lifting the curtain of consciousness. Empowering you to bypass the conscious thinking mind, hypnotherapy allows you entry into the inner mind to resolve and heal past issues and limiting patterns. It can be used to eliminate and change the thoughts and beliefs that are creating detrimental effects and to introduce positive statements that will empower you to manifest what you desire. Through hypnotherapy, you can also become aware of forgotten memories, even past-life memories, and release fears and phobias. During a hypnotherapy session, you have the opportunity to heal your past and create a fulfilling future.

In recent years, nontraditional and innovative therapies and healing modalities have become more widely used to understand the unknown and buried memories, emotions, and beliefs that affect and influence behavior and experiences. Among them is BodyTalk, a holistic system of healing that reveals and heals the communication connection between the body and the unconscious. Various types of energy healing—such as meridian-tapping techniques, which free the body of emotional energy blockages, and Matrix Energetics, a transformational healing technique that uses the principles of quantum physics—have also become more popular.

Accessing the deeper unconscious enables your authentic self to freely emerge and express your goodness and joy.

*I am willing to explore my subconscious mind
to discover more about my authentic self.*

62. Use Affirmations

Your emotions and thoughts are powerful. Do you know in your heart what is real and true for you? Does your life reflect this? Do you feel that you are able to express the true you? As you become aware of your authentic self, you may at times find that your day-to-day life is not always conveying your inner truth.

You can break free from the grip of continually attracting and manifesting what you do not want and create experiences that are better aligned with your truth. One of the most effective ways to create and manifest your core truth is through the consistent use of affirmations.

An affirmation is a short and concise positive statement that, when repeatedly spoken or written, attracts and creates the conditions and experiences that you most desire. Replacing self-defeating thoughts and beliefs through the use of affirmations empowers you to manifest your authentic self.

For an affirmation to be effective, here are a few basic guidelines.

Create a short "I" statement that directly expresses the truth that you want to manifest in your day-to-day life.

Always express this statement in a positive way.

Make sure the statement is in present time.

Use one statement at a time.

Repeat or write down your affirmation seven times, seven times a day, for seven, fourteen, or twenty-one days. This is my personal formula that has worked quite well for me. Seven is a powerful number that reinforces and connects you to your highest potential.

When you speak or write an affirmation, visualize an image of yourself manifesting and experiencing what you desire. Feel the positive emotions and feelings associated with this image. Open your heart and surround your affirmation with love.

Keep in mind that negative thinking neutralizes the effect of an affirmation. If you find yourself complaining or becoming negative, repeat the affirmation seven times.

When you begin to use an affirmation, it is not uncommon for thoughts to surface that are in opposition to what you are affirming. This means that the affirmation is working. As the new thoughts are accepted, the beliefs and old patterns of thinking that oppose the affirmation will surface. When they do, make the choice to no longer accept them as your reality.

Eventually the statement will sink deep into the inner mind and you will automatically begin to experience the affirmation.

At the end of every entry in this book, there is an affirmation. Here are a few more. You can use these or create your own.

I manifest opportunities to fully live my purpose.

I confidently express my authentic self.

I attract a loving, emotionally and spiritually mature partner.

I receive financial abundance.

I am healthy and full of energy.

> *I use affirmations to attract opportunities*
> *and experiences that express my authentic self.*

63. Depression and the Authentic Self

Depression is a dark cloud of energy that feeds off the soul. It is a hungry destroyer of the light and has no essential purpose in this world but to feed and survive. Unlike the emotions of sadness, grief, heartache, or despair, which allow for the presence of other emotional states and feelings, depression is a hungry ghost that consumes all other emotions and quietly seeps into every aspect of an individual's being and takes control. Depression is a psychological, mental, emotional, physical, and spiritual cancer that usually creeps in without notice.

Depression begins with the small dismissals of our personal truth. It often takes root in a childhood where truth was replaced by manufactured smiles and compliancy. When a child's feelings, emotions, and thoughts are ignored or ridiculed, the authentic self is numbed into silence and nonexistence. Gradually and throughout life, this denial of the true self only intensifies. As we are socialized to live according to outer expectations and be who others want us to be, layers and layers of the false dim our inner light. We compromise, ignore, and suppress who we are and what we feel. This creates an energetic vacuum that allows the energy of depression to settle deep into our heart, our bones, and our soul. Without the light of our truth and the power of our spirit, we are vulnerable and defenseless. We become immobilized, and with severe depression, we can no longer find our inner light. We cannot hear the voice of our soul, and we live within the prison of darkness.

Signs of Depression

True depression is more than feeling down and sad. Feeling the highs and lows that come with life is natural and normal. Depression is a lack of feeling and a deadening of the spirit. If you experience several of the following signs and symptoms that do not go away, you are likely depressed:

+ Changes in sleep; sleeping either too much or too little
+ Experience exhaustion, fatigue, and loss of energy
+ Feelings of worthlessness and self-loathing
+ Experience physical aches and pains
+ Feel hopeless and helpless
+ Unable to control negative thoughts, no matter how much you try
+ Inability to concentrate and difficulty performing simple tasks
+ Loss of appetite or continuous eating
+ Feeling irritable, aggressive, and short-tempered
+ Engaging in reckless behavior, consuming excessive amounts of alcohol, or illegal drug use
+ Thoughts of suicide; life is painful and you will do anything to stop the pain.

Reclaiming Your Light

If you struggle with depression, you cannot ignore it and hope it will go away. Although depression may intensify or subside, if it is lying dormant within you, it will surface. Know that the true you is buried deep within and you must do everything you can to activate its presence and power. Everyone experiences depression a bit differently, and your path out of depression will also be unique to you. Here are some strategies.

Talk to someone. As difficult as it might be to acknowledge that you need help, reaching out to another begins the healing process. Start with someone you are comfortable with. This may be someone in your family or a friend. Be honest and express what you are experiencing. Depression loves isolation, and once you begin to share what you are feeling, you invite new energy into your life.

Seek out professional healers. You are in need of healing. A part of you will resist getting help. This is the depression talking; your mind, body, and emotions are being held hostage. Do not give in to this thought. A good medical doctor, psychiatrist, psychologist, counselor, or therapist can make a significant difference. In addition, consider seeking the assistance of credible energy healers. Depression is a dark and negative energetic vampire that is feeding off your energy. It is essential to open and clear your subtle energy body and remove any negative attachments. Depression can make you vulnerable to attracting other negative thought forms. Find a healer who can detach these energies, clear your subtle energy body, and strengthen your aura. This may be an energy healer, a Reiki practitioner, a shaman, or someone who works with the angelic realm. Get a referral from someone you trust. If a healing practitioner tells you that they can heal you for an astronomical amount of money, find someone else. A true healer will charge a reasonable fee for their services.

Create the conditions for a breakthrough. It is essential that you create a way for your authentic self to emerge. Inner and outer movement will stimulate and allow healing life force energy into your mind, body, and spirit. Take some form of action.

Do yoga, get a massage, or sit in a hot tub, sauna, or steam room. Get outdoors and walk, run, bike, or do any other physical activity. The sun, wind, moon, stars, trees, and flowers all emit source energy. If you cannot exercise, then sit outdoors, close your eyes, and breathe in the natural world. Create art or go to the movies, to a play, or to a live concert. Hit a mattress with a tennis racket. Sit in front of a fire. Yell, scream, climb a tree, or plant a garden.

Eat healthy and drink clean water. Natural whole foods contain vital life source energy. The energy of the earth and the sun are absorbed within and will revitalize you at a cellular level.

Help others. We tend to open our hearts and give more to others than we are willing to give to ourselves. Get the love within flowing outward. Volunteer at a homeless shelter, soup kitchen, or any environment where others are in need. Talk to others, look in their eyes, and listen to their struggles. Feel your heart open and give. It can also be helpful to work in an animal shelter or with rescue animals. Be sure to do this with others or with a group. Remember, depression loves isolation. Absorb the energy of those who freely give their love, time, and attention. Be this kind of person. As you give, you receive. Sharing your unique talents and love dispels depression. It cannot exist in someone who is in their truth and whose light shines.

Know who you are. Listen within, meditate, and make a commitment to live in a way that is true to you. Whatever it is that makes you uniquely you, do it. It does not matter what others think, what you have been told about you, or the past roles that you have played. Get rid of the false. Live only in your truth and keep digging deep inside and expressing who you are, no matter what anyone else says or thinks. Be the authentic you.

You can heal. There is nothing outside of you that is more powerful than what is within you. Although depression is challenging and can feel overwhelming, the universe and your own soul flow in the direction of goodness and love.

I seek help with depression.

64. Absolute and Relative Truth

Our thoughts change and evolve. What you believe today may only be temporary. A new thought or insight may soon emerge and become your truth. It is not being false or indecisive to change your mind, your opinions and beliefs. Knowing the difference between absolute and relative truth will help you to better appreciate the continual reshaping of your truth into new awareness and perceptions.

Most of what we know as our true thoughts and beliefs is relative. They are likely to change and do not describe the ultimate and eternal truth.

For instance, I grew up believing that I had to work hard to receive any degree of success and security in life. This was the truth that I acted on. After working hard for many years, my beliefs began to change. I realized that hard work alone does not always guarantee success and abundance. As I learned more about metaphysics and my understanding of the laws of the universe increased, I began to perceive things differently. I challenged my beliefs and feelings and became aware that the universe flows in the direction of positivity and abundance. I realized that I could flow within this current and not against it. My old truth and belief was replaced with the truth that abundance is natural and I can receive it with ease.

Unlike relative truth, absolute truth is eternal and never-changing, as it lies beyond our thinking mind. We may be intellectually able to understand absolute truth, but the full experience of knowing ourselves and all of life in this way is rare. However, in moments of illumination and intuitive insight, we can catch a glimpse of our eternal self and feel our soul power and potential.

Whatever your truth may be in this moment, accept it and live it. Do not be shy about claiming your beliefs and thoughts. What is true for you today is an essential stepping stone on the road to reaching your highest potential. Your truth cannot just be known. It must be embodied and integrated into every area of your life. Speak your truth and share it with others. Act on it and be aware of new insights and awareness that continue to unfold. Most of our truth is transitory and fleeting, but do not devalue it for this reason. Be true to yourself today and be willing to peel these layers off when your thoughts and beliefs no longer support and best express the authentic you.

I claim my truth.

65. You Are Love

Just as there is relative and absolute truth, there is relative and absolute love. The kind of love that we desire from another is absolute love. This love is divine, all-forgiving, compassionate, and healing. Yet the kind of love that we usually experience in our relationships is personality-based, or relative love. Relative love is experienced through the lens of our beliefs, emotions, judgments, biases, and experiences. We generally experience relative love in our relationships, and it can be clouded by fear, defensiveness, jealousy, and need.

Love in its absolute form is divine life force energy. It is at the authentic core self of every living being and is an electrifying energy. It unifies and speaks to us of our oneness with all of life. To penetrate into the presence of this pure form of love, peel away the layers of false love and allow the light of absolute love to emerge.

Through acknowledging and letting go of our less-than-attractive emotions such as jealousy and fear, we ascend into the higher vibrations of love. Listen to your feelings and emotions and do not judge them or yourself as good or bad. Be a curious observer and allow your emotions to move through you. As you do this, you will begin to experience their transitory nature. They come and go and they intensify and subside. Feel all of your emotions, even those that are difficult and distressing. Do not blame others for your less-than-positive feelings. Own them and realize that they are messengers that have come to tell you more about yourself. If you frequently experience feelings such as anger, sadness, fear, anxiety, stress, or depression, ask yourself what you need to pay attention to and listen within.

Meditate on the purest energy of love within you. Close your eyes and imagine your heart opening and unfolding like the petals of a rose. Continue to breathe and exhale any stress and tension. As you do this, imagine your heart opening and, from its center, absolute love pouring through you. Keep breathing and allowing pure love to move through your body, mind, and spirit. Rest and absorb this love.

Become comfortable with experiencing love in its many different forms. Feel the power and presence of absolute love deep within you, ever ready to emerge. As you come to know yourself as love, you attract this kind of absolute love from others.

I feel my emotions and they lead me to the core of absolute love.

Chapter 5

THE INTUITIVE YOU

There are many ways to know who we are. Our thoughts, feelings, beliefs, and experiences reveal the multifaceted aspects of our nature, yet some part of us still remains hidden. It is through our natural intuition—the surprising insights, gut feelings, and the quiet inner voice—that we connect with our more soulful self. This chapter encourages you to listen, feel, and trust your intuitive inner self.

66. The Quiet Truth

During my long career as a professional psychic and medium, the authenticity of psychic ability and mediumship has been debated and denied by some and accepted and relished by others. When I first started giving readings in the southeastern part of the country, there were still laws that made clairvoyance a crime. Although psychics and mediums are now more mainstream, there are still many people who view the ability to access nonphysical energy information as delusional, an impossibility, and possibly a scam practiced by con artists. Yet there is also much more acceptance of intuitive and psychic ability than ever before.

Whatever your personal views and beliefs about the validity of intuition may be, you are intuitive. You may not care to be or you may have a particular idea of what it means to be intuitive that does not fit in with your experiences. Either way, it is as much a part of you as your other senses. Intuition is not something that you can acquire or obtain. It is a core aspect of who you are. It is the living and communicative nature of your mind, body, and spirit.

Your intuition is the voice of your authentic self. It communicates your innermost truth and cannot be manipulated or influenced. It will let you know through feelings of expansiveness and joy when you are in alignment with your inner truth. It will also send you intuitive messages letting you know when you are going against it. For instance, in a relationship you may disregard your own needs in favor of your partner's. With a desire to maintain relationship harmony, you may continually compromise your true thoughts and feelings and over time lose your sense of self. However, as much you may deny the negative effects that overcompromising is having on your self-esteem and self-worth, your intuition will not be quieted so easily. Persistent gut feelings, unsettling dreams, or a quiet inner voice will likely alert you as to when you are not being true to yourself.

We often argue against the truth of our intuitive insights. The conflict between our intuitive knowing and our human reasoning can create confusion as to what part of ourselves to listen to. Much of the time, human logic and reasoning is louder and gets our attention more easily. Because of this, it usually wins out over the more subdued intuitive signals. Yet when we do listen to our intuition and act on what we receive, we never regret it. Even though your intuition may seem elusive and difficult to trust, it always works for your highest good.

I trust the power of the quiet inner truth.

67. Intuitively Attuned

As you peel off the layers of the false self, you become more intuitively sensitive. The thoughts, feelings, and beliefs of others may begin to affect you without your knowledge. Have you ever walked into a crowded room and felt a wave of sadness come over you? Has a friend ever left you a voicemail message and simply by looking at their number on your phone, you know what they want to talk about? Have you ever been caught up in another's enthusiasm and done something against your better judgment? These and other similar types of experiences are usually spontaneous intuitive insights. Although we all intuitively absorb the energy of others, some people are more likely to intuitively pick up on the thought and emotional energy of others and the environment.

Intuitively attuned people are often unaware of the full extent of their intuitive receptivity. Although being intuitively attuned can be empowering, helpful, and enlightening, it can also cause emotional, mental, and even physical confusion and distress and keep you from discerning and knowing your authentic self. When you are not aware of the source of the thoughts, feelings, premonitions, and sensations that you unknowingly absorb from external influences, you can experience and act on them as if they are your own.

For instance, imagine that miles away a family member is struggling with financial problems. You wake up at night feeling anxious and stressed about your finances, even though there is no reason to be. You toss and turn, unaware that you are intuitively receiving the emotional stress of a loved one. Not only do we absorb others' thoughts and feelings, but we can also experience their physical aches and pains as our own. For instance, let's say your office coworker struggles with arthritis. Even though she takes medication, she still feels tightness and pain in her joints while at work. Although she does not complain, you feel empathy for her condition, so much so that you, too, begin to experience joint pain and stiffness in the same areas where she is afflicted.

Here are some other types of phenomena that you may experience as you become more intuitively attuned.

Feel and See Spirit Presence

Do you ever see orbs, a glow of energy around another, or streaks of light? Do you ever feel that you are not alone? Have you ever felt a touch on your shoulder or hand, a warm embrace, or waves of coolness or warmth? These are often signs that you are in the presence of a loving spirit. Trust your intuition. If you feel as if a family member, angel, or spirit presence is with you offering love and support, try not to get caught up in doubt and question yourself. Feel the presence and listen and tune in to any messages you may receive.

Have Premonitions of Personal and Global Events

Have you ever felt feelings of fear, stress, or grief and a day or so later a natural disaster or large-scale tragedy occurred? Intuitively attuned people are precognitive. You may not always know what, when, and where an event will take place, but you may feel and know that something is off or is going to happen. Quite often, the emergence of sudden and intense emotions only makes sense several days later when a positive or tragic event takes place.

Intuit Through Your Dreams

Oftentimes your intuition will first surface through your dreams. Because dreams are usually metaphoric and symbolic in nature, it is not always clear when a dream contains intuitive insight. If you suspect that you are having dreams that foretell future events or provide you with previously unknown information about others or events, write them down. Keep a journal of your dreams and be alert to events and experiences that confirm its contents.

Heightened Awareness with All Five Senses
Bright lights, noise, smells, and even tactile sensations can be irritating and overstimulating. Artificial lighting might give you a headache. While others might enjoy the scent of a fragrance or perfume, you may feel overwhelmed and lightheaded or dizzy from it. You become anxious at the sound of constant or loud noise. You need periods of silence and quiet to relax and unwind. You prefer wearing all cotton or other natural fibers. Polyester and other synthetic fiber clothing can cause you to itch, scratch, or break out.

Sensitive to Others' Needs
You know when others are in pain, sad, depressed, or struggling and what will help them. You are often drawn to those who are in need and have a knack for saying exactly what they need to hear. You are caring, warmhearted, and sensitive to the needs of others. Oftentimes you would rather suffer than see those around you in pain.

Feel Tired and Exhausted and May Have Trouble Sleeping
Sometimes it all becomes too much. You may feel overwhelmed by this chaotic, overstimulating, and demanding world, but you do not always know how to take care of yourself. When you should be resting and recharging during sleep, you may instead feel restless and toss and turn. If you are an open intuitive receptacle, others' thoughts and feelings may pour in while you sleep. In an effort to shut out the demands of others and decrease your sensitivity to your environment, you may try to shut down and cut yourself off from your innate sensitivities. Unfortunately, this may only increase your feelings of exhaustion and inner stress.

Have Spiritual Depth

You may not be religious or follow a particular spiritual path, yet you have a sense of knowing and a connection to a greater force of love and wisdom. While others may discuss and theorize about the existence of God or a spiritual force, you may not always want to join in. Your sense of spirituality is lived and experienced. You are likely to notice opportunities to act in kind and loving ways toward others. You give more than you ask for and expect from others. In your heart and soul, you know that your life has purpose. You may not always know what it is, but you know that you are here to be of service to others and the world.

If you are intuitively attuned, it is important to acknowledge, accept, and learn how to use this innate gift for your highest good. Instead of being intuitively bombarded by the energy of others and the environment, you can use your intuitive sensitivity to be a light of insight and service to others.

I understand my intuitive sensitivity.

68. Care for the Intuitively Attuned

If you suspect that you are intuitively attuned, you probably are. You do not have to receive clear intuitive messages or even know when you are receiving energy information to be naturally intuitive. Instead, you might experience feelings and sensations or instantaneously know something and not know what it means or why you are experiencing it. There may be a vague murkiness and fuzziness about what you are feeling and sensing, without any further understanding or meaning behind it. This tendency to feel odd sensations, to sense and know things, may just seem to be one of your quirks, and you may not give it too much thought. Or you might be highly motivated to better understand your intuitive sensitivity and further develop and use it for yourself and others. Either way, the more you know about how to tune in to and work with your intuitive sensitivity, the better able you will be to make choices and steer your intuition in the desired direction.

Here are a few suggestions that will help you navigate the often confusing intuitive landscape.

Accept Your Intuitive Nature as a Natural Gift
You receive intuitive information because you can. If you go outdoors on a sunny day, you will feel the sun's warm rays. Energy information is all around us, all the time. There are times when you will be more intuitively aware than at others. There are many factors that will affect your intuitive receptivity from one day to the next.

Keep Track of the Intuitive Information You Receive
It can be helpful to keep a journal of or record your intuitive impressions. In time you will notice patterns as to when and how you are

picking up information. It will also become easier to discern and interpret what you are receiving.

Observe and Be Patient

Approach intuitive insights and occurrences with curiosity and detached interest. Sit with whatever you receive, and allow its significance to unfold and become clearer. You do not have to rush to interpret or understand it. Many sensations, feelings, moments of inner knowing, and dreams become clearer with time. If you feel that you receive intuitive messages or information about another, you do not have to tell them or get verification. Be patient with the process and let yourself be led.

Maintain Good Boundaries

If you are intuitively sensitive, you need to create and reinforce intuitive boundaries so as not to be bombarded with intuitive energy. The good news is that this can be done quickly, easily, and effectively.

Begin by stating an intent either aloud or within, something like *I intuitively receive only loving and positive emotions or thoughts.* Or *I intuitively receive only those emotions and thoughts that are in my highest good.* Repeat this intent several times. As you do this, visualize in your mind's eye white light energy completely surrounding you like a cocoon. Imagine this white light as a web of translucent energy that shields you from negative, confusing, or unwanted energy.

Spend Time Alone

Release and let go of intuitive energy that you have absorbed from others. It can be helpful to get away from the chaos, noise, and demands of the world. Have quiet time to yourself where you can clear your mind and recharge your batteries. Close your eyes and draw your awareness through your body from the top of the head to your feet.

Breathe, relax, and make the intent to let go of and release any energy that you have picked up from others or from your environment.

If you can, spend time outdoors or in nature. The natural elements—the sun, trees, sky, and water—can help you to release unwanted energy that you may have absorbed from others. Breathe and relax.

Attract Positive Energy

You are more likely to attract and receive intuitive information to which you have a personal connection. If you harbor old resentments, emotional pain, or fears, you will likely intuitively attract this same energy from others. Do what you need to do to release and heal unproductive and painful emotions. Limit the amount of time you spend with negative people or in situations that promote stress and anxiety. You might also want to avoid violence on television, in video games, or in the news.

Notice the positive in yourself and others. Be with people who support the authentic you and allow you to be yourself. The more you love yourself and express love and gratitude to others, the more you will intuitively attract positive energy.

I accept and care for my intuitive nature.

69. Your Intuitive Type

The process of coming into the full awareness of your authentic self takes time. As your beliefs, thoughts, emotions, feelings, and attitudes are embraced, examined, shed, and released, you become better able to identify and claim your true self. Becoming aware of your authentic self and expressing it in the world is an intuitive process. Listening within and trusting your innermost self moves you beyond reliance on the outer world. Your innate intuition empowers you to connect with the depth and vast territory of your authentic self. It is your intuition that lets you know when you violate your inner truth and when you are in alignment with it.

Everyone is intuitive. Your intuition is as much a part of you as your thoughts and emotions, your physical body, and your other five senses. Intuition is the gut feeling that you experience when making decisions, the dream that inspires you, the sudden awareness of a solution to a problem, and the sense that you are not alone. Connected to the most real part of who you are, you can trust your intuition to direct you to your highest good.

To better harness the power of your intuition to discern and live your truth, become aware of how your intuition naturally emerges. We make many assumptions about what intuition is and what it is not. Some people feel that to be intuitive it is necessary to see visions, communicate with those on the other side, or know the lottery numbers and be able to accurately predict the future. Intuition is much less glamorous and more subtle than that. It is the quiet, persistent voice, a gut feeling, and the nagging sense that something is just not right.

Intuition surfaces through four primary modalities or types. You may naturally intuit energy information through your thoughts, your feelings, your physical body, or your energy field. An emotional intuitive receives energy information through their emotions and feelings.

A mental intuitive intuits through their thoughts, while a physical intuitive absorbs energy information into the body. A spiritual intuitive receives energy information through their aura or energy field. You are likely a combination of two or more of these types.

Once you know the way that you are already intuiting information, it becomes easier to recognize when your intuition is communicating to you and how to better utilize it. Knowing your intuitive type provides you with energy information about others and your environment. It also provides you with insight into the vast depth and mystery of who you are and is the voice of your innermost soul and spirit.

In my book *Discover Your Psychic Type*, I discuss the four intuitive types in further detail.

I pay attention to the way my intuition naturally surfaces.

70. The Intuitive Heart

Have you ever tried a new activity, heard a new song, or imagined yourself in a different career and felt a spontaneous opening of your heart? If you intuit primarily through your emotions, you are likely empathic and heart-centered. When your words or actions violate your true self, you may feel frustration, guilt, and disappointment with yourself. However, when you act on and speak from your core self, your heart opens and you likely experience feelings of elation, love, and happiness.

By paying attention to what uplifts you, opens your heart, and fills you with love, you will be guided to what is real and true for you. In the same way, if something closes your heart and produces fear and stress, it is a warning sign that you are not in sync with your authentic self.

To use their intuition effectively, it is important for an emotional intuitive to become aware of past wounds and repressed emotional energy. Stuffing away difficult emotions and unresolved emotional pain is like the static on a phone line that prevents clear reception. It makes it more difficult to receive clear intuitive messages. Uncovering and healing past emotional issues and forgiving oneself and others expands and strengthens the heart's intuitive receptivity.

On a daily basis, emotional intuitives tend to feel and experience a wide range of emotions. Being able to distinguish externally intuited emotions from personal and authentic feelings and emotions may be a constant challenge.

The following short meditation will empower you to better tune in to and listen to your heart. The heart is a doorway through which your true self speaks to you.

Find a quiet place and begin to take cleansing breaths—long, deep inhales and relaxing exhales. As you breathe, imagine that your heart opens like a flower, petal by petal. Continue to breathe and open your heart. Allow any feelings and emotions to surface and breathe into them. Release them and continue to breathe. When you feel a sense of quiet inner peace, draw your attention inward and listen. Remain open and attentive.

Inhale and say to yourself, *Love is within me.*

Exhale and say to yourself, *I feel the love that is within me.*

Pause and allow any emotions, feelings, or thoughts to surface. Accept all that emerges. Listen and fully receive it all.

Feel love opening you to a new level of self-awareness. Pay attention to whatever surfaces. Continue to breathe and listen.

When you feel as if you have received all that you can at this time, open your eyes.

If you are an emotional intuitive, focusing your meditation on the essence of love will reveal your innermost truth.

I listen in quiet contemplation to my heart.

71. Self-Care for the Empath

As your self-awareness increases and you live and act from the core of your authentic self, your openness, insight, and sensitivity to the emotions and feelings of others also increase. These feelings of expansion and compassion for self and others often activate empathic abilities.

An empath is an individual who, knowingly or unknowingly, is able to tune in to another's feelings and emotions. Empaths tend to absorb the emotional energy of others. This can cause confusion, a feeling of being out of balance, and can even affect physical health. When we are unaware that we are feeling another's emotions as our own, we lose touch with our own authentic feelings.

Empaths tend to be sensitive souls who are able to perceive the good in others and their positive potential. Nonjudgmental by nature, they accept others for who they are and do their best to support and help those who need it. They go through life openhearted yet vulnerable. Unfortunately, it is for this reason that they are often taken advantage of.

Although empaths are correct when they sense and feel the positive potential and goodness in others, they often disregard the unfortunate truth that there are those who would seek to take advantage of and deceive them. Because empaths tap into the core love and beauty of others and desire to be of service, they can be easy to fool and manipulate.

For instance, Anna is a sensitive empath who would like to be in a long-term relationship. Looking forward to meeting someone she could build a life with, she was intrigued by a gregarious man she met at a company picnic. Underneath his outward confidence and sense of humor, Anna sensed Jed's vulnerability and felt that he, too, knew what it felt like to be alone.

What Jed perceived within Anna was quite different. Glancing at the buffet table, he saw a shy and attractive woman with kind eyes. He inched his way into line behind her and started up a conversation. It was easy to get her laughing, and he knew that if he played into her gentle warmheartedness, he would have her hooked by the time their plates were full.

What Anna did not know was that Jed had no desire to enter into a relationship. She was correct that, despite Jed's look of confidence, his self-esteem was suffering. Yet what she did not know was that he had recently been rebuffed by a woman he had asked out. He was just looking for someone to boost his ego and remind him just how attractive and charming he was. As he talked to Anna, he was already feeling better. Her attention and kindness were just what he needed. She was the kind of girl he knew he could fall back on when his dating conquests and adventures fell flat. He knew how to gain her sympathies and trigger her caring and concern for him.

If you are an empath, it is important to understand and care for your warmhearted emotional and intuitive gifts. Here are a few suggestions.

Pay attention to others' actions, not just their words. Do others follow through with action on what they say and profess? Your intuition may be spot on as to their deeper inner self, yet if they choose not to relate to you with honesty and integrity, your kindness will be taken advantage of.

Remember that you, too, have needs. Make sure that those you invite into your life pay attention to your preferences and needs and reciprocate your kindness and support.

Do not make excuses for another's behavior. Don't blame their childhood, boss, past relationships, or circumstances for their attitude, choices, or actions and certainly not for how they treat you.

Be very careful when you begin to feel sorry for someone. Stop in your tracks, take a deep breath, and remind yourself that we all have ups and downs in life. Ask yourself if your sympathies are making it easier for another to not take charge of their life or treat you with the love and respect that you deserve.

Talk things through with someone you trust and who can give you an unbiased sense of what you might not be seeing in your connection with another. When you are confused, uneasy, or unsure of someone else's intentions, get a second opinion. Trust your intuition when you feel that something is not adding up. Know that while your empathic abilities make you sensitive to others' emotions and potential, you might be unaware of their ego-based motives.

Accept that not everyone chooses to act on their potential and innate goodness. You cannot make anyone do this. No amount of love will change someone's mind if they only want to take advantage of you.

Help and support those who are doing all they can to heal and become whole. Give to others in equal measure to the amount of effort and resources that they are willing to expend on themselves. Healing is always an inside job, without exception.

As an empath, you will want to reach out to those who are suffering and in need. Yet you must make self-care a priority. Don't give away your power to take care of yourself. This is not selfish. It is necessary to keep your light shining brightly.

I value my empathic abilities.

72. Your Intuitive Truth

Do you sometimes know something without knowing how you know it? Do you have an abundance of new and stimulating ideas? If you intuit primarily through mental thought energy, you are a mental intuitive. Not only are you able to intuit others' thoughts, but you are also attuned to the energy vibrations of truth.

A mental intuitive knows what is true and real for themselves through an inner sense of knowing. When a mental intuitive is not in sync with their authentic self, they have the persistent awareness that something is off and just not right. However, they often talk themselves out of trusting their intuition. An emotional intuitive will violate their inner truth to fit in and be loved. A mental intuitive can argue against their intuitive knowing if it does not fit in with their logical reasoning. Reality is pliable and changeable for a mental intuitive, and they can become confused and overwhelmed by their own reasoning and rationalization. The key to connecting to their personal core truth is to trust their nonlogical intuitive knowing more and their analytical thinking less. A mental intuitive can also become an open channel for collective thought energy. Their mind is often full of conflicting and overwhelming intuited and self-generated thoughts.

If you are a mental intuitive, it is necessary to cultivate the ability to differentiate between mind chatter and intuitive messages. In this way, you can learn how to better tune in to your intuition with as much clarity as possible. It can take practice and consistent awareness to clear the mind.

The following meditative exercise will empower you to better identify and intuit your inner core truth.

Begin by becoming comfortable and closing your eyes. Inhale long, deep, relaxing breaths and exhale any stress and tension. Continue to breathe and relax. When you feel an inner sense of calm, invoke the wisdom of your authentic self with an open-ended question, such as *What is in my highest good? What is my truth?* or *Who am I?*

Use one phrase at a time and repeat it as you continue to breathe and relax. Listen within as you repeat the statement. Mental intuitives often receive intuition through an inner voice and sense of knowing. Listen and trust what you receive, without overthinking, analyzing, or arguing against your impressions. The intuitive voice will be persistent and steady and may seem almost obvious. Continue to breathe and listen.

When you have received all the information that you can at this time, open your eyes and write down your intuitive impressions.

In time, you will better trust your intuitive sense of knowing. Your ability to discern your truth will become natural and automatic.

I listen to the intuitive voice of my authentic self.

73. Your Intuitive Body

Do shivers of energy running up your spine act for you as an intuitive antenna? Do the hairs on your arms stand up when you feel a connection to something or someone? Do you experience your intuition as a gut feeling? If so, you may be a physical intuitive. A physical intuitive's body is their intuitive energy conduit. They experience intuition as a feeling or sensation in their gut, tingles of energy that move up and down the spine, and feelings of power or uneasiness in their solar plexus.

A physical intuitive has a special connection to the physical world. They are attuned to nature, animals, plants, and all natural life forms. They tend not to be overly mystical or dreamy. Instead they have a down-to-earth and practical approach to life. Because of their straightforward nature, they are not always aware of their inner intuitive functioning. Their truth is easily stated and not complex. They are more the "what you see is what you get" kind of people. One of their challenges is to explore their multidimensional nature. By listening to their intuition, they can access the deeper recesses of their authentic self.

Because of their innate connection to the physical world, a physical intuitive can benefit from physical activity and being in nature. Walking, running, swimming, dancing, yoga, or a similar kind of activity can help to promote a meditative state. This calms the mind, releases stress in the body, and allows repressed emotions, beliefs, and thoughts to surface and be released.

Meditative walking can be especially helpful in stimulating intuitive insight. If you are a physical intuitive, try the following meditative exercise.

A path in nature or a park can be the most conducive for intuiting. However, you can also try walking through a neighborhood or a more densely populated area. Walk alone at a moderate pace. Breathe in long, deep breaths and exhale any stress and tension. Pay attention to your breath. Listen to the sounds of your environment. Take in the colors and scenery.

Listen within. Notice the thoughts and feelings that surface without over-focusing on them. Continue to bring your attention to your breath, and tune in to the external environment and your inner self.

When you feel calm and relaxed, scan your body. Where in your body do you feel stress, tension, or tightness? Breathe into the tension and release it as you exhale. Imagine that the tight and tense areas can communicate with you. What are they saying? Take your time and listen.

Where in your body do you feel relaxed, open, and expansive? Breathe into these areas and allow the feelings of relaxation to spread throughout your entire body. Imagine that the relaxed parts of your body can also communicate with you. What are they saying?

Your body may communicate to you through feelings, through a sense of knowing, or through sensations of openness and expansion and feelings of freedom and power. Keep tuning in to your body's wisdom. Trust the information you receive.

For a physical intuitive, the body is the center of self and will impart wisdom and direction for authentic living.

I listen to the intuitive wisdom of my body.

74. Centered in Your Spirit

Do your dreams ever reveal surprising intuitive information? Do you ever see orbs, streaks of light, or color in the air or surrounding others? Have you ever felt as if an angel or spirit is guiding you? Spiritual intuitives intuit through the energy field, or aura, which is an electromagnetic orb of energy that completely surrounds the body. The aura of spiritual intuitives is a cosmic intuitive receiver that enables them to receive energy information through dreams, through communication with spirit beings, and through spontaneous insight and visual images.

A spiritual intuitive is usually comfortable with the elusive, intangible, and mystical. Some spiritual intuitives are religious and adhere to their faith's principles, while others have a more eclectic and nonreligious spiritual orientation. Either way, most spiritual intuitives view their soul and spirit as the center of their authentic self.

Unlike the emotional intuitive, who tunes in to their heart center; the mental intuitive, who hears the still, small voice of truth within; or the physical intuitive, who intuits truth through the physical body, the spiritual intuitive's true self is perceived as essence. Their means of intuiting can be more elusive and mystical than that of the other types.

Many spiritual intuitives feel as if they do not fit in with the status quo, and some feel odd and unusual. With a need for more freedom and independence than the other types, they often have difficulty finding their place in the world. A spiritual intuitive needs to know that there is meaning and purpose to their lives. Without this, their true self may remain dormant and unexpressed.

Spiritual intuitives tend to intuit through inner sight, commonly called clairvoyance. In the following meditative exercise, use your imagination to create images to help you to better receive intuitive guidance.

Close your eyes. Inhale long, deep breaths and exhale any stress and tension. Continue to breathe and relax. When you feel an inner calm, imagine breathing vital life force energy down through the top of the head. Send this breath through the body and exhale. Breathe another breath down through the top of the head, move it through the body, and imagine exhaling it through the heart. Breathe in this manner a few more times. As you do this, imagine that an orb of vital life force energy surrounds you. Continue to breathe in this way. With each exhale, imagine that the orb surrounding you becomes stronger. You are safe and comfortable within this cocoon of energy. Allow your spirit to expand into this orb. Continue to breathe, and imagine that you can move outside of the confines of the physical body and fill the orb with your spirit and essence.

Ask yourself one of the following questions or create your own.

- *What is my purpose?*
- *What is my truth?*
- *What gives my life meaning?*

Repeat the question, then pause and listen. As you do this, pay attention to your feelings, thoughts, and sensations and allow any images to emerge. Keep inwardly repeating one of the questions and paying attention to whatever surfaces. Use your imagination to give form and color to what you are intuiting.

Continue breathing, relaxing, and listening. Trust what you receive and take your time interpreting it. It may take several days or weeks to fully understand the images that you receive.

When you have received all the information that you can at this time, open your eyes and write down your intuitive impressions and images.

For a spiritual intuitive, finding purpose and expressing their authentic self provides them with a sense of connection to others and inner peace.

I tune in to the images that I perceive with my inner sight.

75. Listen and Act

It is not always easy to live authentically and act on our personal truth. Too often we take the path of least resistance and become complacent, conform, and do what is expected. Yet sometimes an intuitive revelation that something in our life or within ourselves needs to change or transform is so strong that we are motivated to step out of our comfort zone.

For instance, you may become increasingly aware that there is something else in life that you are meant to be doing other than your current job. Your intuition may nudge you that it is time to sell your home and move to a location where you have always wanted to live. Feeling exhausted, you may become intuitively aware that you need to change your diet and eliminate certain foods.

To strike out into new territories of thought and behavior, we have to break the momentum of the status quo. The human part of us tends to be a creature of habit and resists change. Fear is the primary emotional motivator of human nature. It will lead you to make decisions based on the need for safety and security. Your spirit speaks a different language. It desires freedom and expression and motivates through love and joy. It yearns to evolve and create new experiences. To better hear and follow through on the inner promptings of your truth, it is necessary to strengthen and increase your conscious connection to your spirit.

The quiet voice of spirit always speaks your truth, whispering and nudging you to pay attention. Focus on listening to it and taking action when you feel led to do so. Here are some tips to guide you in intuitively listening and taking action on your truth.

Understand the power of the moment. Allow yourself to be led by the inner voice of your spirit. Nurture and honor this small seed of awareness and it will blossom magnificently.

Don't talk yourself out of your intuitive impressions. Instead, use your thinking brain to plan, strategize, and devise doable goals to manifest your truth.

If you feel led to make significant changes in your life, take your time. Don't rush and try to create change too quickly. Take care of yourself and take it one day at a time.

Don't overshare your plans with others, especially those who do not support you. Your unconscious translates your speaking about action as taking action. Have you ever noticed that people who talk a lot about their plans do not always follow through by taking action? This is because they have unknowingly released their creative energy into the world prematurely. Hold the energy within. Let it germinate and express itself as action and not just words.

Know that your spirit is connected to a powerful current of life force energy that supports your efforts and guides you. Release yourself into this invisible but powerful stream of energy.

Meditate and read inspiring and spiritual literature to strengthen your connection to your spirit.

Truth is always accompanied by positive and uplifting feelings. The sensation of power in your belly, the electrical shivers that move up your spine, the hair on your arms tingling with energy, an open heart, positivity, strength, and sure knowing are some of the ways that your spirit communicates messages to you. Breathe, relax, and take in these signs from your spirit that you are on track.

I take action on what I know to be true for me.

76. Dreaming the True You

At night while your conscious mind sleeps, the true you speaks to you through your dreams. Alerting and informing you of your true feelings, thoughts, needs, wants, and desires, your dreams can be a form of intuitive self-awareness.

Dreams never waste your time. They are created from the soulful place within that invites you to take another look at your thoughts and feelings, who you are, and your innate wholeness and interconnectedness with all of life. At times dreams can seem to be too bizarre, silly, or complex and make no sense. Although they may be difficult to decipher and understand, when you engage with your dreams, you will find that they offer you insightful wisdom and transformative energy.

There are many different ways to work with your dreams to better understand and derive more insight and meaning from them. Most dream-interpretation techniques involve deciphering the symbols and images contained within them. However, understanding a dream's symbolism does not always reveal the depth of personal insight that it contains.

The *conscious dreaming technique* provides a framework to use a dream as a tool for self-awareness. It stimulates deeper and often unconscious thoughts and feelings to come to the surface. With this technique, it is not necessary to interpret and understand a dream's symbols. Instead, it allows you to become aware of what is hidden and repressed within.

To begin, write down your dream as soon as you wake up. If you wait too long or get involved in other activities, you will likely forget parts or all of it.

For instance, in a recent dream, I am in my house alone. Someone comes to the door and I am not sure who it is. Then the scene changes and I am outside on a tall mountain peak and I hear my name being called. I then find myself looking down on the scene as if I am a bird. I see how little I look in comparison to the tall mountain and the surrounding hills.

After you have written down your dream, sit back and relax. Take a moment, close your eyes, breathe long, deep breaths, and recall the dream. Invite it into your consciousness.

Now write the dream down again, but let it change as you write it. Let it unfold as if you are dreaming as you write. Use the dream as a jumping-off point to consciously dream.

My dream example: I am in my house alone. I notice light coming in from the window, but it feels cold in the house. Someone comes to the door and I don't want to answer it. I look out the window and I see a man who I am surprisingly happy to see. I have been waiting for him. He seems warm and friendly. He wants to take a walk with me. We easily walk through a valley, then up the mountain. He wants me to see something or someone. We get to the top of the mountain and it is beautiful. I can see forever. I lift up into the skies as if I am flying and I feel supported, understood, and loved.

Can you feel the shift that happens when you first recorded the dream and then when you allow the dream to actively unfold? There will be more engagement and emotional connection to the symbols and what is happening. Although you may still wonder what the dream's symbols mean and how the dream fits into your everyday life, using the conscious dream technique strengthens your ability to form intuitive connections.

Allow your dreams to reveal their meaning and message.

Be the Dream

Every symbol and image in a dream comes from within. Dreams represent personal characteristics and aspects of who you are, and every symbol can reveal new and surprising information about you. The dream interpretation technique called *Be the Dream* allows you to communicate with a dream's symbols and images.

Begin by writing down a dream and picking out a perplexing or intriguing symbol. Then speak as if you are the symbol as you recall the dream. Relate to the other dream symbols and content through the symbol in the first person. Allow yourself to be spontaneous and flow freely with what feels right to you. It can be especially insightful to become each of the symbols one at a time. As you become one of the symbols, the dream will likely change from its original form. Let this happen. Use your imagination and go with it.

As an example, I will use my same dream from the conscious dream technique.

I am in my house alone. Someone comes to the door and I am not sure who it is. Then the scene changes and I am outside on a tall mountain peak and I hear my name being called. I then find myself looking down on the scene from the sky. I see how little I look in comparison to the tall mountain and the surrounding hills.

Using the Be the Dream technique, I become the person at the door.

I come to the door of a house of someone I love. I want her to know that I understand her and I want her to see herself in a different way. I invite her to take a walk with me and am so glad that she agrees to go. We easily climb a mountain. It is a clear and beautiful day. I tell her to let go and allow the warm winds to support her. She does this and lifts up into the skies, and all of her troubles and worries slip away. She feels her interconnectedness with all of life.

You can also become a nonhuman dream aspect or symbol.

For instance, in the same dream I become the mountain.

I am the mountain. I feel the power within me that reaches deep into the earth and up into the skies. I am peaceful and I give sustenance to the flowers and trees that adorn me and to the birds and animals that make their home with me. I am part of all of life, the sun and moon, the streams and rich soil and all the life forms that I nourish.

As you become aware of each symbol within the dream, notice how you feel and the transformative energy that moves through you as you allow it to speak through you. Feel your heart, mind, and spirit integrate the new aspects of your true self as they emerge. Invite every aspect of the dream to be a part of you.

As you explore the rich tapestry of your dreams, your authentic self comes to life. Our dreams bring us insight, healing, and the awareness that within us is a vast network of intelligence and love.

I recall and listen to my dreams.

77. Four Misunderstood Intuitive Signals

When we listen to our intuition, something magical happens: unexpected and often surprisingly useful help comes our way. Despite the conditions and difficulties that confront us, a way is made, a door is opened, and the wisdom and grace of the universe flows into our lives. We are so accustomed to using logic and reason to make choices and decisions that we all too often disregard subtle intuitive guidance.

Intuitive insight gives us more than practical and concrete guidance and direction. It reminds us that we are more than we believe ourselves to be. There is a subtle and often mysterious transcendent presence that moves through our heart, mind, and spirit. It connects us to one another and to a greater wisdom than our thinking minds can fathom. Intuitive awareness gives us insight about ourselves and the universe. It is the doorway through which our most soulful authentic self emerges.

Our intuition continually sends us signs and signals. Some we notice, but many we disregard and are oblivious to. We are inclined to believe that receiving intuitive guidance is markedly different from the way we receive information through our other senses. Yet intuitive insight is intertwined throughout our moment-to-moment thoughts, feelings, and experiences.

Here are some often misunderstood ways in which your intuition can surface.

Your Thoughts

Although there often seems to be a discernible difference between thinking and intuiting, intuitive messages often emerge through our thoughts. Intuitive thoughts come into our awareness complete and as a cohesive whole. Finite mind-chatter thoughts stream into our consciousness in a more linear way. One thought leads to another, then another. They may cause confusion and doubt or leave us with more questions. Intuitive thoughts are aha moments that assure us with a flash of knowing of their accuracy and truth.

For example, while driving the car or doing another repetitive task, the sudden surprising awareness of the solution to a pressing problem is likely an intuitive thought.

Your Feelings and Emotions

With a little awareness and focus, you can become aware of the difference between an intuitive emotion and one that is being generated through biological and physiological responses. Most of our emotions and feelings originate in what we think and believe or are prompted by physical or mental unconscious triggers. Intuitive messages that emerge through our emotions are often sudden and all-consuming and may seem inappropriate to the situation. They quickly shift us into unexpected feelings and emotions that are unrelated to our current thoughts.

Intuitive energy information may move through you as unexpected feelings of comfort, love, and compassion that seem to contradict your current situation or emotional state of being.

For instance, in the midst of grief and loss, a sudden comforting feeling of peace and love that heals our heart and soul is most likely an intuitive emotion.

Emotions such as fear and stress may also be intuitive messages that come to alert you to be cautious and extra aware of your environment or other conditions.

For instance, feeling surprising stress about driving your usual route to work one morning despite no recent issues or problems is likely an intuitive message.

Physical Sensations

Physical sensations can be triggered by intuitive energy information. A tingling up your spine, the hair on your arms standing up, a feeling in the pit of your stomach, or a buzzing in your head are common intuitive signals. They differ from physical sensations derived from normal biological processes such as digestion or muscle twinges in that intuitive physical sensations usually come with an instantaneous awareness, knowing, or feeling.

For instance, the gut feeling in the pit of your stomach that something is not right about the contract you are about to sign is likely an intuitive message.

Unexpected Changes

Intuitive messages often show up in our lives through events and conditions that unexpectedly fall apart or bring us good fortune and positive benefits.

For instance, have you ever done everything you can to organize and execute a plan or project and then something seems to come out of nowhere to put an end to it or to divert the expected outcome? Has a spontaneous opportunity or a surprising success ever easily and unexpectedly come your way?

These kinds of situations are a type of intuitive message that come into our lives to inspire and align us with our true soul path. They differ from plans that fall apart through lack of hard work and preparation or opportunities that come to us that steer us away from our highest good through wishful thinking and empty illusion. Outer intuitive messages that emerge through changes in our current plans and direction transform us on a deep level. We inwardly sense that what has occurred was not an accident or lucky chance. Recognizing this as a call to a new path, we are given the choice to trust our inner knowing or continue to ignore the signs. When we choose to pay attention and accept the wisdom of the message, we are never sorry. Good things come, even if we are initially frustrated or resistant.

Intuitive messages come to you from the core of your authentic self. They are the voice of your heart and soul. As subtle as they may appear to be, trust the little voice inside of you that always recognizes truth.

I notice and listen to subtle intuitive messages.

Chapter 6

RELATIONSHIPS:
MIRROR OF SELF

When we love soulfully and deeply, all of who we are surfaces. It is through our relationships that we discover more about ourselves and what we are capable of. We can feel uplifted and encouraged by our capacity to forgive, devote ourselves to another, and put aside our needs. We may also be surprised by the emergence of unacknowledged fears, jealousies, and desires. In this chapter, further explore the you that surfaces through your relationships.

78. Pushing Your Joy to the Surface

Along the journey to discovering and living your truth, you will be tested not once, but many times. This is a world of shadows that seeks to dim your clear light of awareness and enlist you into the ranks of conformity. It is in your relationships that you will be most tested, tempted, and challenged to know who you are.

To be in harmonious and happy relationships, it is essential to be true to yourself and allow your friend, partner, family member, or lover to do the same. When we are not true to who we are, relationships simply do not work. Even if there appears to be compatibility and coupled unity, sooner or later the slippery slope of losing self proves to be too much. You feel invisible and resentful and must scramble to rediscover and claim your truth.

Relationships are the playing field where we learn how to be selfless and support others and at the same time be loving and true to ourselves. While we desire to both retain our individuality and fully connect with another, the balance between these two is not always easy to achieve and maintain. We can all too often merge and allow others' wants and needs to take priority or erect walls to protect our sense of self.

Like a posable Gumby doll, relationships pull and stretch our heart, our boundaries, and our concepts of love. We are challenged to love others and still say no when no is called for and learn how to compromise. Being true to self while being kind and simultaneously present to another can test the best of us.

The not-so-secret secret is that relationship happiness does not necessarily come from being with another. Happiness is always an inside job. It doesn't spring from an outer source, and we cannot catch it flitting across the sky and descending on some and not others. Happiness and harmony come from within, from the heart and soul. Always in a state of constant renewal, the happiness and joy that we seek is always available. The best of relationships push and prod our soulful joy to the surface. In our willingness to love another and let go of our selfish ego desires and expectations, the best of us comes forward. We bear witness to the love within us, warmheartedly share it with another, and give our partner the space to do the same. In this way, we unlock our inner joy.

I share my love.

79. Your Many Roles

There are many ways that you show up in the world. You may be a mother, father, sister, brother, daughter, son, grandparent, employee, friend, lover, husband, wife, boyfriend, girlfriend, pet owner, or any of the many other roles that make up your outer identity. Each role emphasizes certain aspects of your personality and either supports your true self or detracts from it. For instance, you may enjoy being a loving and caring mother but dislike being the organized office manager.

Different roles empower us to experience the depth of our personality and promote our emotional, mental, and spiritual growth. Yet it is important to remember that there is an inner you that cannot be defined and known through a role. When you overidentify with one aspect of your being, you can lose your connection with your authentic self. When you are out of touch with your core truth, you look to others to validate and tell you who you are. As much as others attempt to support you, insecurity and a lack of confidence are inevitable. You become the role you play in an attempt to fill the empty inner void of the loss of self. This only leads to an increasing sense of uneasiness and a feeling of being off-center.

The roles that we play give us the opportunity to experience new ways of being and interact with others in unique ways. But no matter how gratifying a role may be, it is important not to completely dissolve into it. When you have a firm sense of self, you can experiment with different roles and ways of being. Secure with who you are, you are centered and able to be there for others in ways that they need and desire while still being true to you.

I learn more about who I am through the many roles I play.

80. Being Misunderstood

Staying true to yourself and being understood and acknowledged by others for your unique self can be challenging. Others perceive you through the lens of who they are. They will not necessarily be able to see you in the same way that you see yourself. It is likely that you will at times be misunderstood. It is essential to know, honor, and love yourself despite how others perceive you.

When you stand in your truth despite external expectations, some will recognize and admire this and some will feel threatened and insecure. Many people experience a sense of safety, security, and control by playing it safe and fitting into family, cultural, and societal standards. When you are strong and determined enough to think for yourself, you break through the invisible ceiling of conformity that many are trapped in.

From early childhood, we are taught to follow rules and adjust to what and who our parents, teachers, caregivers, and friends would like us to be. Individuality is noticed but not necessarily celebrated. Fitting in, being like others, and conforming to unspoken expectations is met with positive feedback, good grades, and praise. Although you may initially feel a sense of connection and bond with others when you adjust yourself to their expectations, the feeling is usually short-lived. If you cease living your truth, eventually you will feel empty and without an anchor.

Although it can be frustrating and induce feelings of loneliness when others do not understand you, there have been many exceptional people throughout time who have been misunderstood. Among the unique individuals who were misunderstood and went on to achieve greatness are Jesus, Martin Luther King Jr., Abraham Lincoln, and Vincent van Gogh.

The sting of not being accepted and being out of step with others is only temporary. You shine a bright and clear light when you are you. You naturally attract those who are able to see and connect with the true you. In the meantime, if you have to go it alone, love and honor yourself. Seek out groups and activities that interest you and speak to who you are. When you are being true to you, lasting and authentic friends and community eventually gather around you.

I accept that I will at times be misunderstood.

81. Take Back Your Power

Is there someone in your life with whom you feel you cannot be yourself? You hear their voice or become aware of their presence or even just start to think of them and you lose the ability to think for yourself. You become who they want you to be and hold on to the hope and wish that they approve of you. Maybe you want to impress them. Perhaps you fear that you will be criticized, laughed at, or rejected, so you do your best to be who you think they want you to be as a protective shield.

In this reactive state, it may feel as if you have no power. The good news is that you can break this spell and reclaim yourself.

When you feel yourself slipping into invisibility or becoming who another wants you to be, ask yourself what is triggering these feelings. What do you most fear, and is it reasonable? What will happen if you are criticized or rejected? What keeps you playing the game of compromising your true self?

Some people stir up strong and confusing emotions within us. Fear is triggered and your true self shrinks deep within. Most likely the feelings that motivate you to take on a false persona do not make sense. They may be connected to early childhood experiences and false beliefs about your safety and security that are buried deep in the unconscious.

As you explore the origin of your emotional reactions, you begin to take back your power. Self-awareness moves you back into the center of your being. Feel your feelings and know that you can take care of yourself with people who trigger you.

I take back my power when I feel my authentic self slipping away.

82. Affairs and the Unexpected

Living an authentic life, becoming aware and listening within, is an accelerated path of growth and evolution. Sometimes this journey inspires peaceful, joyous, and lofty thoughts, feelings, and experiences, but not always. Along the way you may experience times of sudden and unexpected change and confusion. This is inevitable and not a failure.

I recently saw a client, a woman about to turn forty, whose world was turned upside down by an overwhelming and unexpected attraction to another man. The last time I had seen Vicky was a couple of years previous to our session. At that time she was happily married with two young children. Now confused and ridden with guilt over her affair, Vicky wanted to understand why she was drawn and magnetized to another man and what to do now that her life was in shambles.

Vicky is not alone. This kind of experience is more common than we would like to imagine. Many people are jolted out of their predictable life by unforeseen and unexpected people and events. This might be spurred on by the arrival of someone who stirs up unexpected feelings, a partner or spouse who suddenly leaves the relationship, being betrayed, or finding out upsetting information about a loved one. These life-altering occurrences ignite and stir up confusing feelings and emotions that keep us off balance. We no longer know who we are, why the unexpected is happening, and what to do about it.

The root of these life-changing events is within you. What we believe will bring us joy and happiness does not always work out the way we think it will. Unexpected change comes to our door when we are not in sync with our innermost truth. When we make choices and decisions based on what others think we should be doing or when we become attached to an empty dream and desire, our truth emerges in an attempt to set us back on course. When our current reality crumbles, we are forced to look within and rebuild our lives around a more authentic sense of self.

Vicky, like many others, was not intentionally living a false life and suppressing her true thoughts and feelings. She was doing the best she could to be a good wife and mother. She loved her family and was not looking to have an affair. Yet unexpected changes occur when we settle into a false life, even when we are not aware that we are doing this. Change comes as a wake-up call to jolt us into a renewed and heightened state of self-awareness. Life shows us, often in unpleasant ways, what lies deep within our soul and psyche. Taken into places and situations that we would normally avoid, we are directed away from the safety of our comfort zone and, like a baby bird, thrown out of the nest.

Under normal circumstances, we would not choose to be tested in difficult ways. We avoid change and do all we can to control our day-to-day circumstances. Yet we often come to know who we are only when we are pushed and prodded to change and grow.

I look deeply into myself during times of change.

83. What to Do When Unexpected Change Comes Your Way

Change is inevitable. When you are on a conscious path of authentic living, it is likely that you will experience surprising and uninvited opportunities for change and transformation. Although change often comes to us disguised as unwelcome loss and chaos, greet it with confidence and the assurance that despite its appearance, you are being guided and ushered into a more authentic life.

If you find yourself in the midst of sudden change, here are a few helpful suggestions.

Do not try to control what is happening. As much as you may not understand why and what you are going through, surrender and let go. When we resist and try to control ourselves and life, change only becomes harder. Once change is in motion, go with the flow.

Keep the focus on you and your process. As tempting as it is to blame or become preoccupied with outer events and other people, what is happening is about you. New circumstances and conditions come along when we are ready. When we need a wake-up call, our soul creates the perfect experience to get our attention. Conditions will right themselves as you accept your lessons, evolve, and transform.

Take time for yourself. Instead of trying to figure out what you may not yet be able to understand, accept your confusion and give yourself some time. If you do not know what to do, don't do anything. You may need solitude to reflect and listen within. Reconnect with your inner self and be honest. Trust your heart and your intuition.

Have compassion for yourself and the people in your life who are affected by what you are going through. Compassion is the ability to fully accept, love, and care for yourself and at the same time recognize the pain that another is experiencing without judgment.

Listen to others and accept the fear and confusion that they may be experiencing. Listen to your own fear, doubt, and stress and keep loving yourself.

Forgive yourself and forgive others, even if you do not feel forgiving and especially loving. Use positive affirmations that support and spark the emergence of your wisest and most loving inner self.

Take baby steps and constantly assess how you feel. Know that it is all right to make mistakes, change your mind, and feel differently from one moment to another. Do not make commitments or long-lasting decisions unless you feel a calm inner assurance that you are on the right path.

Notice new aspects of your personality and inner self that are emerging. For instance, a change in your financial status may motivate you to look for another job. You apply for a job that you might not normally be interested in and are hired. This new job brings out more of your latent leadership abilities and you find that you enjoy it. Take a chance on trying new activities, developing new skills, and meeting and networking with new people.

Know that the confusion, the tumultuous events and changes, will pass. Wait out the storm. Clarity, renewed energy, and a higher state of well-being and inner peace are on the way.

I gracefully accept change.

84. Recognizing Emotional Vampires

Emotional vampire is a term that describes a person who is an expert at eliciting emotional attention from others and using it to their advantage. Attracted to loving and caring individuals who are willing to give of themselves, emotional vampires feed off of positive energy. If you feel unusually tired, anxious, stressed, and irritable after spending time with certain people, you may have been in the company of an emotional vampire.

In a close relationship with an emotional vampire, you are likely to lose your sense of self. Their needs, wants, and desires take priority over your feelings and needs, and eventually yours are discounted altogether. Their constant emotional demands will leave you with little energy to focus on yourself.

Emotional vampires do not have a healthy sense of their core truth. Instead, they are focused on the external world of appearances and boost their low self-esteem by taking on and mimicking the positive attributes of others. They need constant validation and people in their lives whom they can control and manipulate. Without this, they feel as if they are shadows and ghosts who do not exist. Because they are out of touch with their genuine thoughts, emotions, and individuality, they create drama and crisis wherever they go. In this way, they receive the attention they desire and temporarily fill their inner emptiness. Yet this strategy never works for long. The constant craving for emotional energy never ceases. They continue to seek more and more attention and emotional energy.

Emotional vampires lack empathy and the ability to be emotionally present to others. Unable to reciprocate the amount of love and attention they require and often demand, they are extreme takers with no ability to give. If you are in a relationship with an emotional vampire and hope that one day your love and care will heal and bring your partner into wholeness, you will be disappointed. No amount of love will ever be enough. You will never receive as much as you give. Instead, you will likely become drained, resentful, and confused. When you are finally unable to give any more, the emotional vampire will seek out another source of emotional sustenance.

If you feel that someone is draining your energy, they likely are. When you suspect that you are in a toxic relationship, take some time to listen within. Breathe and tune in to your gut impressions. Feelings of weakness, confusion, or powerlessness are signs that someone is siphoning off your energy. Detach from the person or group that you feel is draining you. Spend time reconnecting with your core authentic self. Seek people you can be yourself with and who uplift and energize you.

> *I take care of myself when others try*
> *to rob me of my positive energy.*

85. Detach with Love

Have you ever ended a relationship but still feel emotionally connected to your past partner long after the breakup? Do you feel as if you lost a part of yourself in a relationship? Are you currently in a relationship and feel as if you no longer know who you are?

In an attempt to harmonize with and understand those with whom we are in a relationship, we all too often allow another's perspectives, opinions, feelings, and needs to replace our own. Over time, we become overwhelmed and lose contact with our own core self. Even long after we have ended a relationship, we may still be energetically connected to the person we are trying to move on from or let go of.

This visualization will empower you to lovingly detach from another. If you are unable to let go of a past relationship or you feel like you have lost touch with your authentic self, you may be entangled and enmeshed in another's energy. This exercise will help you free yourself from another and regain your sense of self.

Begin by relaxing in a comfortable position. Think of the person you would like to release and detach from. Close your eyes and take a few deep, cleansing breaths. Imagine that you are inhaling white light down through the top of your head. Let this breath move through your entire body and relax you. As you exhale, imagine that you are releasing any stress or tension from anywhere in your body. Keep breathing in this manner, inhaling cleansing breaths and exhaling tension and stress.

When you feel relaxed, create in your mind's eye an image of the person you are detaching from. Imagine that the person is standing against a blank background. Notice as many details as you can about them—their clothing, expression, and general demeanor. Now imagine yourself facing this person at about an arm's distance. Pay attention to any feelings that surface as you do this.

Close your eyes, and starting at the top of your head, scan your body. As your awareness moves down your body, imagine that there are invisible connectors that run from parts of your body to parts of the other person's body. Take note of which parts are connected. There may be more than one.

Pick the connector that feels strongest, and imagine what it seems to be made of—perhaps a steel rod, a fleshy appendage, a vibration of light, or a rope. Does there seem to be energy flowing through this connector? If so, in which direction is it flowing? Are you giving your energy away or are you receiving the other person's energy? Do your best to tune in to the energy flow of the connector. If you feel that you are not receiving much information, keep using your imagination and trust your gut feelings.

You now have the opportunity to release this connector. Close your eyes and imagine that you have the power to disconnect yourself from this person. You may want to ask for divine guidance and intervention in order to let go. The other person may not want to disconnect. You might feel as if it is unloving to let go, or you may feel as if you need this connector in order to keep this person in your life. Do not judge or fear what will happen when you disconnect from this person. Let go. When you do let go, don't be surprised if you initially feel sad or confused. It is necessary to feel your feelings in order to release them. You will soon feel more positive energy flow into your mind, body, and spirit.

Once you have disconnected, take the connector and imagine you are attaching it to the highest source of absolute love. Allow this love to flow through you, especially into the areas where the connector was originally attached. Become aware of your authentic feelings, thoughts, and truth.

Release this person to absolute love.

When you are ready, open your eyes and write down your experience.

I free myself of past relationships.

86. Be Honest and Direct

Being around direct and honest people is easy. You know where you stand with them. Indirect people who fear speaking their truth cannot be trusted. Eventually their truth will surface in an indirect and surprising way. If you feel guarded and hesitant with another and do not know why, it may be that they are hiding something about themselves or their motives. It is difficult to form a real connection with someone who hides their truth.

Be the kind of person who is easy to be with. Trust in what feels right for you. Express your thoughts as clearly and honestly as you can. It takes effort and energy to suppress and tiptoe around your truth. You can be kind and honest at the same time. We are often better able to know our personal truth by expressing and sharing it with others. Once spoken, new ideas, thoughts, and awareness surface.

Sometimes we need time alone to tune in to our beliefs and thoughts. At other times we need to share and express who we are and be with others. When others agree with our truth, we feel a bond and connection to them. Being understood and accepted feels great. When others disagree with our truth, we can feel hurt and angry or we can choose to let it go and let them be who they want to be.

Be strong and do not let others shame or diminish you if they do not share your truth. Allow others to believe and think whatever they want. We are all at different stages of growth and self-awareness. We do not always agree with others and they do not always agree with us. If another's truth differs from yours, do not take it personally. Allow others their truth in the same way that you want them to listen and respect yours. What is true for you today will likely change. This is natural and normal and a positive sign that you are growing and evolving.

I am direct and honest in my communication with others.

87. Share All of Who You Are

One of our most compelling needs is to be known and loved by another for who we are. Yet we often repress and hide the depth of our innermost true self in intimate relationships. We are especially prone to withholding and not revealing our true thoughts and feelings at the beginning of a new relationship. At one time or another, we have all been ridiculed or criticized for being ourselves and expressing our true thoughts and feelings. Because we fear the sting of rejection, we hide our vulnerabilities and express only the most positive and pleasing side of our personality.

To develop and deepen a relationship, we eventually need to take the risk and express our vulnerabilities and our true thoughts and feelings. If we continue to limit and measure how much we express and share, this withholding only cripples and eventually destroys intimacy. Relationships need to evolve, unfold, and continually create new avenues for mutual expression. Being true to ourselves while in a relationship is a daily process. Some days, being emotionally available to another and taking care of ourselves is a challenge. It may feel easier to just play along and be and do what others expect of us. While it is important to compromise and be there for others in the way that they most need us to, know when you are at risk of not being true to yourself. The line between being present to a loved one in the way that they want you to be and overcompromise is not always clear. It constantly shifts and forces us to reevaluate our needs and the needs of others.

If you are tempted to ignore your true self for the sake of relationship harmony, try these strategies instead.

When you are confronted with what feels like a choice between expressing your truth or aligning with your partner's preferences and viewpoints, look at this as a win-win instead of a win-lose situation.

Too often our first thought is to defer to what our partner may want and what will make them happy. As noble as this might seem, it is essential to know and share your true thoughts, feelings, and preferences. Do not feel embarrassed or shame if what you want or desire is not what your partner wants. This does not make you selfish, egotistical, greedy, or needy. It means that you are aware of who you are and what works best for you.

When you feel at odds with your partner's needs or desires, ask yourself on a scale of one to five how important it is for you to get what you want. One is not very important, a minor blip on the screen of desires. Five is very important; you feel strongly that being heard and receiving what you desire or need is vital to your well-being. Let go of what is not important and work toward compromise in those things that are crucial for your happiness.

State your feelings and thoughts as clearly as you can. Then be willing to not get your way. There is power in simply expressing who you are knowing there is no guarantee that you will or always should receive what you desire.

When you know what you want, what is real and authentic for you, share your truth. Then really listen to your partner and support the emergence of your partner's true self.

I lovingly express my preferences and opinions to my partner.

88. Karmic Relationships

Have you ever felt a strong connection with another, yet you have a hard time just being yourself with this person? Intense feelings get stirred up, and as much as you want to have a harmonious relationship, you find yourself acting in ways that do not make sense to you. A karmic relationship is the continuation of a past-life and soul relationship with another. The origin of the word *karma* is the Sanskrit *karman*, meaning "action, effect." In Buddhism and Hinduism, it is used to describe the sum total of a person's actions from this and a previous existence.

In a karmic relationship, the existing karma may be harmonious. Two people come together from a previous life where they have worked out their ego-centered challenges and love each other with a pure and compassionate love. In these relationships, both people often come back together to work toward a common goal. Usually this goal is to be of service to others and contribute to the greater good. Their authentic self has been integrated into the relationship and they can freely and joyfully be with each other.

However, most karmic relationships are not easy. Two people are brought together to learn how to unselfishly love each other, heal past-life imbalances and wounds, and express their authentic self. These relationships are usually initially passionate and stir up deep feelings of longing and what feels like love. This irresistible magnetism is usually needed, as these relationships can be challenging. Past emotional wounds, fears, anxieties, and egocentric selfishness often surface. There may be periods of harmony and loving connectedness interrupted by conflicts, power struggles, and unfounded fears. Simply put, these relationships can be confusing. Despite the desire to leave a karmic relationship, the magnetic attraction may keep pulling you back. The soul chooses these difficult relationships because of their inherent potential for healing, growth, and wholeness and to refine and experience real love.

If you suspect that you are in a karmic relationship, it is important to recognize that this in an opportunity for growth, profound healing, and the experience of real love. It is also important to recognize that you are on a challenging journey. Although your authentic self is often hidden behind layers of karmic issues and suffering, it is your strongest guide. To heal and transform a difficult karmic relationship into one of harmony and the truest experience of love, the false must be shed.

Begin with awareness. When intense emotions surface or your beloved acts in ways that cause you distress and pain, realize that as distressing as this may be, it is an opportunity for healing. Feel the intense emotions and feelings that surface. Do not dismiss or disregard them, even if they do not make sense. Sometimes all we need to do to release old karmic emotional energy is feel it. As you do this, you let it go.

Do not let anyone convince you that what you feel or think is wrong or not valid. One of the ways you will know that you are in a karmic relationship is that the intensity of emotions and pain seems out of proportion to what is happening in the relationship. Whatever needs healing, forgiveness, and transformation will surface.

Your authentic self is the inner observer that knows and feels what you are experiencing but does not dissolve into the confusion and relationship drama. Listen within to the quiet inner presence that informs you of what love is and what love is not. Your authentic self moves you forward out of victim and aggressor roles and provides you with the strength and wisdom to heal. Take action on what feels true and right for you. Be kind and loving to yourself. Forgive yourself and forgive your partner. This will free you from negative and difficult karma.

Remember that you can only do your part in the healing process. This is all that you are responsible for. You cannot force your partner to perceive issues the same way that you do or heal in the way that you want them to. Yet something magical happens when you act in loving ways toward yourself and confront and heal your inner wounds. You transform and exert an unspoken but powerful influence on your partner and on the relationship.

Some karmic relationships can be healed and transformed. They become a vessel for divine love where both people evolve and express their authentic selves, freely and joyfully. Some karmic relationships are more short-term. You may have come together with another in order to free yourself from oppression and control. In some karmic relationships, the purpose is not always clear. You may meet another for a specific lesson, and once you learn what you need to learn, heal, or transform, the karma is completed and the relationship ends. When you do your part to heal a karmic relationship, you shed long-term negative and difficult karma. Even if the relationship does not continue, you experience the freedom and joy that come with healing.

I recognize the power of my authentic self
to guide me in karmic relationships.

89. Your Attraction Vibe

The most successful way to attract a loving and compatible partner is to be yourself. Despite the games that both men and women play in an attempt to attract the person of their dreams, being the real you is what works. To attract the most compatible and loving partner, broadcast the strong and powerful bright light energy of your individuality.

The law of attraction states that we create and draw to us what we most think about, feel, and believe. If you act in ways that are not true to who you are or if you hide your true feelings and opinions from others, then you attract confusion and deception. When you know who you are, love yourself, and have confidence in your authentic self, your energy vibe is pure and invincible. How we love ourselves is how others will love us. The invisible beam of who you are magnetizes the similar and compatible energetic light of another.

Dating can be challenging. It often brings out our insecurities and fears. To cope with our vulnerabilities, we often adopt personality traits, behaviors, and qualities that we feel are appealing and attractive to others. Many women spend a lot of money and time enhancing their physical attributes in the hope that it will increase their desirability and attract a partner. If you find yourself contemplating altering your physical appearance, it is important to examine your motives. If you would like to make outer changes that help you feel as beautiful on the outside as you feel on the inside, then your energetic vibration will be harmonious. However, if your motivation is to enhance and change your outer self because you feel lacking and insecure about who you are, no number of outer changes will make you feel truly beautiful. You will likely attract another who believes that dating an attractive women will improve his self-esteem and make up for his lack of self-confidence.

Some other common ways that women lose their sense of self when dating and send out a confusing attraction vibe is by hiding their intelligence or becoming sexual before they are ready. Women may fake an interest in a man's hobbies and pastimes and hide their true thoughts and feelings. All of these types of false behaviors attract incompatible and inharmonious relationships.

It is not just women who are prone to self-doubt and lack confidence when dating. Men, too, have their insecurities, which they may attempt to make up for by acting in inauthentic and false ways. Many men are sensitive about their financial status and feel emotionally vulnerable. Some may present the image of being financially well-off and successful in their career when they are actually struggling to find their way. Others may hide their emotional vulnerability and appear to be confident and strong when they are actually unsure of themselves and want very much to be loved. Some men do not want to ask for help for fear of appearing weak. They pretend to be in charge and immune to the insecurities of dating and falling in love. Acting in false ways and being inauthentic creates dissonance in a man's attraction vibe as much as it does for women. They send out a mixed energetic signal that attracts women who are faking it as much as they are.

If you feel that you are not always confident in dating, that you lack certain attractive physical attributes, or that you do not make enough money, there are others who feel the same way. Your vulnerabilities make you human and lovable. Stepping out into the world just as you are is a courageous act, especially when dating. Love all of who you are. Be kind to those you meet, even those you do not feel a connection to. They, too, are looking for love. Accept your imperfections and others will feel more comfortable and at ease with you.

Being you is the only way to attract harmony and a loving and true partner. You will still likely meet and date a few who are not "the one." But when you are being true to who you are, you will quickly recognize who you are not compatible with and be able to move on. Being authentically you sends out an invisible beam of light that will draw your soulmate to you.

I express my authentic self when dating.

90. Relationships: The Soul's Agenda

The dream of finding our forever soulmate often leads us into the true work of love. Although we imagine days and nights of bliss and heaven-sent, uplifting love, a soulmate often brings us unexpected challenges and provokes deep healing. We would like to believe that there is a perfect partner who will fulfill our needs and make up for any relationship difficulties we may have experienced, but the soul is not here to simply float along in unchallenged harmony. The true work of love is to break us open and move us beyond complacency and into transformation. In our search to find our perfect love, we often discover parts of ourselves that need healing, love, and acceptance. Loving another can be a direct route into our fears and insecurities. In this way, relationships become fertile ground for self-growth and awareness.

When we are highly invested in finding a partner who is the answer to our desires, wants, and needs, we forget that love requires that we let down our barriers and allow the full force of cosmic power to redefine who we are. Not everyone is capable of loving in this way. We all too often settle for a partner with whom we share common interests, sexual attraction, and material security.

As much as we want to find our true soulmate, the soul may have another agenda. There are mysterious undercurrents that attract and magnetize others into our life. Even though there is a purpose to every relationship, we do not always know why someone is in our life and it is not always clear why they leave. When a relationship comes to an end, it is not always someone's fault. Blaming ourselves or others when things do not work out is counterproductive.

Surrender to the flow and current of love. There is a powerful purpose within all of your relationships. When you act with integrity and share your authenticity, you draw from the well of deep, soulful love.

I surrender to love.

91. Navigating Change

When you are on a conscious path of self-awareness and authentic living, time seems to speed up. As your self-knowledge increases, you may find the outer circumstances and conditions of your life changing as well. These changes further accelerate your evolution. To keep pace with your increased self-awareness, your connections with others will intensify and also go through a process of growth and change.

Your relationships are an important vehicle through which continued soul transformation occurs. They provide you with the perfect opportunity to integrate, share, and embody new awareness and insight. To better navigate your way through relationships in these accelerated times, here are a few suggestions.

Let go of your thoughts and beliefs of how a relationship should be. Relationships are not static. They need to flow, evolve, and move into new forms. As you evolve and change, so will your relationship needs and desires.

Know yourself. You are a microcosm of the universe. When you discover who you are, you know all of life. Do not settle for a surface awareness; plunge deep into your heart, mind, and spirit. The better you know yourself, the more you will know and understand others.

Confront and work through your past emotional wounds and issues. Challenge yourself to push beyond your pain. Do not expect a new partner or lover to heal your past and make up for past relationships.

Be honest and speak your truth and encourage your partner to do the same. Look into your partner's eyes and listen to what they are expressing. When your partner triggers uncomfortable feelings such as frustration or anger, practice sitting with these emotions without reacting immediately. Treat your emotions as a guide that provides insight into what within you needs your attention and healing.

Do not become lazy and complacent. Many people are attracted to others who exhibit strengths and characteristics that they feel deficient in. While we can benefit from being with others who embody skills and characteristics that we do not have, this cannot become a long-term substitute for what we feel we lack. Challenge yourself to examine your weaknesses and perceived deficits and take action. An imbalanced relationship will not last.

Trust that your authentic self will guide you as to what is true and right for you and what is not. We often talk ourselves out of what we intuitively know we need in order to get along and keep the peace. While this may create a sense of security, not being authentic will eventually drain your energy and create an unhealthy inner and outer environment.

Depend on yourself and be true to who you are. In this way, you will be able to love others more purely and freely. Relationship success is not measured in longevity. Allow your relationships to draw you into the sacred and true work of love. Bless, love, and forgive your lovers, friends, partners, and all who have shared and continue to share this journey with you.

I continue to grow and evolve in my relationships.

92. Look into the Soul

Has anyone ever looked deeply into your eyes and seen the true you? Not just your vulnerabilities, your hopes and fears, but the light of your soul as well. The best of you that only seems to come to life when another acknowledges it. We live our lives in the hope that the light of our soul shines brightly out into this world and is known. When another has the patience and bravery to see who we are, we are blessed.

Have you ever looked deeply into another's eyes and seen the soft glow of their soul? We shy away from this kind of seeing and being seen. Be brave enough to hold the immense essence of another in your gaze. Give the gift that we crave so much from one another. We want loyalty, love, and devotion, but we also yearn to be seen. Being present to another's truth, without expectation and judgment, fills the empty spot within. Give this to another and to yourself. When you look, really look.

A friend of mine is a beautiful woman both inside and out. By the accepted standards of beauty, she has it all. She is tall, with a great figure, long hair, and sparkling eyes. When people meet her husband, they are often surprised. She once told me that when she introduced him to her coworkers at a work dinner party, a few jaws dropped open. Shorter than his wife, with a receding hairline and a bit of a belly, he does not look the part of the gorgeous blond's husband. Their romance began the day they met at a wine-tasting fundraiser. She went with a date and he was there volunteering for the charity. When he handed her a glass of wine, their eyes met. Accustomed to being the object of men's stares, she did not expect to be truly seen by the friendly man passing out wine samples. Yet when they looked at each other, her stomach quivered and a little shock of energy ran up her spine. A few days later, she asked around and found out that he worked in the same building that she did. Without hesitation, she went down to his office armed with a good excuse and reintroduced herself. Again, she felt caught in the spell of his eyes.

"It was not a sexual look or a look of desire. Men have looked at me this way for most of my adult life," she said. "When he looked at me, something deep within me came to life. My soul leapt up and did a bit of a somersault. I felt like the real me. I still feel this way when my husband looks at me."

Gently look at another in the way that you would like to be seen. Give this gift to those you love and care about and your relationships will naturally unfold with truth and honesty. Be willing to be seen and don't hide yourself away. Give yourself and others the real you.

I let myself be seen and I am willing to see others.

93. Let Love Break You Open

If you have never been rejected, betrayed, disappointed, made to feel like a fool, left, or dismissed by someone you love, you will be. It is inevitable. You cannot love without experiencing the full spectrum of love's bounty. When this happens, be brave. Act with courage and don't sweep your pain under the rug. Let the force of your grief, pain, loss, and sadness flow through you like a raging river. Resist the temptation to hold it all together. Submit and allow yourself to be shattered. Feeling the fear, unworthiness, anger, and despair that come with the loss of love may be one of the bravest things you will do.

Love will break you open and then rebuild you bit by bit, not with the false hopes and fantasies of immature love, but with its raw truth. This love is not for sissies, and it is not for brutes who cannot submit and humble themselves to its power and wisdom. Not everyone is able to enter into love's innermost sanctuary. When you do, the false drops away and you stand naked and vulnerable before the fiery blaze of your soul's passion.

You are here to bear witness to the gnawing, uncontrollable, and unsatisfied hunger of your soul. Though we attempt to quiet and pacify it by believing that a safe and subdued version of love is what we need and desire, it cannot be so easily tamed. Listen to the rumble of your authentic voice in your soul, heart, and gut. It is asking you to become aware of the fears and insecurities that you try to avoid and run from. Love with passion and accept both its frailty and its eternal nature.

You have probably loved many times and you likely still feel that you can somehow lose love. You cannot. Every time you take the risk and love and every time this love seems to dissipate, leaving you empty and searching, your heart opens to a greater depth of truth. Like the petals of a flower that delicately open and reveal a unique essence and fragrance and then fall to the ground and sprout new growth, your love goes through the cycles that are inherent in all of life. Love in human expression is subject to its seasons and rhythms.

The origin of love is the eternal all that is. It can never truly depart or be diminished. If a love relationship ends, wait patiently for love's reemergence. It will reappear in a new form, a new essence, and again capture and work its magic through you. Don't resist the rawness of love. Let it open you with its promise, and feel the sting when it appears to fade. Let your tears flow and nurture the holy ground where the seed of your sorrow lies. If you bar yourself from love's journey, you stay put on dry and empty ground. Dig deep and let your soul have its way.

I love with passion.

Chapter 7

Spirit Mentors, Power Animals, and Guides

We are a mystery to ourselves. Even as we further explore and dig deep into our authentic self, our most soulful truth may seem to elude us. In this chapter, you can explore your connection to the spirit realm. Although this may initially seem to be an unlikely source of self-awareness, the spirit realm knows you well. It can reveal core qualities and attributes and awaken the essence of your true self.

94. Helpers Along the Way

You have many unknown mentors, friends, and allies who support the emergence of your authentic self. Along the journey to claiming your truth, these allies play an essential behind-the-scenes role in creating opportunities and experiences through which to better know yourself. Although difficult to detect, they cross your path and make themselves known in interesting and sometimes mind-boggling ways. They will delight, confuse, inspire, motivate, and open the door and invite you into a reality that you may not have known existed. At times you will wonder if you are delusional and imagining things, but if you trust and follow their signs and guidance, you will discover that you are known and never truly alone.

Among your celestial allies are spirit guides, power animals, and angels. Not limited by the three-dimensional world of time, space, and matter, they are expert shapeshifters. One day they may appear to you as the owl that sits outside your window, and the next they are the cloud that shapes itself into a heart or the sensation of warmth and love that fills your aching soul. They speak to you in dreams and inspire and motivate you to claim your power. When you embark on the journey to know self, they huddle around you, sending warmth, love, clarity, direction, and motivation.

Since these allies operate outside of the limitations and restrictions of what the human world considers possible, trust your intuition to better detect their presence. Through sensations, feelings, aha moments, synchronicities, dreams, metaphors, and unexpected opportunities, they will make themselves known and guide you. Do not expect them to speak to you in the same way that you communicate with the human realm. They will spark your imagination, your intuition, and your curiosity. If you feel as if one of your spirit mentors has given you a message or direction, listen and act on what you receive. Take the chance, even when you are unsure and have doubt. When you know in your heart that you have received a divine sign, follow it with everything you've got. There may be no hard evidence to persuade your thinking mind to trust and go forward. It may feel silly and awkward to put your faith in what appears to be elusive. Yet the more you listen to your heart and act on what you receive and follow where you are led, the more guidance and help will come your way.

I trust that my spirit allies, friends,
and guides are leading and helping me.

95. Spirit Power Animals

The authentic self surfaces through our thoughts, feelings, actions, and beliefs and also through our connection with the natural world. Everything is alive and has inherent wisdom and power. There is an unspoken connectedness within all living things. This includes the human world, the stars and planets, all of nature, plants, birds, and animals. Everything and anything can be a mirror through which we can better see and know who we are. Synchronistic encounters with nature and the animal world can reveal and confirm aspects of your true self.

A spirit power animal can be a bird, reptile, insect, or mammal that embodies and expresses specific characteristics and qualities similar to the traits of your authentic self. Power animals mirror many of your innate gifts and can guide you into greater self-knowledge and awareness. Over time, your power animal may change, with new ones coming into your life when you need to explore certain characteristics or traits that you may not be aware of.

When you become consciously aware of your power animal, you can better absorb and work with its powerful gifts and be inspired to explore the full scope of your authentic self.

Here are a few ways to become aware of your power animal.

Pay attention to the animals or birds that come into your life through synchronicity. For instance, have you ever driven down a road and happened to see a wild turkey, then a few days later you see a painting of wild turkeys in an office hallway?

What animals or birds are you most interested in? Which ones intrigue you the most? When you were a child, what animals and birds did you most want to learn about and see? As children we have a pure attraction to the animals that speak to our essential nature. Remember those animals and birds that you felt a connection to.

What animals have you had either frightening or positive encounters with? Have you ever been bitten, attacked, or felt threatened by an animal? Are there any animals that come close to you or look at you through a window?

Are there any animals or birds that show up in your dreams? In the past, have you had recurring dreams of any particular animals or birds?

With the sincere intent to honor and learn from your spirit power animal, ask your power animal to make itself known. Open your heart and invite the spirit of your power animal to be a part of you. You may feel and receive a personal response, or you may have a sighting of the animal in nature. You may see it through a vision with your inner sight or notice synchronicities, or it may come to you in a dream.

Your power animal picks you and not the other way around. Keep in mind that the animal you desire may not be your power animal spirit. With their deep primal energy, power animals bypass our personality self and connect to our spirit energy. In this way, they help us to know ourselves in unique ways.

Once you become aware of one of your spirit animals, you have the choice to accept its help, protection, and guidance. It is a reciprocal relationship, and just like a friendship, your connection with your power animal needs time, attention, and focus.

I learn more about who I am
through knowing my power animal.

96. Bird Messengers

Birds may likely be the most common animals, beside our pets, that we encounter on a daily basis. Wherever we are, wherever we go, birds are likely to be present. As power animals, birds embody a vast array of characteristics, traits, gifts, magic, and power. Do not let their small size fool you, as power in the animal world is not measured by size. A lion or elephant may be no more spiritually powerful than a crow or sparrow.

Here is a small sampling of the vast variety of possibilities in the winged world. Each bird has specific qualities and traits that can ignite and mirror attributes of your authentic self, especially those that are hidden and important for you at the present time. Power birds can also activate aspects of your authentic self that you have been unable to access.

Blackbird: Indicates latent healing gifts and creativity. You have the determination and ability to focus on developing your innate hidden abilities. Sometimes it is only when someone we care about suffers that we activate our potential. Be proactive and explore one or more of the many forms of healing that may appeal to you.

Bluebird: You have a joyful and happy disposition. Reclaim your innocence and the lightheartedness of your childlike nature. With your positivity and inner joy, you can inspire others and open their hearts.

Blue Jay: You are on the path of true power. Harness your ability to balance and integrate the earthly and spiritual within self. You may confront lessons of power and its misuse in yourself and others in this lifetime. Once you align your power with your spiritual depth, you can experience success in all areas of your life.

Cardinal: You have a royal nature, courage, and the ability to rejuvenate after times of illness and stress. You are able to inspire and encourage others to act with determination. Connected to the heavens, you have the ability to manifest your highest intentions and dreams.

Chickadee: The chickadee is the bird of truth and comes to assist you in putting your truth into words and expressing it to others. You are active, communicative, and expressive and bring a sense of fun wherever you go. Through your enthusiasm and nonjudgmental acceptance, you inspire others to know and express their truth.

Crow: Signifying life, death, rebirth, and transformation, the crow is a bird of magic and initiation. You can constantly change and reinvent yourself. New aspects and unknown qualities of your authentic self will continually surface over and over in this life. You embody intense and transformative aspects of truth and can delve into areas and issues that may intimidate others.

Eagle: This majestic master awakens our highest spiritual knowing. You embody the eagle's purity, innate wisdom, and higher spiritual truth. You have the passion to express these characteristics in your everyday life and inspire these qualities in others. You are a natural leader.

Hawk: You have clear and deep vision and embody a developed spiritual consciousness. With the ability to perceive the big picture, you are a natural problem solver and planner. Hawk comes to activate your soul energy and to help you to better know the deeper aspects of self. Be alert and at the same time patient with the development and emergence of your soul's deepest longings.

Maintain perspective and cultivate your clairvoyant and precognitive inner sight.

Hummingbird: You are a messenger of hope and love to others. A powerful catalyst of miracles, the hummingbird inspires you to be a light in the darkness and to draw from the deep well of love within. Do not get weighed down by others' expectations. Be light and free.

Owl: A symbol of the feminine, the moon, and intuition, owl awakens the unknown and mysterious side of our nature. The seed of the divine feminine is a strong aspect of your authentic self. Owl energy emits and expresses aspects of the goddess energy. If you have not yet done so, it is time to acknowledge the intuitive, psychic, right-brain, and imaginative aspects of your nature. Pay attention to your dreams, as they often foretell the future, provide you with insight into yourself and others, and connect you to the astral realm.

Robin: You have the ability to attract growth, change, and positivity into your life at any given moment. The ability to enjoy the simple things in life, along with the gift of igniting joy in others, resides deep in your soul. Express the love that is in your heart, knowing that this frees you to be you.

Sparrow: You are stronger and more resilient than you may know. Sparrow comes to inspire you to perceive yourself in the most positive way possible. Instilling dignity and heightened self-worth, sparrow supports you through empowering your authentic self. It is time to sing your song, no matter what others think and feel. You have the resourcefulness and inner strength to be who you are.

Through this short list of spirit power birds, I hope that you have come to recognize the unique and insightful gifts that they offer you. There are many books that contain a more extensive list of birds and their qualities and the contributions they can make to your continued journey of growth and self-awareness.

I accept the gifts and lessons of my power bird.

97. How to Work with Your Power Bird

When a power bird offers you an invitation of connection and guidance, accept its energy and work with it. There are several ways to receive its beneficial and powerful assistance. Here are a few.

Meditate

Meditation allows you to quiet the thinking mind and better tune in to and connect with the spirit of your power animal. It is best to meditate and send a message to your power bird early in the morning. Before you begin to meditate, determine how much time you want to devote to the session. When you first begin, ten to fifteen minutes is fine. Set a clock or timer.

In a comfortable and quiet place, close your eyes and begin to breathe. Take long, deep inhales and exhale any stress and tension. When you are relaxed, send a message to the universe that you are ready to know what your power bird is and to work with its energy. Continue to breathe and relax. Breathe deeply and release any stress and tension through the out breaths. Repeat your request to receive the spirit energy of your power bird.

Breathe and relax, and using your imagination, visualize a field or meadow and a vast blue sky. Create this scene with as much detail as possible. Keep breathing and relax. Repeat your request to connect with the spirit energy of your power bird and be patient. Do not try to rush the process or become impatient. It may take several days and sessions before it makes contact with you.

If you make contact with the spirit of your power bird, maintain a receptive attitude. Continue to breathe, tune in to its energy, and pay attention to any sensations, insights, feelings, or thoughts that you receive.

When you feel that you have received all the information that you can at this time, open your eyes and write down what you received and send gratitude to the spirit of your power bird. If you complete the intended time and your power bird still has not entered your meditation, send gratitude to it anyway. Open your eyes and write down any sensations, feelings, or thoughts that you received.

Take a Walk

Go outdoors, in the morning if possible, and walk. It is best to walk in a natural setting or near water. If this is not possible, try to walk someplace where there is not a lot of traffic and noise. Focus on your breath. Breathe in and say to yourself, *I am receiving the spirit energy of my power bird.* Exhale and say to yourself, *I am tuning in to its message for me.* Continue to inhale and exhale, repeating these statements. Be attentive and listen within. New insights, sensations, feelings, and awareness will begin to surface. Notice and listen to what you receive. Keep bringing your awareness back to the breath and maintain a receptive and openhearted state.

Make an Offering

This can be a flower, a ripe piece of fruit, a bird feeder, a crystal or other stone, or an outdoor birdbath filled with clear and clean water. Your offering can be placed close to your home or in the woods near where you live. Find a spot, and before placing the offering, hold it in your hand and say something like *I send you this gift of honor and respect. Please teach me.* Visualize in your mind's eye an image of your bird while you say this.

You can give your power bird repeated offerings. It is best to always place them in the same spot.

Ask for Feathers

Ask your power bird for a feather or other gift. Be aware of and alert to any feathers, eggshells, or nests that cross your path and the songs of birds close by. You can make your request while doing the walking meditation or when giving your power bird an offering. Sometimes the gift will come to you in a dream. Pay attention to your dreams, write them down, and do your best to decipher their meaning. You might also receive gifts in the form of synchronicities and opportunities to act on your new power and awareness.

You have a reciprocal relationship with the spirit of your power bird. Do your part in interacting and being open to learning new ways to communicate and connect. Enter your power bird's world and you will discover more of your own inner truth.

I communicate with my power bird.

98. Become Aware of Your Animal Spirit Guides

Spirit power animals embody specific characteristics and traits that complement and mirror your authentic self. We do not pick our spirit animals. They choose us based on our soul path and the lessons that we have come to the earth to learn and experience. Spirit animals are the benevolent guardians of the earth. This is their home and they love and protect it. We are under their mentorship, and to fully embody their strength and power, it is necessary to become more conscious of their presence. Spirit animals empower us to live our truth. They help us to ground our authentic power and use it lovingly and wisely for all living beings and the planet.

To become conscious of your spirit power animal and further invoke its blessings and teachings is a process of opening and allowing.

Begin by devoting yourself to the natural world. This will get the attention of your spirit animal and demonstrate your sincerity. Volunteer in an animal shelter, rescue orphaned dogs or cats, feed the birds, pick up trash, ride a bike or walk instead of driving, plant a garden, recycle, or invest in solar energy or other earth-friendly energy sources.

Spend time in nature. If you live in the city or in an area that does not have open natural areas, then a park, a garden, an apartment deck, or even a window where you can see a tree, vegetation, or the sky will do. If you are able, spend time in the forest, open spaces, or the seashore and walk alone in silence. Wherever you are, relax in the quiet and soak in the energy of the environment.

Watch animals. This can be squirrels, dogs, cats, birds, snakes, or whatever animal crosses your path. Notice their intelligence. Be receptive to their form of communication. Try not to project human characteristics onto them. Their reality is different from the human orientation, so become more familiar with it. Greet every animal that comes your way as a messenger. Trust your intuition as to what they may be communicating or sharing with you.

Your spirit animal may make itself known through signs and unlikely coincidences, or synchronicities. Be alert to and trust the signs of your spirit animal in your day-to-day life. For instance, you may notice that the man standing in line in front of you to get coffee has a tattoo of a lion on his arm. Later that day, you go shopping and on the box of detergent that you are buying there is a picture of a lion. You go online and a photo of a lion appears while surfing the Internet. Your spirit animal will make itself known to you in ways that defy explanation and do not make logical sense. Trust and accept its presence when you experience these kinds of signs and synchronicities.

Here is a short meditation that you can practice to tune in to your power animal.

Meditate outdoors if possible and invite your power animal to make itself known to you. If you cannot be outdoors, sit near a window. Close your eyes and begin to take deep, relaxing breaths. Continue to breathe, allowing any emotions and thoughts to surface. Release them through the breath. As you continue to breathe, become aware of your environment. Feel the sun and breeze on your skin. Breathe and listen to the sounds that surround you. Take it all in.

Open your heart and ask for the presence of your spirit animal. Invite it to come close and reveal itself to you. You may receive an image or visual glimpse of it. You may feel it as a specific animal close to you. You may hear it or have a sense of knowing what your spirit animal looks like. Be patient and continue to breathe and invoke its presence.

Do not be alarmed if you do not see or become aware of your spirit animal. Sometimes it takes continued meditation sessions to call and make contact with it. Quite often your spirit animal will come to you hours, days, or weeks after your initial request. Although you may not be aware of its presence, it is likely working closely with you without your conscious awareness.

Your power animal may also choose to contact you through your dreams. Sometimes their presence will be powerful, colorful, and unmistakable. At other times it may seem more obscure and faint. Either way, if you dream of an animal, write the dream down and meditate on it for the deeper message.

Your spirit animal has powerful medicine to share with you. Spirit animals can guide us in ways that defy what we know of human reality. Be respectful of their presence and know that they are in charge of the agenda, not the other way around. Don't expect them to do favors for you or fulfill your desires. Instead, seek to learn from their primal and ancient wisdom and power.

I am alert to the presence of my spirit animal.

99. Characteristics of Your Personal Spirit Animal Totem

Your spirit animal is often referred to as your *totem*. A totem is recognized in the Native American culture as the power animal spirit that offers protection, physical and spiritual gifts, insight into the future, and better self-understanding. Once you become aware of the power spirit animal that reflects your authentic self, dormant aspects of your true self come to light. You may or may not initially recognize some of your spirit animal qualities and characteristics as your own. They may seem foreign and unfamiliar, or you may instead identify and feel at ease with them.

The following is a list of power animal spirits and their characteristics that reflect aspects of the authentic self. This is only a partial list that includes some of the most common animal totems.

Bear: You have courage, confidence, and the ability to access the unconscious. Likely grounded and down-to-earth in your approach to others, you are protective of family and friends. You are likely introspective, especially in the winter. Listen to your dreams, as they will guide you throughout your life.

Coyote: You can be a jokester who does not always reveal your depth of wisdom. Adaptable and playful, you don't always let others know how much you truly know. You can keep others off balance by not always revealing the true you. Be careful to penetrate through illusions so that you can perceive the truth.

Deer: You have the ability to move through obstacles and issues with grace and gentleness. Stay connected to your inner child and your innate innocence. Although you may be sensitive and prone to nervousness, you instill calm in others.

Dolphin: Naturally spiritually oriented, you bring harmony, joy, and peace to others. Endowed with a high degree of intuitive awareness, you can use this gift to help and heal others. You are protective of those you care about and will come to their aid when they are in need.

Fox: With your keen perception and ability to see through deception, you are discerning and quick-thinking. Pay attention to your dreams and use them for insight and guidance. Until you are well acquainted with someone, you may hide behind a mask, not allowing others to see the true you.

Horse: With a tendency to be active and a driving force, you can accomplish a lot in life. Male or female, you embody masculine energy. You are passionate, have strong emotions, and may at times experience strong sexual urges.

Lion: With an abundance of personal power, strength, and assertiveness, you are a natural leader. Learning how to use your power and strong emotions wisely and with benevolence and compassion is one of your life lessons.

Panther: Endowed with the ability to explore the shadow side of life, you are able to penetrate into the mysteries of life and death. You embody the vibration of the divine feminine and have the ability to guide and help others better understand their full nature, both the positive aspects and the shadow side.

Sheep: You have an innate innocence and childlike nature. Be careful not to let your gentleness and vulnerability turn into powerlessness and weakness. Because you tend to conform to social and family values, you are at risk of losing your sense of self. Accept your sensitivity and set limits on how much you will adapt to try to please others.

Tiger: Strong-willed and focused, you have the ability to follow your dreams and skillfully execute plans to accomplish your goals. Be sure to use your innate assertiveness and strength in positive ways. Otherwise, your personal power can emerge in ways that cause you and others distress and confusion.

Turtle: Determined and grounded, you are an old soul. Others are likely drawn to your innate wisdom and understanding. In the midst of chaos and disruption, you maintain composure and emotional balance.

Wolf: A free spirit, you need to balance alone time with the company of others. With your sharp intelligence and intuitive perception, you see through appearances with penetrating insight. Trust yourself, even if you lack concrete information to back up your suspicions.

A totem animal spirit may embody qualities and characteristics that you do not readily identify with. If this is true for you, take some time to explore these attributes. Sometimes there are dormant characteristics or aspects of self that have not yet been activated.

I learn more about myself through my power spirit animals.

100. Your Pet Totem

Your spirit animal totem may be a pet. Although it appears that we choose our pets, they instead choose us. Their energy finds us, often before we even desire to bring a pet into our lives. For instance, the thought that comes to you one morning to get a cat or dog may be coming from a specific animal who wants to come into your life. As you look at pet profiles on the Internet or in the paper or as you visit the animal shelter or visit a new litter of puppies, you will notice a certain animal. It will greet you with its eyes and draw you in. You know that this is your pet. Sometimes they show up at our door or are bold enough to stand in front of our car while we barrel down the road, in an attempt to get our attention. Our pet totem comes to us when we are ready to explore dormant aspects of our authentic nature and to magnify and draw out unrealized traits and inclinations. The following is a list of common pets as animal totems.

Cat: You are independent and highly sensitive and may have a tendency to be controlling. With the cat as a totem, you are highly intuitive, psychic, and creative. Yet you do not always reveal your intuitive insights to others and can be private and guarded with those you do not know well. Even those who know you well are often surprised when new aspects of your personality spontaneously emerge. Although you can appear aloof, you are actually highly sensitive to others and to your environment. With a rich inner life, you may need time to process your thoughts and feelings to maintain harmony and balance.

Dog: You have a huge capacity to love. Sensitive, loyal, and a protector to those you love and care about, you are heart-centered. You are here to help others or serve humanity in some way. With your compassion and strong spirit, you may be willing to go through the gates of hell for those you love. You tend to accept others for who they are, without judgment and criticism, and understand the complexities of human nature. Be careful not to allow your giving spirit to be taken advantage of.

Not all dog people fully understand their capacity to love. A dog will often show up when the heart is shut down, wounded, or filled with grief. Dogs act as a catalyst for healing and provide the soothing, gentle balm of dog love magic.

Fish: You are spiritual and sensitive to energy. You tend to bring harmony and a sense of calm to others. Adaptable and able to go with the flow, you can work in difficult and challenging environments. With your innate ability to go along with others' likes and dislikes, being a part of the group can sometimes prevent you from being fully aware of your authentic self. There are often hidden aspects of your personality that may only surface when you spend time alone. With the fish as your totem, you likely have good luck and experience abundance in your work and love life. You are creative and fertile, and whatever you focus your thoughts and feelings on will manifest.

Snake: There is something mysterious and compelling about you. With the ability to sense what others are thinking and feeling, you can draw people to you with your charm and magnetism. Flexible and open-minded, you accept others for who they are and encourage individuality. You are creative and often have a personal sense of style that may border on the unusual and exotic. With an innate ability to change and rejuvenate, you may reinvent yourself over and over throughout your life. Many people with the snake totem are gifted energy healers.

If you are a true pet lover, you likely have and love all kinds of pets. People who have a house full of different animals often embody some of the traits of each type. You share a special relationship with the natural world that can bypass human understanding. If you feel more bonded with your pets than with people, you are likely able to intuitively connect with the animal world. Although you are here in human form, you need animals to feel truly understood, known, and comfortable.

I value my animal family.

101. Natural Beauty for Your Soul

You cannot fully know yourself through the thinking mind alone. In the depths of your soul, you are subtle essence, difficult to grasp and always changing. When your conscious mind and your pure essence intersect, it is always a surprise. It can feel like a vast, expansive opening where you feel the peace and joy of the moment in singular awareness.

To lure your essence into your conscious awareness takes patience, solitude, and compelling quiet. This aspect of your true self often surfaces when you are surrounded by natural beauty. In a forest, garden, or desert or along a seashore, lake, or river, there is an intoxicating perfume that entices the soul.

Be alone in nature, look at the sky, breathe in the energy of nature, and your soul will emerge. If you cannot be outdoors in natural beauty, then fresh flowers, a water fountain, a garden, a starry sky, or the view outside of a window can also have the same effect. Wherever you are, just be. Give yourself time without any expectations. Be in the moment, and whatever your experience is, accept it. Feel the beauty of nature, drink it in, and absorb it into your mind, body, and spirit.

Your soulful essence may emerge for only a moment, then quickly submerge once again, to hide out underneath your thoughts and feelings. But it is there. You may feel it in a variety of ways. It can be a sudden awareness of your connectedness with all of life. You may become aware that everything is in divine order. Your worries, stress, and fears may take flight and dissolve. The light of who you are fills you. Maybe just for a moment, you feel and know the power that resides within you.

If you are fortunate enough to experience your truth in this way, stay in this awareness for as long as possible. It is a sacred and precious awareness that can be all too fleeting. Soon your soul will seem to recede, but the clear awareness of its light will stay with you. Tuck it into your heart and keep it close. Even though you may no longer be consciously aware of this crystal-clear emergence, it is still with you. Behind your thoughts and feelings and emotions, the pure you is present, observing, inspiring, and offering love and wisdom.

I invite my soulful essence to emerge.

102. How Spirit Guides Help

The more we begin to know our authentic self, the more of a mystery we may seem to be. As the layers of our thoughts, feelings, beliefs, prejudices, and desires are peeled away, a rich, timeless inner-core self emerges. This timeless self is spirit. It continues to live long after our physical body passes away. When we live each day from this core truth, we live in joy and freedom.

Spirit guides support and assist us in remembering our truth and encourage and inspire us to live authentically. Beyond our fears, grumpiness, worries, and the mistakes and mishaps that we clumsily make, we are known and loved, even cherished and adored. Most spirit guides have lived many earth lives. However, they have evolved beyond the physical realm and no longer need our earth school lessons. Spirit guides continue to grow and evolve as we do. Through their interactions with us, they achieve the higher purpose of enlightening, loving, and being of service to others. They exist in the oneness of all of life, and at the same time they enjoy soulful individuality.

Even though your spirit guides are close, you may not be aware of their presence. They cannot be known in the same way that you know your friends and family. Instead, your spirit guides are selfless beings whom you may become aware of through the effect they have on your everyday life. Spirit guides are concerned with your growth and development as a soul and use all kinds of methods and tricks to keep you aware of and aligned with your higher purpose.

For instance, the career opportunity that suddenly presents itself on the same day that you decide to leave your current occupation may come to you through supernatural assistance. Being in the right place at the right time and meeting a soulmate or having the courage to face your fears and pursue your dreams may be due to your spirit guide's support and influence. A spirit guide may also protect you by quietly steering you away from certain individuals or by persuading you to make wise and beneficial choices.

Communicating with Spirit Guides

Communicating with spirit guides often begins with a leap of faith. It would certainly be more comfortable if our guides gave us their names and communicated in clear and obvious ways. Instead, their communication is usually more playful, intuitive, surprising, and not always what we would expect it to be.

Investing a bit of your time and attention and inviting them to be an active part of your life can yield surprisingly positive results. One way to begin to connect with your spirit guides is simply to ask for a sign of their presence. Then be attentive, open, and aware of your surroundings. Watch for synchronicities, unexpected phenomena, and anything unusual that crosses your path. The spirit realm is adept at turning electronic equipment, lights, televisions, and phones off and on. They may also attempt to get your attention by dropping bird feathers or coins in your path, waking you with powerful dreams, influencing you to look at the clock at the same time day after day, calling your name, or sending birds or other animals your way.

If you suspect that a spirit guide is present, take a moment, breathe, and listen to your heart. This is where your confirmation will come from. All too often we get into our head and overthink and eventually talk ourselves out of believing that a guide may have something to do with the signs that we are experiencing. Tune in to your heart and feel and trust their warm reassurances. Another common way to connect with your spirit guides is through meditation. Through quiet inner listening, it becomes possible to better tune in to the subtle and gentle whispers of your guides.

Try this simple meditation exercise.

Set aside a period of time when you can be undisturbed and quiet. Find a comfortable spot and close your eyes. Begin to take long, deep breaths and release any tension or stress in the body as you exhale. Let go of your expectations as to how you want your spirit guide to communicate with you.

Send a message to your spirit guide that you would like to connect.

Continue to breathe and relax.

Keep sending a silent message to your spirit guide that you would like to feel their presence.

Breathe and pay attention to any sensations, images, thoughts, and feelings that surface.

You may feel a warm presence, your heart may fill with love, or you may feel a tingling sensation running up your spine or down your arms. Keep breathing and notice whatever surfaces without thinking too hard about what is happening. Just accept what is and breathe. Often guides will give you a message through a thought. You may see an image, a color, or sparkles of light or feel a buzzing sensation throughout your body.

Ask your guide if they have a message for you. Again, allow what is. Do not expect a message to come to you as a clear and concise answer to a question. Tune in to what you feel, sense, or know. Take your time and allow your heart to open.

When you feel as if you have received all the information that you can, send gratitude to your spirit guide and ask for their continued love and support. You may also want to write down all that you experienced. This is a way to ground the information and strengthen your connection to your guide.

Sometimes long after a meditation or request to a spirit guide, you will feel their presence or receive a message through a dream or a synchronistic encounter.

Your spirit guides steer you toward the experiences and conditions that align and help you to better know your authentic self.

I enjoy the friendly love and support of my spirit guides.

103. An Angel by Your Side

Since your birth into the physical world, there has been an angel close by. This is your guardian angel, who protects, comforts, loves, heals, guides, and watches over you. Angels are pure love and compassion and powerful guardians of your authentic self.

You are worthy of angelic love and healing. Whatever you have been through in life, your guardian angel can restore you, mind, body, and spirit. Your angels hold the blueprint of your soul's journey and your individualized divine spirit. They know your purpose for being here and they know when you struggle and when you fall short of your own expectations. Yet they also know you as a wise, loving, and perfect being. When you lose your way or feel overwhelmed by life's difficulties, they are present to help you to get back on track and remind you of who you are. Because they do this in ways that can be hard to detect, we discount their influence and intervention. Yet they are always available to heal and help you to live from the most true and real part of who you are.

Our most loving, wise, and authentic self often lies hidden within us like a buried treasure. At times we get a glimpse of our own pure goodness. But all too soon, our daily thoughts, feelings, stresses, and demands cloud our vision and we are unable to connect with our inner truth. When you are able to feel and be influenced by the goodness of your spirit, you see yourself and life with clarity. All things transform, as does your sense of who you are. Your guardian angel can help you to become aware of and align with the core of your innermost truth that remains untouched and unaffected by outer conditions and experiences.

Communicate with Your Angels

Your guardian angels can empower you to move beyond your self-judgments and false beliefs and know the true you. Open your heart and ask for your angels to restore your awareness of your true self. Earnestly desire to feel and know the goodness, love, wisdom, and joy that are within.

Be patient and alert. You cannot control the timing of your angels' response to this request. You may immediately feel a renewed sense of self. For some, transformation comes slower, sometimes days or weeks after the request. If you do not feel that the angels are responding, continue to ask and be patient.

Let go of expectations. Your angels may not help you in the way that you want them to. They see the big picture and speak to your highest good. Angels work primarily through spirit and emotions. Be aware that instead of feeling the love and healing that you may desire, you might initially feel confusing or difficult emotions. If this happens, breathe into the feelings without repressing or pushing them away. The emotions are surfacing to be released. Ask for the strength to feel and let go of what no longer serves your highest good. Go with the process. As you feel difficult and uncomfortable feelings, love and joy will begin to emerge. Notice yourself and others being more kind and thoughtful. The ability to forgive yourself and be more compassionate and accepting will subtly take root. As feelings of perfectionism, self-loathing, and depression give way, inner light and restored energy surface.

Your angels will likely send you a sign that they are with you. Stay alert to messages and synchronicities that strike an emotional cord within you. If you find feathers, especially white ones, your angel is close. Birds and butterflies that seem to want to get your attention, that fly overhead or near your car or watch you from outside your window, may also be sent from the angelic realm. Seeing the numbers 11:11, 1:11, 2:22, or 12:12 on clocks, documents, bills, etc., can signify the presence of angels and is an assurance of their intervention. Sparkles of light and rainbows, streaks of light in the sky, and light-filled clouds are angelic imprints. You might even be fortunate enough to see an angel as a shimmering, light-filled outline or as a more three-dimensional image that suddenly appears and disappears.

Angels are often felt through feelings of love and warmth that seem to envelop you and bring you comfort. Tingling sensations that move up the spine, a feeling of lightheadedness, or the relaxing knowing that everything is in perfect order and that there is meaning and purpose in difficulties and challenges will let you know that your angels are with you.

I am alert to signs of my angels' presence.

104. Strangers as Messengers

When there is a message that we need to hear, it can find its way to us in a multitude of ways. There is no limit to what the energy of our spirit combined with the love and the intelligence of the cosmos is capable of. One of the more interesting and mysterious ways that we receive guidance is through our interactions with strangers. For instance, while out and about, has a passerby ever gently smiled, opened a door, or helped you in some way at a time when you needed a bit of care and warmth? Has your heart opened or your faith in others been restored through an act of kindness? Have you ever encountered someone who told you exactly what you needed to hear? In the midst of our day-to-day routines and activities, we often ignore or fail to notice the dynamic interactions we may have with those we cross paths with. Our lives intersect with the lives of strangers in casual ways that seem to have little or no significance. Yet if we pay attention, every so often there is a message or guidance that unexpectedly comes our way.

The random kindness and warmth of another can have a profound and positive effect on us. We expect our friends, family, and acquaintances to be helpful, supportive, and there for us in the way that we want them to be. But when a kind word, smile, or helpful act is freely given, with no strings attached and without expectation, something in us wakes up. We feel seen and known and our trust in the goodness of others is restored. Even overhearing a conversation on a subway or in a crowded coffee shop can convey an insightful and helpful message.

Not only can daily random interactions with others provide you with important guidance, comfort, and messages, but you can unknowingly offer insight and wisdom to others as well. The impulse that moves you to give someone your seat on a crowded subway or allow someone to move in front of you in a long line may be more important than you think. A small act can bring hope and comfort to someone who feels tired, weary, or filled with despair. Making small talk with someone or telling them a story or sharing an insight may be exactly what that person needs to hear.

Here are a few suggestions for inviting more stranger magic into your life.

Be Open and Attentive

Even when we are in a crowd, we can feel isolated and alone. Consumed with a litany of personal thoughts and concerns, we notice very little of what is happening around us. Instead of shutting down or closing off when in the company of others, practice opening your awareness to what is going on around you. Be aware of others, and if an opportunity presents itself to engage in a meaningful way, trust your intuition.

Be a Conduit

Allow yourself to be a channel for a higher love and wisdom to flow through you and use you for the benefit of others. Whatever you give to others comes back to you tenfold. Although you may not always know the impact you have on another, kindness is never wasted and never falls flat. Even if the intended recipient does not accept this freely given gift, the energy spreads to where it is needed.

Trust Your Intuition

There is power in allowing yourself to be guided. Although we hide and deny our vulnerability and needs, especially when we are with strangers, keep an open heart and mind in all your interactions. There is good reason not to trust everyone. Taking care of yourself in the world is a necessity. Exercise your intuitive muscle when it comes to others and trust your vibes. If you feel uncomfortable or uneasy or if something feels off, walk away. However, trust your gut when it comes to the positive, too. If it feels right, generous, and safe, then give and receive.

Seek the Unfamiliar

It is not always easy to be truly seen and known in the company of those who are familiar. Your friends, family, and acquaintances cannot always perceive new aspects and qualities of your true self as they emerge. New people we do not know well can sometimes see aspects of our authentic self more clearly than people who we have known for a long time. In the same way, you might be able to perceive in another something special and unique that others cannot see. Unfamiliar situations and people allow us to reinvent ourselves, fresh and new. Look for opportunities and environments that provide you with the chance to try on new aspects of your authentic self. Attend a talk or a weekend workshop, go to the movies, or take a trip, and go it alone. Step out on your own and allow new energy into your life.

You can practice listening and receiving messages and participating as a conduit of love wherever you are.

*I am aware of opportunities to give
and receive kindness and grace.*

Chapter 8

Embrace Your Passion

Creativity unlocks the door for authentic expression. You do not have to be an artist or even artistically inclined to be creative. This chapter provides you with activities, exercises, and suggestions that will bring your inner self to light.

105. Let Your Passion Lead You

One of the biggest yet underrated and hidden challenges that you will confront on the journey of authentic living is expressing your passion. Depending on your perspective, passion can either empower you to feel truly alive or be a blinding force that dulls your awareness of your true self. In some spiritual traditions, passion is viewed as excessive and willful and it is to be quieted and tamed. In our Western culture, passion is associated more with romance and unrestrained desires and feelings.

The kind of passion needed for the emergence of your authentic self transports you from the known into the unknown. This is authentic passion. It is an energy force that moves through your mind, body, and spirit and rearranges and reveals aspects of who you are that you may not have been aware of. It empowers you to perceive your soul connections in the outer world.

When my friend Keli was going through a difficult divorce, it was all she could do to get out of bed, go to work, and take care of all of the grueling details of responding to her divorce agreement. For months she lacked energy and looked listless. One day while on the train to work, she noticed an advertisement for a painting class. She recognized the teacher as an artist who did instructional painting videos on YouTube. The class was not far from her work, and given how much she enjoyed watching the teacher's videos, she signed up. Keli loved the class and discovered within her a talent and passion for painting. Not only did she enjoy the tactical and sensual act of working with paint and canvas, but while immersed in the process she forgot about her problems and stress. The passion that she felt while painting became a doorway through which new life and possibilities began to emerge. It wasn't just distant mountains and ocean scenes that she was painting.

It was the open landscape of her life and the hope of new beginnings that she saw materialize on the canvas.

Whatever your authentic passion may be, listen, follow, and allow it to take you into a new understanding and awareness of who you are. You may not feel led to paint or participate in the arts. Instead, nature, outdoor activities, cooking, yoga, a spiritual practice, books, gardening, writing, collecting antiques, going to flea markets, dancing, volunteer work, traveling, history, learning about different cultures, or a vast array of other interests may be calling to you.

Take a risk, give of yourself, and become comfortable with your authentic passion. Allow it to be a cleansing force that sweeps you clean and leads you into new discoveries and possibilities. On this journey to authentic living, your passion can be a trustworthy guide—not as a distraction that veers you away from self, but as a force that propels you into the places within that you have not dared to acknowledge.

I allow passion to lead me.

106. Do It Now

Do something today that is perfectly you. Sing your favorite song aloud. Wear your most comfortable clothes. Start a creative project that you have been wanting to do or visit an art gallery. Go to your favorite restaurant and try something new. Take a walk in nature, or go to a lake or the seashore. Lie on the couch and read your favorite book. Listen to your heart, feel the boundless love within you, and share it with others. We often lose touch with the small joys.

Give yourself permission to claim what you want and then be willing to receive it. Don't wait any longer. You do not have to do better to receive more. No one has to validate you or give you the stamp of approval. There is nothing that you need to achieve or succeed at in order to be happy. If you have been putting off doing something that you know will lift your spirit, now is the time to do it.

We often feel that we need to wait for good things to come our way, and we put ourselves at the end of the receiving line. There are times in life when we need to be patient and self-disciplined and take into consideration what others need and how we can best help them. But all too often we forget to let out the free spirit within that wants and needs to go a little wild and experience renewal.

Wonderful ideas are born and good things come to us when we take the pressure off of ourselves and stop planning and overthinking. Our creative juices get flowing and we feel reenergized and refreshed. Allowing more freedom and spontaneity into your world reduces stress and allows joy to make its way into your life.

I enjoy my freedom to be me.

107. The Creative Approach

Years ago I started an art therapy program in a treatment center for violent teenagers. I went to the school three days a week armed with all kinds of creative materials, most of which sat untouched. For several months there was little interest in the program. In this austere and cold environment, the teenagers were watched over by adult guards and not encouraged to speak or interact in any way. Creating art presented a bit of a challenge to students and the administration, and I experienced resistance from both groups. Yet slowly this began to change. By my second year in the center, I had full participation and my program was expanded to five days a week and two hours a day. Because art therapy allowed the residents a safe place to express themselves without judgment or expectation, they began to open up and enjoy it. The quality of the art did not matter. Instead, creating was an avenue through which feelings, ideas, and individuality were expressed. It allowed the students to take charge of a part of their lives.

Creativity helps everyone. It does not matter if you feel like you have artistic talent or not. You are a creative being. Although being an artist, designer, or craftsperson requires creativity, this is only one area where creative ability surfaces. Creativity opens up a part of ourselves that is often unknown and dormant. It gives us the opportunity to take risks and express our individuality, and it empowers us to discover, harness, and express our authentic energy.

In my art therapy program, confused and troubled teenagers uncovered and connected with a part of themselves that was safe and good. Creativity gave them hope. We all have parts of ourselves that we need to become more aware of and birth into being. Approach all that you encounter with creative, open-ended awareness. Ask yourself,

How can I see or understand this in a fresh new way? What is my unique perspective and opinion on this? Resist taking the well-worn path and strike out into new territory. Creativity has a place in every area and aspect of your life.

> *I approach all things with creative vision.*

108. Create a Vision Board

Remind yourself of who you are. Contemplate the many things that make you smile and bring you joy. So often, the demands of daily life consume our time and attention. We are bombarded with distractions from morning until night and are confronted with a parade of issues and problems to attend to. The path back to our core self can sometimes seem elusive. We forget, all too quickly, the importance of listening within to our authentic voice.

One of the ways that we can become more centered and be reminded of our truth is to create a vision board. This can reinforce our truth and induce more clarity and peace of mind. A collage of images, quotes, and a personal statement of truth, a vision board can remind us of who we are.

Begin by creating a statement that describes your personal truth at this time. Try to make this as concise and accurate as possible. Remember that your truth can and will change and evolve over time. Here are a few examples:

- *I love and accept myself for exactly who I am.*
- *I live each day with an open heart and mind.*
- *I am free to be me.*
- *I express my truth.*
- *I allow my authentic self to lead me.*
- *I feel joy and abundance within.*

Ask yourself what living authentically would look like. Find images from magazines, the Internet, or personal photos that support your statement of truth. These images can be of experiences that you have had or experiences that reinforce your personal values, dreams, and hopes. Be sure to include inspirational and motivational images as well as photos of beauty. Cut out the photos or, if you find them on the Internet, print them. You can also save images to create a vision board on your computer.

Write down meaningful affirmations, quotes, or passages that speak to your authentic self. These can be statements that motivate you to feel your feelings, share your truth with others, or fully love and accept yourself.

Glue or pin your photos and statements to a poster board or corkboard. If you want to create a vision board on your computer, find a program that will allow you to copy and paste your photos and quotes. You can print it when you are finished or, if possible, use it as your screen saver.

Take a few minutes first thing in the morning and before you go to bed at night to look at your board and meditate on it. As you do this, your subconscious mind will absorb and materialize your truth in the world.

Reinforce your personal truth and focus on what is important and of value to you.

I create a vision of my most authentic self.

109. Choosing Your Personal Style

Our daily choices and preferences help us to know more about who we are. Our likes and dislikes and preferences in all things give us the opportunity to try out and express new ways of being. Our hobbies and interests, the way we decorate our home, and our personal style in clothes, furniture, and cars help us to become more aware of and express our individuality.

This process begins early in life. When we choose a favorite color from the crayon box or pick our most beloved cartoon character, something in us feels an inner rightness and connection. As we grow older, we begin to lose the innocence and pure impulses that we had as children. Our inner barometer as to what feels right for us is all too often replaced by outer influences. We allow others' opinions and beliefs to replace our inner sensors. We adopt as our preferences what our friends have, what is popular, and what advertisements tell us will make us happy, attractive, and successful. Identifying what you want based on others' opinions and choices eventually leads to a disconnection from what feels right for you. You lose yourself somewhere in the backdrop of what you have filled your life with. Although it is important to be open and try new things based on others' recommendations and experiences, ultimately you have to be able to discern and feel what lifts your spirit and brings you joy.

Not listening to your preferences when making small, everyday choices may not seem like a big deal. Yet one choice at a time, you can either become disconnected from your authentic self or strengthen your connection with it. Despite the many claims of fulfillment that come with the various products and services that you are bombarded with on a daily basis, what will truly make you happy is filling your life with what speaks to your authenticity and individuality.

I express my individuality in my personal style.

110. Drawing Your Essence

We tend to know ourselves best through our thoughts, emotions, beliefs, preferences, and physical attributes. It can be a bit more mystifying to know our inner spiritual presence. There are few words that can describe and accurately portray the expansiveness and beauty of our spirit.

Our spirit is hard to grasp and understand. Becoming quiet and listening within enables us to better connect to and embrace our inner essence. Creativity in all forms is another way that our spirit speaks to us. Painting, sculpting, gardening, mixed media, writing, and other types of art, craft, or design work allow our spirit to be expressed in the physical realm.

Try this creative exercise to better tune in to your spirit.

You will need colored pencils, markers, or crayons and white paper.

Get comfortable and close your eyes. Take deep, relaxing breaths, exhaling any stress or tension. Continue to breathe and relax. Ask within to feel and connect with your spiritual essence. Listen, feel, and become aware of whatever feelings, sensations, or images surface. It may feel as if you are making this up. Your imagination is a useful tool with which you can better tune in to pure essence. Be patient, breathe, and tune in to any colors, feelings, sensations, symbols, or images that surface.

When you feel that you have received all the information that you can at this time, open your eyes and begin to draw or paint. Put form and color to the sensations, feelings, or images. Continue to allow new awareness and images to surface while you draw or paint.

When you feel that you have completed the drawing, close your eyes. Breathe into your heart and feel it expand, then exhale through the heart.

Ask for colors or images to emerge that represent the essence of your heart. Use your imagination. Notice any colors, sensations, images, and symbols that surface. Take your time.

Breathe and continue to receive. When you have received all that you can at this time, open your eyes and draw or paint the essence of your heart. Allow more images and colors to surface as you draw or paint.

Once you have completed the drawings, periodically meditate on them. Over time they will continue to unfold and provide you with new insights and awareness. You can also repeat this exercise as often as you would like to continue to tune in to your spiritual essence.

I use my creativity to tune in to my spiritual essence.

111. Writing Your Authentic Self

Creative writing can help you lift the veil of the conscious mind and access the rich potency of your authentic self. Journaling, poetry, prose, and even doodling can help you to better know self.

The key to using writing as a creative tool is to suspend the critical mind that would like to edit and critique while you write. To elicit the voice of your deeper self, adopt a curious and patient attitude and let go of your expectations. Write to simply write and the passion of your heart and mind will use this as a channel for expression.

Stream-of-Consciousness Writing

Stream-of-consciousness writing is a technique that you can use to stimulate and promote the emergence of your true voice.

This technique helps you bypass the common issue of not knowing what to write or where to start. Stream-of-consciousness writing moves you through inner blocks and often elicits surprising raw insights. Do not edit or worry about spelling or grammar while you write.

To begin, have plenty of paper and a pen or pencil. You can also type on your computer. Have a clock or watch close by, as you will write for a specific amount of time.

Stream-of-consciousness writing employs prompts, which are short statements that stimulate and activate your deeper unconscious.

Create an open-ended stimulating statement. Use a favorite quote or one of the following prompts to write about. Use only one statement at a time.

- *Who am I?*
- *What do I need to know about me?*
- *I am love.*

- *I am consciousness.*
- *I am a unique expression of the divine.*
- *What have I come into this life to experience and learn?*
- *What is my purpose?*
- *What do I most need to know about my life right now?*

Determine the amount of time that you will write. Usually fifteen to twenty minutes to begin is sufficient. Stream-of-consciousness writing is continuous and nonstop. Do not lift your pen from the paper or stop writing. Do not review, edit, or correct what you are writing. Write nonstop. If you do not know what to write, write something like *I do not know what to write.* If you feel frustrated, write out your frustrations. Just keep going. Eventually you will begin to feel a sense of flow. Words, ideas, and thoughts will move from within to the paper or computer. Do not read what you have written until you have written for the desired amount of time.

For best results, use steam-of-consciousness writing for consecutive days or weekly. The more often you write, the deeper you will go into self. You can clear out emotional and mental blocks, become inspired, harness your creativity, learn more about yourself, and activate the emergence of your authentic self.

Write a Love Letter to Your Authentic Self

Write a love letter to your authentic self and listen for a response. This process will help you to lovingly integrate the presence of the true you into your daily decisions, thoughts, feelings, and experiences.

Prepare in the same way that you did for stream-of-consciousness writing. Plan to write for fifteen to twenty minutes. Have plenty of paper available. This exercise is better accomplished through writing on paper than typing on a computer.

In this love letter, write without editing, critiquing, judging, or overthinking and without ceasing for the predetermined amount of time.

Prepare yourself by becoming relaxed, breathing deeply, and releasing any tension and stress through the exhale.

Begin by writing the following with your dominant hand (right hand if you are right-handed and left hand if you are left-handed):

Dear Authentic Me,

Express love and support for your authentic self. Let your authentic self know how much you love and support your true inner self. Maybe there have been times when you felt truly free and alive and you would like to send gratitude to your authentic self. You can also ask your authentic self about its perceptions and feelings about any area of your life. You may want to ask what your authentic self might need or want. Write without overthinking and remember that this is an encouraging love letter that will help you to better know yourself.

Once you have opened the dialogue and expressed love and support, allow your authentic self to respond. Let your authentic self communicate to you through your non-dominant hand (left hand if you are right-handed and right hand if you are left-handed). Begin by writing the following with your non-dominant hand:

Dear Conscious Self,

Listen within and write without overthinking or critiquing what you are writing. Give your authentic self permission to say anything. The true you may wish to express love and respond to what the conscious self has written, or you may spontaneously reveal something unexpected.

Continue to write, switching back and forth between your dominant hand/conscious self and your non-dominant hand/authentic self. When the time that you have allotted for this exercise is completed, you can continue to write or end the session.

This is a good exercise to practice when you need to make a decision or when you are unsure if something is in your best interest. The intuitive voice of your heart and soul, your authentic self, longs to express your truth.

I allow my true self to emerge through writing.

112. Authentic Painting

Similar to authentic writing, authentic painting allows you to express your inner self in a creative and spontaneous way. It is not always possible to put into words and clearly understand the evolving mystery of self. We simultaneously exist on multidimensional levels, not all of which are easy to access. Your unconscious self is as much a part of you as what you know as your conscious self. Even though the contents of the unconscious are often hidden, the unconscious self exerts a powerful influence on your behavior, choices, and sense of self and your emotional and mental well-being.

Authentic painting allows the unconscious to surface and frees your creative spirit. It moves you through inner emotional and mental blocks and elicits the positive effects of being in the flow of your spirit.

You do not have to be a painter or even artistic to enjoy and succeed at authentic painting. Use whatever materials appeal to you, such as watercolors, oils, acrylics, and brushes, or paint with your hands. Paint in an environment where you can freely create without worry of splashing or dripping paint. Prepare to get messy. In this process, you can paint for a specific amount of time or simply for as long as you would like. Unlike writing, it is not necessary to use a prompt to stimulate and trigger your inner creative self. However, some people find it helpful to begin by focusing on an intriguing quote, affirmation, or statement. You can use the same kind of prompts as discussed for creative writing. It can also be helpful to play soothing or meditative music while you paint.

To begin, have your materials ready. Sit quietly and take a few long, deep breaths to relax. Breathe deeply and move the breath through the body. If you are using a prompt, repeat the affirmation or statement inwardly a few times. When you are ready, open your eyes and without giving thought to what you are going to paint, pick up your brush, dip it in a color, and begin to paint. Continue to paint and begin new paintings whenever you are ready. Continue to be aware of your breath while you paint. This will keep you centered within. Breathe into your heart and soul. Remember to be nonjudgmental of what you are painting and what it looks like. Develop a curious attitude. What you paint is not meant to hang behind the couch or impress your friends for its technical and artistic qualities. This painting is for you.

When you are finished and the painting is dry, you may want to put it away for a short time. Take it out when you are in a reflective and relaxed mood and allow it to speak to you. You may want to become quiet, notice your breath, and adopt a listening and open state of awareness. Pay attention to any thoughts or feelings that surface from the painting.

I express myself through painting.

113. Declutter Your Home

Let go of the things in your life that no longer have meaning or purpose. Who you are is not dependent on what you have. Long-forgotten material items and accumulated clutter may be a mask that keeps your true self hidden. Holding on to things that no longer reflect who you are keeps you stuck in the past.

When you clear out your physical space, you make room for a new you to emerge. Begin with your home. Make a list of what is most important to you, both what you need in the practical sense, like your kitchen table and chairs, and those things that have sentimental value to you, like your grandmother's porcelain teapot. If you find yourself feeling overwhelmed and not sure of what you need and what you can discard, write those down on another "not sure" list. You can also have a "donate" or "give away" list.

As you go through this process, ask yourself these general questions: *Do I use this? Have I used it in the past year? Will I use it again in the next three months? Do I love it? Does it have meaning for me?*

Take a good look around your home and you will likely come across many things that are no longer "you." These are items that you have had for a long time, things that were given to you as gifts, and other items that you don't quite know what to do with. There may be magazines that you think you may read one day and supplies for projects that you have been meaning to get to. All of this clutter prevents the free flow of energy in your home and within you.

Have a plan in place to discard the clutter. A friend with a truck is always helpful, or call a local charity that is able to pick up and accept large items. When you are ready to purge, start with the bigger items, such as furniture, old bikes, outdoor furniture, fixtures, curtains, or rugs that you no longer use or like. Once the bigger items are moved, you can use the momentum to keep going. Go into each room one by one and move through your list. If you come across items that you are not sure what to do with, use the general questions for clarity.

Keep positive during this process and stay in touch with your emotions. It is likely that you will feel sadness and a hesitancy to let go of some things. Feel your feelings and remind yourself that you can lose track of who you are when you hold on to things. You are not the old tickets to a concert, a pair of pants that no longer fit, a chair that is falling apart, or books that you have already read. Things only contain the value that you give them. Value yourself more and things less.

We often become overly identified with certain objects and believe that they embody aspects of who we are. As you eliminate material possessions, declutter your home, and let go of your emotional attachment to certain objects and things, you will begin to more clearly see the true you. Things get old, break down, become outdated, no longer work, and fall apart. They are not alive. You are energy, always evolving, changing, and discovering new aspects of who you are. The authentic you is beautiful and unique. Don't give these qualities to inanimate objects. Minimize your attachment to things and pour your energy back into you. Your authentic self is priceless.

I let go of things and more clearly see who I am.

114. Simplify

Simplify your life and make space for the true you to emerge. In this busy, multitasking world, we can lose our sense of self. From morning until night, our energy is often focused outside of ourselves on tasks and responsibilities that do not support the truth of who we are. Take back control by focusing on what is essential.

Begin by contemplating what is meaningful and important to you. Make a list of seven things that you most value. What is it that you most want to do in life? What are your priorities? What is your purpose? Write them all down, then list the top seven by their priority.

Think of all the many things you do each day. Write down your commitments and how you spend your time. Write them all down: work, childcare, after-school activities, hobbies, family time, social activities, phone calls, email, Skype, Facebook, playing games, shopping, cleaning the house, watching television, etc.

Compare the two lists. How much of your time and energy is devoted to the seven things that are of most value to you? What are you spending time on that is not reinforcing what is important to you? Eliminate those things that needlessly consume your time and energy. It might feel stressful to let go of commitments to people or activities that you have been involved with.

Here are a few more ways to simplify and enjoy what is important to you.

Learn new ways to let go of stress and relax. Reading Facebook posts, playing computer games, or watching television may give you a break from stress and release tension, but there are other ways to relax that offer you greater rewards. Take a walk, breathe, practice yoga, meditate, read a good book, or play with your kids. These kinds of activities will empower you to relax and reconnect with yourself.

Learn to say no to those things in life that you do not want to do. Feelings of guilt may surface when you take back your power to choose what to devote your energy to. Many of us have been taught from a young age to put aside our feelings and do and give what others expect of us. Learn to tune in to your gut and listen to it. If something does not feel right for you, say no.

Learn to say yes. Become aware of what you want to give your time and energy to and say yes to it. Don't put it off and wait for the perfect time. Life is here for you to live, right now. We often put our true needs at the bottom of the list. When we are done taking care of others and doing what is expected, we tell ourselves that we can then focus on what is important. Yet that time never arrives.

Look at your list of what you most value. Review your current daily activities, then ask yourself if there is a way that you can bring the qualities of what you most value into what you are already involved with. For instance, perhaps being able to help others is one of your values. Is there a way that you can help others at your current job? Can you volunteer time at your child's school?

Commit to spending time and energy doing what is most important to you. Even if it does not seem practical or if you feel that it is too indulgent, take the leap into you and do it.

Simplifying your life allows new interests and possibilities to emerge. As the waves of busyness cease, what is essential and authentic emerges.

I commit to what is truly important in my life.

115. Plant a Flower

Plant a flower as a metaphor for the blossoming of your inner self. The step-by-step process of nurturing a flower from seed to blossoming is similar to the process of nurturing the emergence of your authentic self.

Approach this process with mindful awareness. Begin by going to a garden store and picking out a flowerpot, or use one that you already have. Get soil to fill the pot and flower seeds of the type that you would like to grow. Put the pot in a sunny area in your home or outside, add the soil, and plant the seeds. Water the plant and make sure it gets plenty of sun. Be patient and soon the seed will sprout and grow into a beautiful blossom.

This simple symbolic act of planting and nurturing a flower encourages the blossoming of your authentic self.

Symbolically, the pot represents your physical self. It is the container from which your true self is nurtured and emerges.

The soil is symbolic of all that you have experienced. Your life challenges, losses, problems, and issues are the rich soil from which your true self emerges. Like soil, your past may not appear to possess any outstanding qualities that can support and cultivate the beauty within you. Yet everything that you have experienced nurtures your strength, awareness, and potential. With these qualities, your authenticity emerges.

The seed represents the dormant potential within that has not yet manifested. Even though the seed is small and bears no resemblance to a flower, with the right conditions it transforms. With care and nurturing, you too will experience this kind of transformation. What is unknown and unrealized lies dormant until it is activated.

Water softens the seed and represents intuition and emotion. Trust your intuition and what is in your heart. The sun represents love, power, and energy. Shine your light, love yourself, and have gratitude for the qualities that make you unique. Be patient. You will break open, like the seed, and new life will spring forth. You will blossom and spread your love and beauty out into the world.

I plant a flower and blossom.

116. You Need You

You are your most prized creative masterpiece. Unfortunately, not everyone sees you in this same way. Have you ever been criticized, judged, or bullied for being different or for speaking your truth? Do you ever feel like you have to choose between being yourself or being who others expect you to be?

We all have, at one time or another, spoken our true thoughts, shared our feelings, and expressed who we are, only to be ridiculed or rejected. Sometimes we can easily shrug off another's opinions and commentary; at other times it goes deep. We feel the pain of not fitting in and become fearful of sharing our truth. This apprehension often keeps us locked into a false sense of self. We put aside our natural impulses in favor of doing and being what we feel will be accepted and safe. The stress of not being liked and understood keeps us locked in an isolated inner prison.

Ignoring and detaching from your true feelings and thoughts and ignoring your preferences only leads to loneliness and leaves a void that no one can fill. You need you. It is only when you embrace and love yourself for who you are that you find the safety and security you seek. You are the best friend and ally that you have. Don't alienate your most powerful self. At the end of the day, liking and respecting yourself is what matters most.

Don't give your power to an outer source. Know who you are and dig deep within and create the kind of life that you desire. You are more powerful than what you may believe. Choose what feels right for you. However quirky, different, exotic, or unusual your preferences and tastes may be, if something speaks to you and your heart leaps with delight and wonder, embrace it. Explore the variety of life and new aspects of your authentic self will spring forward. Give yourself permission, without judgment and criticism, to be who you are. Don't ever think that there is anyone more important to please than your most true inner self. This is who you want on your side. There are no substitutes.

I choose what feels right for me.

117. Tarot Cards for Self-Awareness

Throughout the ages, we have sought the reflection of our truth in a multitude of ways. Originating in Northern Italy, tarot cards have been used for generations to gain insight into ourselves, others, and life. They reveal the wisdom of a variety of esoteric traditions, spiritual philosophies, and multiple cultures.

The tarot cards are a deck of seventy-eight cards used for divination. Traditionally, each deck is composed of fifty-six minor arcana cards and twenty-one numbered major arcana cards and one unnumbered major arcana card. The major arcana cards represent the various stages of growth in our search for greater meaning and self-awareness. Through symbolic images, they reveal universal life lessons passed down through the ages. You can use tarot cards to gain insight into your current life lessons and the hidden influences that are either promoting or limiting your highest good.

If you do not have a tarot deck that you use exclusively for self-growth, you may want to purchase a new one. Tarot cards respond to energy. Over time, they begin to acclimate and hold the energy vibration of the purpose that they are used for. I have tarot cards that are used primarily for personal divination, a deck that I use when I work with others, and a deck for spiritual growth and self-awareness. If there is not a bookstore that sells tarot cards in your area, there are many online stores that carry a variety of tarot decks. Purchase the deck that you feel most drawn to, and make sure that it has a major arcana.

To begin, take out the major arcana cards and shuffle them. As you do this, relax, take a deep breath, and exhale any stress and tension. When you feel ready, ask for a card that represents you at this time. Take a deep breath and pick the card that feels right. Place it face down in front of you. Shuffle the cards again and ask for a card that represents an inner aspect or quality of who you are that you need to own and express at this time. Take a deep breath, pick the card that feels right for you, and place it face down in front of you, next to the first card.

Now pick up the minor arcana cards. These cards speak to the more practical and day-to-day aspects of life that have a minor or temporary influence on your ability to express your authentic self. Shuffle these cards, relax, and breathe. When you feel ready, ask for a card that reveals an inner obstacle that you need to confront and release. Pick the card and place it face down in front of you, next to the other two cards. Shuffle the cards again and ask for a card that reveals the gifts and abilities that you can draw from to empower you at the current time. Pick this card and place it face down in front of you, next to the other cards.

Begin to turn the four cards in front of you over one at a time. Start with the card that represents you. After you turn it over, take a few minutes to meditate on it. Look at the symbols that the card contains, then listen within and trust your intuition.

When you are ready, turn over the card that represents the aspect of your authentic self that you need to own and express at this time. Again, take a few minutes to meditate on the card. What feelings and thoughts surface as you look at the images on the card? Trust your gut feelings and intuition.

Now turn over the two minor arcana cards one at a time, and pay attention to the images on them and your intuitive impressions. Write down what you receive. New insights will continue to unfold.

Most tarot decks come with a booklet that provides insight and an interpretation for each card. Consult this for further understanding and insight into what your cards reveal. There are also a variety of books that can help you to further tune in to the symbolic meanings of your cards. Llewellyn Worldwide offers an extensive collection of tarot cards and books at www.llewellyn.com.

I meditate on tarot cards for deeper self-awareness.

118. Learn Something New

Do you ever become bored and restless with the familiar daily routines, but you are not sure of what to do to create positive change? Sometimes we sense that it is time for something new in our lives, but we are not sure where to begin. We have been taught to live life safely, to follow the sure and predictable and not take risks. Although it is natural to seek security and stability, we are here to create and experience new ways of being. To be truly alive, we must continually grow beyond ourselves and challenge our complacency.

If you feel as if it is time for a change, it is. One way to break out of familiar routines and discover more of who you are and what brings you joy is to learn something new.

If there is something that you have always been interested in but have not had the time to pursue, give it a try. We often put off learning new things because there does not seem to be any practical reason to do so. Taking a class about European history may be interesting, but you may not find it to be useful in your everyday life. You might also use this argument to persuade yourself not to pursue similar activities, such as poetry, calligraphy, drawing, or theater. Another common reason for not learning and participating in a new activity is that we believe we may fail or not be very good at it. Although it feels great to quickly learn and excel at new things, if you judge your performance as either good or bad, you will eventually be disappointed. When we do things for external validation, we limit the magic of self-discovery and the joy of being fully present to what is.

Learning and participating in new activities can be inspiring and increase our creative potential. When we challenge our self-perception, new doors open. This is what happened several years ago when I took some computer programming classes. I had been working as an intuitive and an artist for a short time and I began to doubt that

I could make a living in my preferred profession. On a whim, I enrolled in a course to learn how to be a computer programmer. Every class was a struggle. I barely passed and have never worked a day in my life as a computer programmer and probably never will. Yet learning computer programming helped me to better understand myself in new ways. One surprising insight had to do with intuition. Never a math or science scholar, I relied heavily on my intuition to guide me through what felt like a maze of computer language and code. To my surprise, many of my classmates also seemed to follow their hunches and were unknowingly using their intuition. I came to a better understanding of the diverse ways that we use our intuition and how much we use the more logical left brain when we intuit. This insight and others inspired me to teach intuitive development a bit differently than I had been and to eventually write the book *Discover Your Psychic Type*.

Shake up your routines and self-perception. Activate the emergence of a new you. Learn a new language, take up a sport, or learn how to fly a plane or parachute from one. Whether it is a cooking class or a course in how to make wine, grow herbs, run the rapids in a kayak, or survive in the outdoors, explore the natural world and your connection to it. Join a theater group, take acting lessons, learn how to play a musical instrument, or take voice lessons and sing in a band. Learning something new is learning about yourself and having fun in the process.

I commit to learning something new.

Chapter 9

YOUR SPIRIT, ESSENCE, AND ENERGY

You are energy and spirit. In this chapter, you can come to know yourself in this way. Through exploring your subtle energy, your aura and chakras, deeper self-truths are revealed. Although it may seem to be a less tangible way to know yourself, your energy is the core of the true you.

119. Perceiving Your Essence

Where does the authentic self live within you? Is it in your brain, heart, or belly? Within all of these areas and spread out beyond your body, your true self is alive and active. Your authentic self is more than what you have done, your beliefs and opinions, your thoughts, your emotions, and your body. It is energy. Your authentic self is the meeting point of your essence and your soul and spirit. It is the central hub where all of you comes together.

Your authentic self receives energy vibrations from a higher source of love and wisdom. Some call this God, divine being, divine presence, Spirit, positive energy, or the All That Is. However you choose to describe this unseen and benevolent presence or whatever your conscious experience of it has been, it is always with you.

As you become more aware of and work in unison with this powerful source of love and wisdom, you attract and receive more positivity and vital life source energy. You can use this energy in every area of your life. When confronted with problems, pressures, and challenges, remember to draw from this energy.

Become comfortable with the intangible and with essence. We can have a hard time discerning and believing in things that exist outside of the material and physical. To accept and truly know your authentic self requires a revolutionary step into the unknown. You are a mystery and a truth that cannot be fully grasped.

Try this simple practice.

Close your eyes. Take a full, deep breath and ask yourself, *Who am I?*

Then pause, breathe, and listen within. Repeat the question a few times. Each time, pause, breathe, and listen within.

Then ask yourself the following questions:

- *Am I my body?*
- *Am I my feelings and emotions?*
- *Am I my thoughts or my beliefs?*
- *Am I my past, my future, or my possessions?*
- *Who am I?*

As you ask yourself these questions, pause after each one. Quietly listen and feel.

Eventually you will begin to feel a presence, an energy. It may be subtle and you may not be able to define or grasp it. Just allow it to be present. Become more comfortable with knowing yourself in this way. Perceiving yourself as energy is transformative.

I am spiritual presence.

120. You Are Energy Frequency

In your purest state of being, you are an individualized expression of pure divine energy. There are many layers of truth that define you. Your authentic self comprises your feelings and emotions, your thoughts, and your spirit and soul self. At the most basic level, all of these are energy.

In 1905, Albert Einstein proved that physical and material matter broken down into minuscule components exists as indestructible energy. Never static and always in motion, these minuscule particles of energy vibrate at different frequencies and create your individualized energy pattern. Like a snowflake, you are a unique and one-of-a-kind energy formation. There is no one quite like you.

You are constantly changing and transforming your energetic frequency. Emotions such as love and compassion have a high energetic frequency. Fear, pain, depression, and other similar emotions have a low energetic frequency. Negative thoughts have a low frequency, and positive thoughts have a higher frequency. When your overall frequency is low, you attract and create negative experiences. Loving yourself and being kind and forgiving to yourself and others, along with thinking positive thoughts, elevates your vibrational frequency. A higher vibrational frequency empowers you to attract and create positive experiences, love, abundance, and well-being.

Yet it is not only your everyday thoughts and feelings that contribute to creating and attracting what you experience. Unresolved emotional wounds, repressed anger, and traumatic memories and past experiences also send out an energetic signal. These powerful but often unconscious energies attract negative, disruptive, and confusing experiences and people into your life.

The more you release and heal the past and choose to live in positivity, the more you live from your authentic self. From this center of high frequency vibration, you naturally attract and create the pure path of love, abundance, and purpose that you are meant to be living.

I choose positivity.

121. Your Subtle Energy Body

Your authentic self is birthed from pure energy. The seed from which your individuality takes form has its roots in the unseen. Although we identify who we are primarily through our five senses and our thoughts and emotions, we are so much more than this. As you develop a sensitivity to your true self, you will be able to better perceive the nonphysical aspects of who you are.

Your subtle energy body is an intricate, pulsating web of energy that both extends beyond the physical body and vibrates from within it. The aura is the outermost egg-shaped web of the subtle energy body. It is made up of energy vibration and undulating layers of color that expand and contract with graceful fluidity. The aura contains seven inner layers of energy, each serving a specific function. These energy layers are the interface between the physical body and cosmic life force energy. Each of the seven layers filters and regulates the interaction and interconnectedness between an individual's spiritual, mental, emotional, and physical energies. The aura also protects the body from toxins and detrimental energies and acts as an antenna to attract and receive positive and life-giving pure energy.

The seven layers of the aura are connected to the chakras. Chakras are spiral discs of energy that act as receivers and distributors of pure life force energy throughout the body. There are seven major chakras located from above the head to the base of the spine. These seven chakras are each encoded with seven varying levels of vibration, which absorb and process our emotional, mental, spiritual, and physical experiences and life lessons. Each chakra contains a diary of information about our present and past-life challenges, karma, and soul purpose and potential.

Your physical, mental, emotional, and spiritual health and well-being directly correlate to the health of the chakras. Highly sensitive to our thoughts, actions, feelings, experiences, and spiritual purpose, the chakras are influenced and affected by all that we experience. When we deny our feelings, harbor negativity and critical judgments, stuff away our pain, and detach from our personal power, our chakras absorb all of this material. The chakras are never in denial. They embody all that we think, feel, and experience as well as our higher soul purpose and individuality. The heavier energy vibrations of negativity, pain, and powerlessness block and restrict the chakras from distributing the necessary flow of vital life force source energy to our organs and physiological systems.

It is important to become aware of the subtle energy body to fully understand our authentic self. Although tuning in to the subtle and nonphysical aspects of self may seem difficult, our energy make-up provides us with insight and important information about who we are. When you define yourself only by the more concrete parts of who you are, you limit your potential. Your innate power goes unrecognized and lies dormant within. Understanding your subtle energy body provides you with greater opportunity to unleash the power and potential of your total being.

I am vibrant high-frequency energy.

122. First Chakra: Rooted in Your True Self

Your seven chakras are spinning vortexes of vital energy that extend from above your head to the base of your spine. Each of your chakras is a power center that embodies the lessons that you have come into this life to learn and your thoughts, feelings, and experiences associated with these lessons.

The first chakra is the root chakra, or base chakra. It is located at the base of the spine. This chakra is energetically coded with issues of survival, our sense of belonging, our instincts, and our ability to live our purpose. The function of this chakra is to empower us to fully live our divine purpose in the physical material world. When we are unable to identify and make choices that demonstrate our highest good in a concrete way, this chakra loses its necessary energy fuel. We experience fear and insecurity and lack the ability to take care of ourselves. However, when we are conscious of and live in alignment with our authentic self, our first chakra empowers us to manifest positive opportunities and supportive people who assist us in living our purpose.

The root chakra also connects us to the earth and to the people, animals, and living beings we can enjoy a compatible relationship with. Without a genuine connection to others in the physical world, our soul becomes adrift, with no anchor. Like a limb cut off from a tree, we lose the necessary energy we need to fulfill our purpose and maintain a healthy mind, body, and spirit.

The intuitive information contained in the first chakra has to do with our early family issues and experiences, our ability to connect with others and the environment, and our capacity to move forward and make concrete changes in our everyday lives.

Ask yourself the following questions to better understand if your first chakra is supporting your authentic self:

- *Overall, am I satisfied with my current relationship connections to my family and friends?*
- *What recurring patterns and challenges do I continue to confront that originated in my family of origin?*
- *What are the blessings that I have received from my family?*
- *What and whom do I feel most connected to? What and who is my spiritual family?*

When your authentic self is known and appreciated by others, you are supported in living and expressing your purpose and truth. If you do not have the kind of connection with others that you need, spend time cultivating relationships with those who can know and appreciate the true you.

I am connected to the earth and to all living beings.

123. Second Chakra: Giving and Receiving

The second chakra is the sacral chakra, which is located in the lower abdomen, below the navel. This power center is concerned with creativity, sexuality, finances, and issues of control. This is the Johnny Appleseed of chakras, as it empowers us to spread the seeds of creative life force energy out into the material world. This chakra teaches us balance through give and take, sharing and receiving and manifesting and experiencing.

Empowering us to draw from the well of cosmic energy within, the sacral chakra motivates us to create and manifest our true self in the world. When we expect to be taken care of by others and do not rely on our inner source energy, we negate the power of this chakra. Compromising our authentic self by becoming a victim to unfulfilling relationships, unsatisfying work or career choices, and empty physical distractions and pleasure weakens the health of this chakra. However, discovering your inner goodness and casting the seeds of positive energy out into the world strengthens this chakra and produces positive manifestations.

This chakra teaches us the lessons of karma and cause and effect. What we send out into the world comes back to us in the exact measure that we set in motion. Before we can manifest fulfilling experiences and abundance, we must act in integrity with our truth.

The intuitive information contained within this chakra includes issues of material success, finances, and relationships and our ability to express and share our creativity and manifest our passions and dreams. Issues with sexuality, reproduction, childbirth and the ability to express physical and sexual intimacy can also be found in this chakra.

Ask yourself the following questions to better know if the second chakra is clearly broadcasting the energy of your authentic self:

- *In what area of my life do I most use my creativity?*
- *Do I need and want more intimacy in my relationships?*
- *Am I comfortable with my sexuality?*
- *Am I confident that I am able to take care of myself financially?*
- *Is my career satisfying?*
- *Do I feel that others and the world owe me something?*

Meditate on these questions and continue to nurture the seeds of positive energy within.

> *I spread the seeds of love and abundance in the world,*
> *and what I give returns back to me tenfold.*

124. Third Chakra: Your Personal Power

The third chakra is the solar plexus chakra. It is located between the navel and the base of the sternum. This chakra is the power center of your authentic self. Listening to and supporting your truth, respecting yourself, and maintaining healthy boundaries with others strengthens this chakra and heightens your overall vibrational frequency.

The third chakra is the center of our personal power, self-esteem, and physical intuition. When we listen to our gut intuition and allow it to inform us of what is right for us and what conflicts with our integrity and sense of honor, we come into the full awareness of our authentic self.

This chakra transmits life force energy into personal power. It is the energy distribution center for integrating the spirit into the personality self. When our personality or ego self listens and acts on the direction and guidance of our spirit, we flow within the current of higher-vibrational energy. Fear dissipates and we outwardly express confidence and inner strength. However, when our ego self believes that it is its own source of power, we experience insecurity, stress, and anxiety. We develop a false self to hide our vulnerabilities and fears.

The intuitive information contained in the third chakra has to do with our personal power, insecurities, fears, self-esteem, personality, ego, and ability to listen to and trust our most basic instinctual and gut intuition.

Ask yourself the following questions to better understand if your third chakra is supporting your authentic self:

- *Can I trust my intuition and act on what I know is true for me?*
- *Am I comfortable with my personal power?*
- *Where in my life do I feel the most powerful?*

- *In what area of my life does my self-esteem need improving?*
- *Do I need the approval of others?*
- *Do I choose what is right for me even if others do not always agree with my choices?*

The center of your authentic self, the third chakra is your inner compass, guiding you through your everyday decisions and choices.

I trust my gut intuition.

125. Fourth Chakra: True Love

The fourth chakra is the heart chakra. It is located in the center of the chest, near the heart. This chakra is the energetic spiritual and emotional axis of love. It absorbs all degrees and expressions of emotional energy along with the higher vibrations of divine love. Its function is to assist us in learning how to integrate the higher divine attributes of love, compassion, forgiveness, and kindness into our everyday lives and relationships. The ability to heal the self and others and transmit cosmic healing energy into the world is also centered in this area.

When we are unable to forgive or commit to loving ourselves or another or when we value material things more than emotional well-being and compassion, the heart chakra contracts. Giving love without being able to receive it or expecting to be loved without returning love to others also creates an imbalance of the fourth chakra. Having a difficult time loving self and others or being fearful of acknowledging and expressing authentic emotions limits the flow of vital source energy through the fourth chakra, the heart, and consequently the entire body.

The center of divine love and compassion, the fourth chakra also contains our emotional fears and vulnerabilities and our relationship wounds and resentments. This chakra reveals our capacity to create a balance between the love and care that we give to others and the love and care that we give to ourselves. The lessons associated with the fourth chakra have to do with our ability to release the lower-ego emotions of anger, jealousy, and fear and receive and embody the energy of unconditional divine love. This chakra also empowers us to be true to our feelings and emotions. Being present to all of our emotions, the positive ones as well as those that are more stressful, allows for the emergence of our innate loving goodness.

When we love ourselves with the deep and pure energy of divine love, our authentic self blossoms and expresses itself fully and completely.

Ask yourself the following questions to better tune in to your capacity to love yourself and others:

- *Who from my past or present do I still need to forgive?*
- *Are there any past relationships from which I still need to heal?*
- *Do I have loving and supportive relationships?*
- *Can I be vulnerable and safely express my emotions and feelings?*
- *Do I love myself?*

Love and embrace all of who you are.

I heal my emotional wounds and receive divine love.

126. Fifth Chakra: Express Yourself

The fifth chakra is the throat chakra, located in the neck and throat area. Empowering us to speak and express our truth, this chakra supports us in living and speaking with integrity and honesty. It assists us by funneling life force energy into our authentic self and then motivates us to express and share our truth with others. The ability to discern your truth, make choices, and align your will with higher wisdom and guidance is also connected to this chakra.

We constantly weigh what we want to share with others and the world and what we would rather suppress. When we express and share our authentic truth and individuality, we flow within the powerful currents of life force energy. What we stifle and repress causes energy blockages and creates dysfunction. Expression creates movement. The spiritual challenge of this chakra is to release our self-judgments, surrender to what is, and trust and allow the moment-to-moment emergence and expression of our personal truth.

The lessons associated with the fifth chakra have to do with the ability to communicate and express ourselves, our fear of being judged, and our judgments and criticism of others. Allowing others to exert control over you or controlling others and your environment creates an imbalance in this chakra.

To further understand if your fifth chakra is fully supporting your ability to express your authentic self, ask yourself these questions:

- *Do I harbor negative self-judgments?*
- *Am I overly critical of myself or others?*
- *Can I accept what happens in my life, or do I have a need to control outcomes?*

‣ *Do I allow others to control my thoughts, feelings, and actions?*
‣ *Do I speak my truth?*

Fill your lungs with air and breathe. Express and speak your truth and release your need to control how others perceive you. Just be and allow others to speak their truth.

I express my true self to others.

127. Sixth Chakra: Authentic Truth

The sixth chakra is the brow chakra, or the third eye chakra, and is located above and between the eyes. This chakra is the gateway for cosmic wisdom. It channels the energy of enlightened thoughts and higher consciousness and empowers us to become aware of possibilities, ideas, inspiration, and cosmic vision. Our thoughts, attitudes, beliefs, and judgments are meant to evolve. As we accept and contemplate higher truth and wisdom, we are renewed and transformed. We live as spiritual beings, empowered beyond the confines of physicality. When we stay stuck in our negative judgments, attitudes, and limited thinking and knowledge, we restrict the flow of life force energy. Our brain and mental functioning withers, shrinks, and short-circuits.

It is through the sixth chakra that we become aware of the spiritual realm and consciously commune with spiritual influences. This chakra is also the gateway for the psychic skill of clairvoyance, the ability to visually see energy information.

An inability to let go, negative thought patterns, excessive mind chatter, lack of self-evaluation, rejection of new ideas, and feelings of inadequacy all impact the health of this chakra. The energy information associated with the sixth chakra includes our acceptance of higher truths, our ability to become aware of spiritual reality, and our trust in the love and benevolence of higher forces.

In the sixth chakra, your authentic self is expressed as consciousness and pure awareness. To better understand if your sixth chakra is supporting your authentic self, ask yourself the following questions:

- *Is my mind filled with constant mind chatter?*
- *Am I able to allow my perception of my truth to evolve and change as I grow in awareness?*
- *Do I meditate and allow a higher vision of my authentic self to unfold?*

It is through the sixth chakra that you perceive yourself as a spiritual being. Your authentic self takes on a new, expanded dimension that supports and nurtures you in the here and now.

As I receive divine wisdom, I grow and evolve.

128. Seventh Chakra: The Eternal Self

The seventh chakra is the crown chakra, located an inch or two above the head. States of pure spiritual illumination, acceptance of grace, and enlightenment emerge through this chakra. Concerned with our soul plan and its integration in our day-to-day lives, this chakra converts higher life force energy into three-dimensional, workable phases. Keeping in sync with our soul's evolutionary agenda, this chakra is the bridge between timelessness and time. It empowers us to evolve through attracting and creating those opportunities that adhere to the lessons, challenges, and joys that we have come into the physical life to experience. This is the chakra that is responsible for disrupting the status quo and initiating change in our daily lives. When we are not living our soul plan, the seventh chakra takes charge and sees to it that in one way or another we begin to pay attention. Unexpected events, such as being fired from your workplace, confronting a life-threatening illness, divorce, or financial collapse, are the calling card of the seventh chakra.

The seventh chakra is the portal through which you can access higher-vibrational energy and guidance. Your spirit guides and angels and other benevolent spirit beings communicate and influence you through this chakra. Past-life influences and your soul plan and life script can also be accessed here.

The seventh chakra can also bring miracles and blessings into your life. Stagnation and resistance to change, unwillingness to surrender to your higher purpose, denial of spirituality, the inability to trust life, and selfishness create disharmony in this chakra. When this chakra is unbalanced or not open to life force energy, you will feel that you are out of sync with your life purpose. You may also experience discord in your everyday affairs and have unfulfilled aspirations and dreams. When you generate positive energy and listen and act on spiritual guidance and your personal truth, this chakra manifests as opportunities and experiences of goodness, love, and abundance. This chakra empowers you to contribute to the common good and to become spiritually aware.

Ask yourself the following questions to better understand if your authentic self is receiving the nurturing life force energy:

- *Can I tell the difference between higher guidance and my ego-based desires?*
- *Do I regularly find ways to be of service to others?*
- *Am I often surprised by unexpected changes and challenges in my everyday life?*
- *Am I willing to let go of what I want my life to be and allow myself to be led?*
- *Do I see beauty and the hand of divine grace in my everyday activities and experiences?*

The seventh chakra transmits your individualized spirit and soul plan into your authentic self. Without this awareness, we feel as if we are limited and powerless humans roaming the planet at the mercy of outer forces. In truth, you are divine presence.

I open myself to the higher vibrations of divine energy.

129. Exploring Past Lives

Many years ago I lived in a small town in rural Georgia. I moved there from Southern California to help my mother, who was the director of a children's home in the area. It was quite a culture shock. In California, I was involved with a metaphysical healing center, where I regularly went to workshops and classes and explored my own psychic and medium abilities. In Georgia, I felt as if I had stepped back in time. I was in Baptist Bible heaven. Psychics and anything New Age were viewed with skepticism by most people and as the devil's work by many. After about a year of not trying to ruffle anyone's feathers, I was in need of a New Age fix. With a strong desire to uncover a past life through hypnotic regression, I began to look for a hypnotherapist. The few people whom I asked for a referral all mentioned an older Methodist minister who lived on the outskirts of town. I called him and we set up a meeting to discuss a hypnosis session.

We met in his small, wooden, white-washed chapel. He was a kind man who seemed surprised that I was interested in hypnosis. As we sat for a few minutes engaged in small talk, I told him that I was specifically interested in accessing a past life. To my surprise, he seemed to take it in stride. He told me that he had never done hypnosis for this purpose but was willing to give it a try.

The following week, I came in for my appointment. While I reclined in a big, comfortable chair in his office, he calmly induced me into a relaxed hypnotic state. I quickly began to see images of a different time and place. I was a man and a priest in what I knew was Egypt. I was standing in a large colosseum about to give a speech. Although I cannot recall exactly what I said, I know that I challenged the current spiritual beliefs. What I said was not well received. I was almost immediately cast out of the city, never to return.

For the remainder of that life, I lived in a small hut along the banks of the Nile River.

Accessing this life was of tremendous help to me. There were similarities in the challenges that I confronted in that lifetime and the feelings and choices that I was making in my current life. Understanding my soul history and the meaning and purpose behind my present challenges inspired me to become more aware of the lessons that I was learning and to heal.

In the many past lives that I have since explored with my clients and on my own, it has become clear that our current life lessons and challenges are similar to those that we have encountered in previous lives. The circumstances, places, and physical characteristics may change, but the deeper lessons do not. We evolve along a soul-path continuum that continuously offers us the opportunity to evolve and grow by experiencing the effects of our choices. Past-life regression empowers us to better identify the areas where we most need to grow and what needs healing. It offers the ultimate big-picture view of our journey as a soul.

One of the most important benefits that I have received in my past-life regressions is the ability to experience my authentic self in another body and another time. We are not our body, our mistakes, our socioeconomic status, or our current circumstances. Past-life regression provides us with the opportunity to experience the core self within. It puts us into contact with a part of ourselves that is true, wise, and eternal. This is the authentic you.

I am not my body or my circumstances. I am eternal.

130. Little Ball of Light

You come into this world a pure being of innocence and love. Your angels escort you through the love and bliss of the heavens and into the waiting arms of the physical world. Filled with courage and hope, your spirit arrives with all it needs to fulfill its earthly destiny. Yet this awareness and knowing are quickly forgotten. The thoughts, emotions, beliefs, and illusions of the world take over. We assume a position of powerlessness, unaware of who we are and what we are capable of.

Although you may not always remember that wisdom, courage, and eternal joy are alive within you, this is your core being. Reclaim your true essence and free your spirit. Embrace the possibility that you are more than you believe yourself to be. Go backward; forget what you have been told and the assumptions that you have made about yourself. Close your eyes and imagine yourself as the little ball of light that came soaring into this galaxy on its way to birth. Feel the energy and luminosity of yourself as light. Warmth, knowing, confidence, abundance, and joy radiate from the depth of your spirit.

Find a picture of yourself as an infant or young child, or recall as best you can an image of yourself as a child. Look at you. Look in your eyes for the light. It is there. Become aware that it has never left you. Dialogue with the young you and tell yourself that you remember. All that you need is within you. Relax and allow it to surface.

I feel the light within.

Chapter 10

YOUR ARCHETYPAL GIFTS: LIVING YOUR PURPOSE

One of the most common questions that I am asked during an intuitive reading is *What is my purpose?*

We have an inner knowing that we have come here to give and share of ourselves in a unique and meaningful way. Your purpose is an innate aspect of your authentic self. This chapter empowers you to become aware of and express your innate gifts.

131. Recognizing Your Purpose

An inner soulful drive compels us to find out what we came into this world to do, give, and experience. Even though our purpose is not always easy to discern, it is always winding in and out of our day-to-day life. When you live authentically, it naturally surfaces.

To better identify your purpose and apply positive energy and effort to making the most of it, consider the following.

You have more than one purpose. You may have a purpose that lasts for a lifetime and others that last for a few years, months, or just weeks. In every aspect of your life, there is a purpose that you have come here to explore.

For instance, relationships are endowed with purpose. People come into our lives who are part of the overall plan through which we can express and live our purpose. You may be in a relationship with someone with whom you have a karmic debt. You may need to extend generosity and help to this person, or they may be in your life to support and care for you. You may also need to learn how to own your power and love and care for another without compromising yourself. A relationship may also come into your life for the purpose of providing you with the experience of a deep and committed love and passion. Your purpose may be to let down your barriers to intimacy and truly give and share of yourself.

There are also special abilities and skills that you have developed and refined in past lives and your present life that you have come here to express and share. This is your opportunity to contribute to the overall good of others and the planet. Sometimes your purpose in the world is easy to recognize. When you work for an organization that directly helps those who need assistance or for a group that cleans up polluted lakes and rivers, your contributions are visible and tangible. At other times, your purpose may be less obvious.

When you work in a supportive or clerical position within a group or organization that is involved in assisting, helping, and caring for others or the environment, your purpose may not be as evident, but it is no less important.

Your purpose is not necessarily specific to your career. Instead, it may emerge though the arts, your spirituality, your intuitive or healing gifts, or your kindness and ability to inspire others to forgive and love. Remember, your purpose cannot be measured purely by worldly criteria. When you are aligned with your authentic self, your positive contributions are always significant.

In every area of your life, there is a purpose that is specially designed for you. Let go of your expectations as to what you believe a purpose should be. Look within your heart and feel what brings you a sense of connection and inner satisfaction. Become aware of the challenges that you seem to continually confront. Feel your passion and let it guide you. Let go and know that your purpose seeks you. Be available and attentive to its emergence. As you become aware of your authentic self and express it in your daily life, you are living your purpose.

When I experience joy, I am living my purpose.

132. Your Gift Archetype

Expressing and sharing your authentic self with others is an important dynamic in fulfilling your purpose. You have come into this lifetime with innate talents and abilities or gifts. Giving and sharing them with others is an essential part of your purpose. Sometimes our gifts are obvious, but not always. Surprisingly, they often lie dormant within, ignored or undervalued.

One of the ways to recognize the special abilities and innate strengths that you have come into this world to give and express is through understanding and working with archetypes. Archetypes are universally understood patterns of behavior. They are the basic blueprint from which all of humanity develops, grows, and evolves. The origin and basis of archetypes dates back to Plato, who observed and developed what he called the *theory of Forms*. Carl Jung developed a similar understanding of the universal and ancient patterns and images that govern the psyche. In 1919, he began to refer to these as *archetypes*. In the 1940s, Joseph Campbell brought to our attention the archetypes embedded within myths and stories and their importance in our personal and collective growth and evolution.

Archetypes Throughout History

Archetypes influence all areas of our lives. They emerge through our personality, our personal preferences, and our soul energy and through the innate gifts that we share with others. Since the beginning of recorded time and in all cultures across the globe, there has been a prominent belief in the exchange of gifts between humans and a greater divine source of power. This relationship has formed the powerful, potent structure and content of archetypal gifts.

For instance, there were many gods in ancient Egypt and all of them bestowed both earthly and spiritual abilities, talents, and gifts.

The goddess Isis was associated with the gift of healing as well as pregnancy and birth. The god Anhur bestowed upon warriors the gifts of strength, courage, and cleverness, while the powerful Bast gave the gift of music and joy to mortals.

In Greek mythology, gods are responsible for the origin of the earth and its inhabitants and both the good and evil aspects of the human experience. Gods provided not only good crops, protection, and health but also the gifts of prophecy, magic, and special powers. Athletes, warriors, philosophers, and artisans received their power and talent from the gods. Medicine was also thought to be a gift from celestial beings. In the Christian faith, gifts play a central role in God's relationship and interaction with the earthly realm. Gift giving is so common in the Bible that the words *give, giving,* and *gift* and other such words occur at least 2,100 times throughout the scriptures.

Since the beginning of time, the importance of giving and receiving gifts has been a cornerstone in understanding ourselves and the greater cosmos. Although archetypal gifts originate in the cosmic realms, they empower us with practical and useful skills here in the material and physical world. Through your archetypal gifts, your soul finds expression in the everyday and mundane world. When you consciously tap into their archetypal energies, you are supported beyond your individual experience and efforts.

There are hundreds of ancient archetypes imprinted in our collective unconscious, and most of them, including the leader, healer, and artist, are familiar and play a dynamic role in contemporary culture. To better recognize your gifts, I have identified seventeen predominant gift archetypes. Some may be expressed through a career, others through hobbies and interests, and many through more subtle everyday interactions with the world and with others. The predominant gift archetypes are the warrior, innovator, teacher, misfit, healer, seer, artist, magician, sage, patron, athlete, entertainer, shaman, leader, monk, channel, and alchemist. As you tune in to your archetypal gifts, your dormant abilities, skills, talents, and subtle faculties and capabilities come to life.

Your gifts are at the heart of your authentic self. Knowing and expressing them empowers you to live in harmony with your most empowered and eternal self. The seventeen gift archetypes are described in the following pages, with tips and advice on how to identify your gifts at the end of the chapter.

I express and share my special gifts with others.

133. Warriors

Throughout time, one of the most recognizable archetypal gifts has been that of the warrior. When the archetypal energy of the warrior moves through you, your authentic self is on fire. The warrior is active, passionate, and courageous. Warriors are able to move through obstacles, confront negativity, dispel illusions, and alert and inspire others to do the same. Warriors courageously face reality, know it for what it is, and confront and conquer their inner and outer demons.

If you are a warrior, you likely are attracted to environments where vigorous change is needed. You may enjoy professions that provide you with the opportunity to be active and create change. Not content to be quietly complacent and on the sidelines, warriors are likely to join the military or the police or fire department or to seek political office. Often community-minded, warriors champion the rights of those who are poor and disenfranchised, become environmental activists, or work from within the system to improve and challenge the policies and practices of traditional institutions. The accountant who insists on rechecking receipts, the parent who speaks out at school board meetings, or the taxi driver who calls city hall to complain about broken street lighting in poorer neighborhoods may all harbor the gift of the warrior. Many warriors help others to work through limiting beliefs or inspire them to make changes in their lives and follow their dreams.

Warriors can provoke strong reactions in others. Unlike healers, teachers, and even shamans, warriors are not always diplomatic and sensitive to individual needs. They are catalysts who often wonder why others are complacent and idly sit by and allow negativity or corruption to flourish. The warrior's heart is connected to justice and power. An archaic energy that has been expressed in a multitude of ways throughout time, modern-day warriors are still inspired by and connect to raw and primitive power.

Many people are repelled by the idea of power. It is often associated with manipulation, force, control, and selfishness. Power for power's sake, as we all know, can be dangerous. Since the beginning of time, power in the wrong hands has caused more suffering and devastation than any other demon that we know. For the warrior, the dance with power must be connected to the highest vision of justice, peace, and equality for all. Without this intent, their innate relationship to power will at the very least lead to aggressive and self-centeredness and, in the worst-case scenario, become destructive and damaging to self and others.

Power in the hands of the enlightened and balanced warrior can be sublime artistry. The warrior can be a prophet in motion. If your gift archetypes include the warrior, aim high and allow your authentic self to be expressed through positive and vigorous constructive action.

The archetypal gift of the warrior
motivates me to take positive action.

134. Innovators

Innovators see a new way. Not content with the familiar and expected, they often seek new paths and ways of doing things, for the sheer joy of it. With intuitive and insightful awareness, they quickly detect outdated methods and wasteful expenditures of time and energy. An innovator would much rather be finding their way through chaos and uncharted territory than following the known. Innovators feel that because something has always been done a certain way, that is enough reason to change. They are bored with the norm and are inspired by the challenge of blazing new trails.

Innovators can be found in a multitude of environments and in all walks of life. Many are drawn to traditional areas of science, engineering, construction, and technology. In these areas, physical necessity and desire catapults them into creative action. If your gift archetypes include the innovator, you may be a bit of an inventor. If you have a multitude of ideas and perceive possibilities for new gadgets, new technology, or futuristic healing or scientific instruments or inventions, you embody the gift of the innovator.

With this diverse gift, innovators can be found in any environment that allows them to do things their way. Many artists, musicians, writers, and teachers are innovators. Mothers and fathers who entertain their children with interesting games and inspired ways to learn or the office employee who devises a time-saving computer network for sharing information are likely innovators. So is the farmer who creates an environmentally sound method of fertilizing plants or the young college student who launches a successful media business that speaks to a current need.

The innovator creates new systems and cutting-edge ways of dealing with old problems. What is seen, known, and utilized repels them. With one foot in the pure, vibrant energy of the unseen, they long to put into physical form what lies just outside of our reach. Blending and combining the abstract and concrete, they are eternal pioneers who move us out of our patterns and habitual approach to life. Their greatest joy may be in giving physical expression to what is necessary but elusive.

If we cripple the heart of the innovator, we will lose our collective soul. As much as we need the innovator, we are at times at odds with their genius. As a culture, we have rigid expectations and fixed ideas of what is desirable, and we are repelled and suspicious of the new and different. Our schools teach conformity, our places of business expect their employees to adhere to specific standards, and we dismiss what is not popular and not yet proven. The original, unique, and unusual are sidelined by the trendy and fashionable, but the innovator does not live in the past. All of the things that promise you prestige and popularity today are, for the innovator, already relics of the past. The message that innovators persistently whisper in our ears is that reality is out there somewhere in what can only be imagined. If you think that you have found the way, think again. Truth runs along a very thin high wire that extends into the unknown.

If one of your gift archetypes is that of the innovator, keep reaching into the beyond. Allow yourself to indulge in what can be while keeping your feet planted firmly on the earth. Your authentic self is expressed through your innate ability to bring into physical reality that which is not yet seen or believed. It is through this passion that you feel most alive.

I allow new and original ideas to flow through me.

135. Teachers

When you have been bestowed with the archetypal gift of the teacher, you cast a compelling and magnetic spell far and wide. Your authentic self embodies wisdom and gifts you with the ability to dispense knowledge and understanding. By unraveling the mysterious, simplifying the complex, and explaining the essential and important, the teacher provides what others need to know and cannot easily grasp on their own.

Some teachers are professionals who can be found in the classroom or as instructors in various fields of study. Others teach through cyber technology, mentoring, or coaching or as speakers and trainers. Those with the archetypal gift of the teacher likely lined up their dolls or pets as children and explained the ABCs or the mysteries of the universe to them. With the gift of the teacher comes the passionate ability to share knowledge and enlighten. Teachers have a natural magnetism that engages others, and they often contribute their time and money educating those with a desire to learn. Teachers not only are able to decipher the complex but can also reach deep into their student's soul and wake and stir their unacknowledged intelligence and drive.

Many with this archetype teach in less than conventional ways and places. For instance, you might find a teacher driving a taxicab, expressing their enlightened philosophy to their riders while careening down a busy street. Your hairstylist, landscaper, mechanic, checkout attendant at the grocery store, patient, child, or dog walker or the homeless man standing on the side of the road may all be teachers. They may, of course, not recognize this gift in themselves, yet they all have one thing in common. The archetypal pattern of the teacher is working through them to share and provide the knowledge and information that others need to know or experience. Some teachers are strong-willed and assertive and freely share their beliefs and philosophies. Other teachers are more subtle and intuitively tune in to what others need to know and learn. They may teach through offering suggestions or insight or sharing their own stories and struggles.

No matter what kind of formal education teachers have, a great number of them have acquired knowledge through the school of hard knocks. Many with this gift have had to confront and learn through their own difficult and challenging life circumstances. At an early age, they may have been motivated to seek deeper knowledge as a way to understand and cope with their own confusing and complex issues.

The God Icarus

If your authentic self embodies the gift of the teacher, it is essential to balance your innate connection to wisdom with the humble attitude of a novice. In Greek mythology, the saga of the god Icarus represents the inherent challenge of the teacher. Icarus attempted to escape Crete by flying over the sea with wings that his father constructed from feathers and wax. Icarus was warned not to fly too high or too low. The sun's heat, he was told, would melt the wax on his wings, while flying near the sea's dampness would weigh down and damage his feathers. Yet Icarus ignored these instructions. When he flew too close to the sun, the wax of his wings melted and he plunged into the sea and drowned.

This is an important lesson for those who embody the archetype of the teacher. Their role is not to accumulate knowledge and wisdom for its own sake. Instead, like Icarus, the teacher must travel and act as an intermediary, receiving the higher light and vibrations of wisdom, symbolized by the sun, and then giving this knowledge to those in the darkness and in need, symbolized by the vast sea. The teacher's home is in this in-between place, between wisdom and ignorance.

I learn by teaching what I know.

136. Misfits

When your authentic self embodies the archetype of the misfit, you have a powerful but often hidden purpose. Most misfits are painfully aware from an early age that they are different. If this is one of your archetypes, you most likely do not consider it a gift. Instead, you may feel inherently out of step with those around you and misunderstood by many. It takes time and deep understanding to fully appreciate this gift and yourself.

Many misfits do not feel like they fit in with their families, workplace, or community. They may struggle with loneliness, self-acceptance, and self-confidence. Their life lesson is to become a light unto themselves and accept the positive impact that their uniqueness can have on others.

The soul elects to embody and express the archetypal pattern of the misfit to learn and teach transformative lessons. Divine energy moves through the misfit to shake and move us out of our humdrum acceptance of what we consider the norm and the way things should be. The impact that the misfit can have on others can be subtle or astronomical. A misfit may unknowingly be the catalyst through which another opens their heart, comes to a new understanding, or embraces self-acceptance.

The child who is born with a facial disfigurement, the artist who works as an accounts receiver in a corporation, the man or woman who struggles with gender identity, or the brawny, macho-looking biker who worships the Goddess are a few of the varied expressions of this gift. Through their mere presence, they break the mold and present a new way of being. Fully realized misfits can change the course of history. Every great enlightened teacher had the gift of the misfit. Jesus broke through the religious limitations of his time and brought forth an evolutionary world teaching. Siddhārtha Gautama, also known as the Buddha, gave up a life of ease and wealth to seek the true path to enlightenment. Noah, Moses, Ralph Waldo Emerson, and modern-day challengers of the status quo such as Steve Jobs all embody the archetype of the misfit.

In Greek mythology, the ultimate mythical misfit was Prometheus, who was charged with the task of molding humankind from clay. In an attempt to better the lives of the mortals, he risked his standing as a god by stealing the best food from the gods' lavish feasts to nurture the mortals. In direct rebellion to Zeus, he also gave humankind fire. Creating upheaval in the prevailing status quo between the mortal and godly realms, Prometheus suffered a punishment that was quick and harsh. He was condemned to be pecked apart by a giant eagle for eternity. Yet as a misfit, he transformed humanity.

Many misfits, either knowingly or unknowingly, go against the tide of the accepted norms. While their opposition may come through their own innocence or by way of helping and enlightening others, they often pay the price. They may be shunned, misunderstood, falsely accused or suffer the isolation that often comes with being different.

Misfits challenge the status quo and provide opportunities for growth and the expansion of consciousness. They alter our preconceived notions of how things should be and allow room for alternative viewpoints and behaviors. The hardened box that we might unknowingly confine ourselves within slips away bit by bit when we are given free passage to new perceptions and ways of being. Although misfits can often be annoying or perplexing and invoke fear, misunderstanding, awe, or disdain, they can also strengthen our ability to be our most authentic self and help us to know ourselves in new ways. When we accept the gift of the misfit, we set ourselves free.

I accept and celebrate all that is different about me.

137. Healers

When your authentic self seeks expression as a healer, you are a conduit of love and healing to those who suffer and are in need. You have an innate ability to tend to those who are ill, transform pain and toxicity, and restore emotional, mental, spiritual, and physical well-being. True healing is always a mystery and takes place in a variety of ways. The manner in which this archetypal gift is expressed varies from individual to individual.

Many healers work primarily with the physical body and within traditional settings as conventional doctors, nurses, physical therapists, or chiropractors. Social workers, counselors, psychotherapists, and life coaches focus on healing emotional, mental, and spiritual issues. Some healers harness the higher vibrations of divine healing energies and become hands-on healers. They may work with healing touch, Reiki, or the laying on of hands. Others may practice acupuncture, homeopathy, massage therapy, or one of the many other types of alternative healing. Some healers do not work in a professional capacity. Instead, they offer their gifts of love and healing to friends, family, neighbors, and even strangers. They may heal through prayer and send healing energy to another or to a group or nation. Some healers quietly heal through listening to the sadness and grief of another or being present and compassionate during times of hardship and trauma.

No matter what form of healing those with the gift archetype of the healer utilize, they allow a greater power and wisdom to flow through them, to others and to the world. Many healers do not always recognize that they embody this gift. However, if you are a healer, you will likely experience some of the following common characteristics.

You naturally and usually unknowingly form relationships with those who are wounded or in need. An invisible radar attracts those whom you can help. The less conscious you are of your gift, the more likely it is that you will unconsciously attract friends, lovers, partners, and strangers who need healing. You are likely able to compassionately listen to another's misfortunes and troubles. Thought of by your friends and family as the giver, nurturer, and listener, you easily open your heart to others. Attuned and sensitive to emotions, you easily feel what others feel. Many are attracted to your calm and nurturing presence.

Healers are often clairsentient. This is the ability to intuit the emotional feelings and physical sensations of others. Waking at night feeling sad, stressed, excited, or joyful for no known reason is common. Tuning in to the emotional energy of loved ones, even those thousands of miles away, may be a frequent occurrence. Healers might also absorb the physical aches, pains, and bodily condition of others. They may suddenly experience an intense pain in their chest only to later discover that this occurred at the same time a family member had a heart attack. Since this ability is not limited to serious illnesses or pain, a healer might also feel another's headache or digestion issues.

Healers may also feel the emotional energy of a tragic or an uplifting event before it happens. Many people have told me that they felt a sense of doom and fear and woke during the night feeling profoundly anxious, sad, and stressed prior to the terrorist attacks in the US on September 11, 2001. This was also true of the tsunami in Japan in 2011. Many people reported to me that for days preceding the event, they felt waves of grief, fear, and stress.

Healers can intuitively absorb the energy of others while riding on a subway, sitting in a classroom, or watching the news on television. Moving through the day with an acute awareness of others' moods, feelings, stress, wounds, and pain can be tiring and confusing. The drive to assist others who are in pain is so powerful that healers may experience an inner pressure and almost compulsive need to give, share, soothe, comfort, and uplift. When you are not conscious of being a healer or your gift is not recognized by those in need, you likely will unconsciously absorb their negativity and pain. This can cause long-term mental, emotional, spiritual, and physical issues and problems. When we take on others' pain, stress, illness, and fear, we suffer. If you suspect that you have the archetypal gift of the healer, acknowledge it and seek a positive avenue through which you can be of service. The more conscious you are of your gift and the more you are able to harness its potent energy, the less you absorb unwanted and detrimental outer influences.

I allow healing energy to flow through me.

138. Seers

Within the archetypal gift of the seer is the intuitive ability to discern the cosmic order, patterns, and wisdom inherent in all things. The soul elects to express the archetypal gift of the seer to bring insight and understanding to chaos and confusion. The seer taps into the deep well of all-knowing and reveals the truth with clear awareness. Seers are driven to know and understand and are often frustrated by conventional explanations and definitions. Trite answers will never satisfy the seer. They need to experience the aha knowing of intuitive insight to be fully convinced.

Seers can be found in all kinds of careers and jobs. However, they are most fulfilled when they are able to intuit and dissect unknown and unseen patterns and energy information that can help and enlighten others. For example, many psychiatrists, therapists, and life coaches can perceive the underlying influences hidden within another's behavior and attitudes and help them to understand these unconscious patterns. Many seers are drawn to teaching, research, and writing. Scientists who discover the cause of illness and disease and develop medicine and treatments likely have the energy of the seer as one of their archetypal gifts. The engineer who can discern the patterns and organization inherent in structures, both physical and theoretical, shares the gift of the seer. This gift can also be found in many architects and builders who are able to perceive the blueprint of a skyscraper or the complexity of technology and computer science.

Whatever their job or career may be, most seers eventually become restless with conventional information and knowledge. This inner discontent often leads them to explore the mysteries of self, life, and the cosmos. Through contemplation and intuitive insight, the seer seeks a truth that they can feel within their heart and soul.

The seer enters the door to a more celestial wisdom, often felt as piercing insights and revelations. Yet the truth that seers often stumble upon is not always easy to accept. It may be counter to their personal beliefs and previously accepted understanding and challenge them to accept new perceptions and views of reality. This, too, is a gift that the seer shares with others. As they break down the old forms and systems of belief, they accept a higher understanding of universal wisdom and inspire others to do the same.

Many seers have an interest in working with the traditional tools of an oracle. They may be professional intuitives, astrologers, or tarot card readers, or they may work with runes or discern the wisdom of the I Ching. Seers are driven to share their gifts with family and friends and provide insightful guidance and advice. They are the people others go to when they are confused and need clarity and a sense of direction. Others know that the seer's penetrating intuitive awareness can skillfully unknot the ball of confusion, revealing the clear strands of truth and a course of action.

One of the beginning signs that the archetypal gift of the seer is flowing through you is the desire to understand and make sense of your life. Seers expend time, energy, and attention in thought, generating new ideas and going beyond appearances. Once the archetypal energy of the seer is activated within the psyche, seers vigorously listen and look within to fully know their authentic self.

I perceive the patterns and cosmic order behind appearances.

139. Artists

When the archetypal gift of the artist emerges through your authentic self, the world becomes a magical playground of color, shape, music, form, and sublime sensory expression. Life wakes you up and pulls you into another reality transposed over the seemingly inert material and mundane world. You see, feel, hear, and touch with the skill of the divine. Because you are misunderstood and often disregarded by the busy, security-minded general population, your task is not an easy one. The creative divine is seeking expression through you, and when you feel its energy and fire, you cannot rest. Your purpose and mission is to free yourself from limitation and capture the essence of the sublime and give birth and form to it. You are here to call others into the mystery of the creative, to move hearts, open minds, and be the springboard from which others leap into glorious, freewheeling expression.

Artists express their authenticity and creative fire in limitless ways. They may, for example, be painters, woodworkers, weavers, potters, writers, musicians, metalworkers, poets, actors, cake decorators, film makers, or costume designers. The list is endless. However, there are many artists who do not draw or paint, did poorly in art class in school, or have never been motivated to pursue a particular artistic genre. Your artistry may not be expressed through a specific talent or form. Instead, it may surface through what you wear or how you decorate your home, wrap gifts, or garden. Whether it is through writing, dance, choreography, swallowing swords, or telling jokes, artists express their unique gift wherever they may be. Whatever their creative expression, artists are always reminding us of the pure genius at the core of their being. When you respond and fully accept the artist archetype, the gates of creative freedom open wide in sometimes subtle and sometimes momentous ways.

The beginning sign that signals the presence of the artist archetype is the sensitive awareness of a beauty and perfection that others do not perceive. You see, feel, experience, notice, respond to, and are moved by a subtle but persistent impulse that cannot be adequately defined. In a ray of sunlight slanting across the horizon, your spirit rises. You feel a rhythm travel up through the earth, and your body spontaneously moves in unison with it. Colors jump off of a work of art. They play with your senses and you become mesmerized and enchanted. You perceive the perfect love in the face of a child. A flower dips slightly in the dew and you feel a oneness with all of nature. Within the sound of the wings of a bird in flight or the buzz of a bee, you hear the heavens sing. You not only long to participate in this wonderful melody of heaven and earth, but are compelled to express it to those who are denied access. The artist within flares up and moves you to create this bliss.

Claiming Your Artistry

Not all those with the archetypal gift of the artist engage and align with their creative desires. Many are not aware of the gift that longs to move through them. Their artistry may stay focused in keeping up with current trends of what is popular and the opinions of others. Instead of listening within and being motivated to reach greater creative heights and go beyond the conventional, their vision is mediocre. Often frustrated and unsatisfied, always searching for the new and novel, the artist within becomes restless. Some with the artist archetype may be aware of the creative and artistic impulse, but they do not participate in their deeper calling. The risk of letting go into creative freedom and creating original and unique forms of art that may not fit in with the current popular norm may be too great. They may fear being ridiculed and having their work misjudged. Some artists feel that they need outer recognition and financial guarantees to pursue their artistry. Whatever the obstacle may be, the biggest limitation for most artists is the fear of letting go into the unknown and living in the now.

The archetype of the artist is not simply about what you do, produce, and materially create. This gift calls you to accept and receive the creative force of the universe and then to interpret and express its mysterious rhythm as best you can. The perfection of this calling is not simply in what is produced, but in your ability to absorb creative energy and express it in your own unique way.

The artist lives in present time and responds moment to moment with creative originality. When a soul elects the archetype of the artist as their gift, the authentic self expresses itself in fluid and constantly changing ways. What is true today may change tomorrow or a few minutes from now. The artist is constantly being pulled by an invisible muse that demands full allegiance. Artists may be unconventional, appear to be spacey, do things their own way, and disregard convention and the current norms. This is part of what they offer us: a way out of the familiar and acceptable. They prod us to explore another vision of truth. However distant and elusive this vision may be, the artist confidently leads the way.

I flow with the power of the creative.

140. Magicians

The magician is a unique and original creator who acts with courage and inner assurance. When your authentic self flows with the energy of the magician, you are driven to shift, change, and transform both what is seen and known and what lies outside of physical laws and limitations. The elements of the heavens, the earth, and everything in between are the tools of your trade.

The magician archetype has its roots in the mythological practice of the immortal deities who granted otherworldly gifts to the human realm. It is this mysterious exchange that drives and motivates the magician. Sailing beyond what can be measured and defined by physical standards alone, those under the influence of the magician use their innate instincts and intuition to create and produce the practical from the unexplained.

Modern-day magicians seek to redefine and defy those physical laws that confine and limit. Often drawn to work in cutting-edge science and technology, they imagine and conceive of possibilities that may seem unattainable to others. The magician is not content with purely theoretical potential. Instead, with tenacity and determination, they go about building and implementing their vision into concrete reality. Modern magicians are presently involved in such pursuits as creating clothes that carry enough of an electrical current to power an MP3 player, and designing underwear embedded with electromyographic sensors that can inform an athlete of the intensity of their muscular workout. They have created eyeglasses that turn a computer or iPad into a three-dimensional game board and robots that are controlled by thought. Closely linked to the gift of the innovator, who empowers original thought processes and inspires new ways of doing things, magicians are not as interested in what has been. Instead, the magician has an innate intuitive awareness of natural power and seeks to combine elements and forces to unleash possibilities.

Although the fields of science, technology, and engineering are dominated by magicians, people who embody this archetype can be found in whatever career or pastime offers them the opportunity to pursue and manifest their futuristic visions. They often work silently in their garage for hours, patiently designing and building a tool that perfectly shells a pistachio or captures the power of the wind and sun. As parents, magicians engage their children to experiment and discover new ways of doing things. They are the friend or family member whom everyone turns to for help with understanding and figuring out the latest technology and gadget. Magicians may also be interested in modern-day magic, puzzles, gambling, or playing cards and they may design and play video games.

Some magicians still practice the ancient arts. Many are Pagans who follow the Old Religion and seek to live in harmony with the natural forces. They may spend years learning how to harness the power of the earth, moon, sun, and stars to become effective practitioners. Casting spells with clear intent and deep self-awareness, the magician channels life force energy and directs it into positive forms.

Magicians can influence and affect others in profound ways. What they present to the world can send shivers down the spine, seduce us into wordless states of awe, and release us from the prison of normalcy and convention. Like wizards and magicians throughout time, present-day magicians harness an elusive power, then offer to our wearied minds the gift of magic.

I perceive the magic of life.

141. Sages

The archetypal gift that may best embody the power of the authentic self is the sage. The sage is the master of self. If this is one of your gift archetypes, then you have the courage and curiosity to know self, and in knowing self, you know the world.

The journey of understanding ourselves begins by identifying our many varied and multidimensional aspects. Like a spiral, one knowing leads us to another and another, until you encounter your core authentic self, whose center is the heart of goodness. There is a powerful force within you that wants to reach out and love others. When you encounter the magnitude of the love that is within, you become aware that you are part of a greater whole. The journey into self continues until there is no longer a boundary that separates you from others. It is at this juncture that the sage archetype comes into its full power.

With transcendent intuitive and psychic abilities, such as precognition, clairvoyance, and telepathy, the sage taps into the mystery of the divine. These special abilities emerge along with the desire and drive to further develop them. Once their intuitive and psychic abilities are fully developed, the sage seeks to inspire others to better know and understand their core truth.

The sage walks through the world quietly and often unnoticed. Although they are sprinkled throughout all professions and careers, they are most comfortable in the role of guide, advisor, consultant, expert, or director or in any position where they can see the big picture and help others to perceive their gifts and effectively utilize them. Sages can be found in conventional careers such as finance, politics, or law or as philosophers and writers. They also populate less conventional areas. Many spiritual guides, professional psychics, intuitives, life coaches, and counselors also embody the sage archetype. Yet the sage doesn't always express their gift through a profession. They are the friend or family member who offers timely wisdom and insight or the waitress at your favorite restaurant who shares a bit of advice when you most need it.

All of the gift archetypes have a shadow side. When you are in denial of your gift and do not consciously develop and follow its inner direction, aspects of the gift emerge in confusing and often negative ways. Self-awareness and conscious self-development are essential for the gift of the sage to fully blossom into its most positive expression. When the lower ego drives impede the natural emotional, spiritual, and mental maturation process of the sage archetype, difficulties arise. Instead of crossing the bridge of personal truth into the rich waters of objective and universal truth, they may feel that their way is the only right way. They may lack compassion and ridicule, criticize, and judge others harshly. Their ability to deceive and to justify their behavior allows them to exert control over others and use them to their advantage. The shadow side of the sage archetype can show up in the policies and actions of groups and governments. Tyranny has its roots in a lack of emphasis on personal self-development and self-awareness.

Embrace the journey of the sage. Layer by layer, peel off the false and that which does not ring true to you. When what is left is your personal truth, you will dive into the sea of all and discover that there is no separation between you and others. This is your freedom and the gift of the sage archetype.

I seek truth.

142. Patrons

The archetypal gift of the patron is expressed as freely given, altruistic, and devoted service to those in need. If this is one of your archetypal gifts, you are likely the friend or family member who is always available to lend a hand and help others. If common activities include things like mowing your busy neighbor's lawn, cooking meals for your sister's family when she is ill, or answering the phone at 2:00 a.m. to talk to a friend who had an argument with her boyfriend, you are expressing the gift of the patron.

Mythological deities created the original archetypal pattern of the patron through their devoted service to the human realm. Certain gods and goddess ruled over specific areas of human need and activity. For example, the god Apollo ruled over music and healing, Aphrodite was the goddess of love and beauty, and Demeter was the goddess of the harvest. These deities devoted themselves to the care and nurturing of their specific domains and the humans who were a part of them. This celestial and benevolent care is also at play with patron saints, such as Archangel Michael and Mother Mary, who protect and guide those in need. When the archetypal gift of the patron is influential within your authentic self, pure compassionate and gentle strength flows through you to those in need.

Much of the charitable and selfless work in the community and the world is undertaken by those who have the patron archetype as one of their gifts. They support positive causes, movements, and activities with their time, money, loyalty, and effort. The patron is often able to manifest large sums of money and attain positions of power through which they accomplish their higher purpose. Through their infectious altruism and empathy, they attract others who follow their example. They are heart-centered compassion in action. Some patrons work on the local scale through bettering schools and advocating for the needs of people who are poor, mentally ill, or disenfranchised. They may also be fundraisers for medical and health initiatives and social projects. Many patrons can be found working on a national or global level, enlightening others about political or social conditions, challenging the misuse of people and resources by corporations, or protecting those who have no power and voice. Yet for all of their selfless giving and sharing, the patron often goes unnoticed. With little need to be in the spotlight or be publicly acknowledged for their efforts, patrons give because it feels so good and right to do so.

The supernatural gift of the patron often shows up early in life. The child who notices and responds to the needs of others might very well be a budding patron. Through lemonade-stand sales, donating clothing, and giving their toys to children who have less, they have a natural and spontaneous desire to give. Children who embody the archetypal gift of the patron are often innocent and a bit naive. Their drive to give and support others can be so powerful that as they grow older, they are at risk of being taken advantage of and possibly duped, fooled, or exploited by those seeking an easy victim. For this reason, it is important that children who exhibit this gift learn discernment and who to trust. Otherwise, they can become easy prey and may eventually shut down the impulse to give, robbing them of the tremendous joy that comes from being in harmony with their gift.

Through their deep, empathetic drive and devoted commitment and passion to help and be of service, patrons inspire and motivate others to do the same. The patron has a compelling aura that others notice and want to be a part of. They are not easily intimidated, repelled, or discouraged, and they do not give much credence to the word no. Capable of moving mountains and inspiring others to follow their vision of possibilities, patrons exude magnetism and power. When you come into contact with one, you can sense their inner strength and devotion. In the midst of obstacles and overwhelming conditions, the patron is patient and works day to day, transforming frustration, anger, and fear into passion and drive. The authentic self of those with this archetypal gift tends to be uncomplicated, as they do not overthink their heart-centered impulses. They are action-oriented and are motivated by a higher vision of unity and equality.

I generously give to others.

143. Athletes

The archetypal gift of the athlete flows through the authentic self as the desire to excel, triumph over physical limitations, and express the strength of one's spirit through awe-inspiring physical feats. This gift exists within those who participate in sports, physical exercise, and training. The athlete archetype also exists in those who overcome physical limitations, health challenges, and illness. The ability to defeat physical frailties and imperfections through inner resolve and self-will exemplifies the gift of the athlete.

The Olympic Games are representative of the archetypal beginnings of this gift. Although the first documented Olympic Games was held in Greece 776 BCE, the original games were said to have started as early as 1232 BCE to honor the god Zeus. By defeating Kronos in a wrestling match, Zeus was said to have won dominion over the earth.

The archetype of the athlete is not solely a gift given to the individual to enjoy and develop their athletic prowess, strength, and skill. Instead, there is something mysteriously magnetic and compelling about athletes. They possess an unspoken connection to a raw and organic presence and power that we long to embrace. Spirit speaks through the athlete and reminds us that we are not simply bones, blood, and finite matter. Within every act of physical excellence, the power of the spirit is apparent. Great athletes thrill and excite us and get our adrenaline pumping by pushing the body to act and participate in ways that seem to defy what is physically possible. The message that we, too, are greater than what we appear to be sinks deep into our psyche when we watch an athletic event. This archetypal gift is also present in those who confront debilitating illness or who, either through birth or accident, struggle with a disability. When the power of the spirit victoriously shines through as determination, a positive attitude, and victory over physical limitations, we are humbled and reminded of the power of our spirit.

Just as the first Olympic competition was held in honor of Zeus, we still perceive and absorb the radiance and vigor of the gods in our present-time athletes. We put them on a pedestal and want to absorb their special magnetism and expert abilities. Although current-day athletes for the most part do not want to be role models when it comes to their behavior and choices outside of their sport, we are hard-wired to perceive them as having a higher status than the rest of the general population.

Many young children who compete in sports tap into the archetypal energy of this gift. They boost their self esteem and confidence by testing their skills and abilities against their peers. Seeing the happiness and pride of their parents as they defend a goal or hit a home run may be one of the first experiences they have in being admired for their prowess.

If you have the athlete as one of your archetypal gifts, you may not be a professional athlete and you may not struggle with an illness or disability. Many of those with this gift go to the gym, run, swim, or work out on their own with no applause and with no visible benefit to others. Yet their devotion and drive to touch the heart of this gift within themselves strengthens their spirit and endows them with the ability to positively impact others. For instance, the woman running down the street at six o'clock in the morning may encourage her neighbor, who spots her from the window, to work out and take better care of herself. The father who coaches his child's soccer team may feel more alive while watching his team's attempts to learn new skills while running down the field. The lonely and awkward adolescent who receives praise and attention for winning and breaking records in his high school cross country races might give hope to others who are awkward and lonely.

When the archetypal gift of the athlete is expressed in one of its many forms, your body, mind, and spirit aspire to move with the magic of the gods. Feel this energy and accept the raw vital life force energy that pulsates through your authentic self.

I exercise and enjoy physical activity.

144. Entertainers

When the archetypal gift of the entertainer expresses itself through your authentic self, your aura sparkles and activates a response in others. If you can evoke laughter in even those with the driest and most serious demeanor or if you can naturally spin a dramatic story that captivates those around you, the archetypal gift of the entertainer flows through you. This gift enables you to stir the heart and invoke emotion in others.

Entertainers are fairly easy to spot. They are seldom shy wallflowers who hide in the background. They are widely seen on television, movie screens, stages, and church pulpits and at political rallies. Some entertainers make a career with their gifts, but most do not. Many who embody the gift of the entertainer are not in the spotlight or in front of large audiences. These entertainers might be the class clown in school, the office employee whose jokes break the tension of a serious meeting, or a salesperson whose sales skyrocket because of their ability to make others laugh and relax. Entertainers are everywhere, and although they may not be media stars and become wealthy, their contributions are endless. They are the parent who parades around like their child's favorite storybook character to help the child learn how to read or the friend you can count on to see the humor in life's most difficult events. Entertainers brighten our day and help us to laugh, take ourselves less seriously, and enjoy the daily grind of life.

Entertainers have played a prominent but often misunderstood role in every culture and place on earth. The ancient Romans loved storytelling, theater, and plays. In China, operas complete with elaborate costuming and masks have kept the country's cultural and spiritual history alive. Court jesters helped maintain calmness and just rule in the Middle Ages. In our society, professional entertainers are more popular and admired than those in almost any other occupation.

Actors, comedians, musicians, vocalists, producers, dancers, and performers have some of the highest incomes and are the most gossiped-about people in our culture. Despite our advancements in science, technology, medicine, and engineering, we fall under the mesmerizing spell of the entertainer, who yields tremendous influence.

Many entertainers unknowingly use their intuition to know what their audience, even an audience of one, is feeling and what will make them laugh, cry, and feel deeply. Many of those with the gift of the entertainer are able to dissolve their personal boundaries and identify deeply with what another is feeling.

We love entertainers in part because they exude a special magic that we cannot control, contain, and fully grasp. When we sit in rapt attention listening to the harmonic chords of musical interments all blending in unison, our worries slip away. Our hearts race during a suspenseful scene of a movie thriller, and we forget our judgments and isolation when a comedian evokes laughter in our shared everyday experiences. Entertainers move us out of our incessant thinking and into the moment and pure presence. They invoke authentic reaction and emotion.

The purpose of the entertainer is so much grander than the personal quest for accolades, praise, and honor. The archetypal energy of the entertainer is not concerned with the egotistical, irresponsible, and pleasure-seeking pursuits of many present-day entertainers. All too often they trade their dance of laughter and joy with the divine for the vain applause of the mundane. Within the gift of the entertainer is the ability to be a force of unification for all of humanity. Their gifts can only be fully realized when they accept that their greater purpose is in what they give and not in what they receive. For all of their magnetism, charisma, and spontaneity, they are, after all, one of us.

I openly and freely express myself to others.

145. Shamans

Within the archetypal gift of the shaman is the ability to perceive the true essence within all of life. If being in nature, hearing a bird's song, caring for a pet, or working in the garden helps you to feel a oneness with all of life, then you may have the gift of the shaman. This gift empowers you to be a bridge between the natural world and the human realm. Your task is to become conscious of the grace and power that this gift endows you with. With the gift of the shaman, you open to the greater essence of nature. The spirit of the plant, the rock, or the animal reaches out and invites you into a more intimate relationship. This unique connection with the natural world empowers you to learn its secret wisdom and mysteries.

Shamans are commonly thought of as intermediaries who, while in a state of trance, provide healing and wholeness to others through communication with the spirit realm. Yet the archetype of the shaman includes a much broader range of interaction and connectedness with all living beings. Not all shamans act as traditional indigenous healers who enter into altered states in order to help others. Instead, many with this archetypal gift express it through their ability to perceive the energy of the divine life force at work within physical form. For the shaman, the dandelion, the squawking crow, the rolling river, and the starry night all flow with the essence of spirit. They tune in to, understand, and communicate with all of life, and all of life seeks to commune with them. Each plant offers its perspective, birds warn of what is to come, stones reveal old wisdom, and snakes bring the gift of transformation. Shamans come to express and share nature's secrets.

It is no surprise that the emergence of the shaman begins with a deep and abiding love for nature and all of its inhabitants. From a young age, shamans have an affinity and fascination with the natural world. From a pet dog or cat to fish, insects, dinosaurs, caterpillars, and elephants, the young shaman is fascinated by all creatures. They love to be outdoors, playing in the sunlight and in the mud, with their pockets full of stones. Whether they are watching ants carrying off bits of cracker crumbs or gazing into the sky and speaking to the clouds, the young shaman's connection with the spirit within physical form is natural and intuitive. As the shaman grows older, their interest with nature matures into devotion. They are likely to rescue dogs and cats, learn about herbs, spend time gardening, camping, or walking in nature or contribute financially to organizations that preserve the natural world.

At this crucial time in history, as we confront the potential destruction and decline of Mother Earth, it is more important than ever that shamans embrace their gift. Since the beginning of time, the inherent power within all living beings has been recognized and honored. In times past, indigenous cultures have had a reverent and sacred relationship with the plants, trees, water, wind, sun, moon, and all creatures large and small. We understood our dependence on the natural world and sought ways to invoke its continued sustenance and grace. The role of the shaman to please the spirits of the natural world and ask for their blessings was essential for survival. This is no longer the case. We ignore, disregard, and feel more powerful than any other life form. With our arrogant sense of entitlement, we have brought ourselves to the brink of environmental disaster. Although its usefulness and importance are often ignored, the shaman archetype is still present and working within the psyche of many. More than ever, we need the shaman to act as an intermediary between the spirit of the natural world and the human realm. There is an unrecognized, powerful alchemy that occurs when we listen to nature and act in response to its rhythms and wisdom. When we reconnect with the earth through our spirit and heart, healing is possible.

If you have the gift of the shaman, recognize its power. Listen within to your heart and spirit, and you will be guided to where you can have the greatest impact and be of service. It does not matter whether your contribution is big or small. Your authentic self will be strengthened and your purpose clearer as you open your heart to all living beings.

I am one with all living beings.

146. Leaders

Do your friends and family look to you for direction and sound advice? Do you have a natural ability to bring people together for a common cause? Are you fair and can you put aside your self-interests for the greater good? Can you harness the collective energy of a group and focus it toward a common goal? If you have these abilities, you may have the archetypal gift of the leader. The leader is an empowering archetype that enables you to bring people together, create change, and accomplish goals.

Magnetic personalities with an underlying seriousness about their role and responsibilities, leaders can be found in all types of environments and occupations. Politics, business, the military, and the fields of eduction, religion, science, and technology all attract leaders. Capable of initiating reforms and creating change, leaders often work outside of the norms and conventional roles. Leaders such as Martin Luther King Jr., the civil rights champion; Mahatma Gandhi, who led through nonviolent civil disobedience; and Nelson Mandela, who fearlessly led others through personal sacrifice, became the change that inspired their followers. No matter how big and daunting their opposition may be, leaders believe in the power of the individual, and they often find themselves living this truth at their own expense.

There are many inspired leaders who do not gain fame and public attention. Naturally humble and not seeking the spotlight, most leaders work quietly and discreetly. For instance, a leader might be the family member who steps out of the dysfunctional family patterns, heals, and then inspires and helps others to do the same. In the workplace, the leader is the employee whose integrity, kindness, and strong work ethic cast a wide net of influence that sets the tone for others to follow. Unlike leaders who are motivated by selfish and egotistical motives, those who accept the soulful archetypal energy of the leader can unite disparate groups and work toward unifying solutions. They are rugged pragmatists who lead with inner confidence and knowing and are able to confront the raw realities of life. The world, with all its chaos, conflicting viewpoints, confusion, and ups and downs, does not intimidate the leader. Their purpose is fixed in the innate belief that they must go forward despite opposition. With piercing insight into what needs to be accomplished, they inspire others to go beyond their self-defined limitations. In religion, business, politics, or whatever field they are involved in, their bliss is in helping others to discover their personal talents and work toward common goals. The leader is similar to the magician or alchemist in their ability to harness collective power and energy and focus it toward a common dream. Wherever they are, their sense of purpose and charisma attract attention. They tend to be passionate individuals who others innately trust. Without much overt effort on their part, their thoughts, opinions, and views influence and guide others to new levels of self-awareness and effective action.

Throughout history, leaders have played an essential role in shaping and controlling human destiny. There have been benevolent leaders who have inspired, enlightened, and moved us toward positive reform. Other leaders have been more ruthless and domineering and have led us to prejudice, war, and death. If your archetypal gift includes the leader, you may be tempted to use your natural magnetism and charisma for personal gain. The archetypal gift of the leader unites, draws people together, and directs individual power and effort toward the common good. Self-centered leaders who violate the archetypal pattern separate themselves from its magical aura. If you embody this gift, it is essential to align yourself with the impulses of your highest integrity and wisdom and heart-centered love. Otherwise, the temptation to abuse your gift may be too great. Be worthy of this gift and share it wisely.

I use my leadership abilities for the common good.

147. Monks

Those with the archetypal gift of the monk live from the inside out. Their inner sense of connection to the presence and love of a higher power is of utmost importance. Do you send love, prayers, and healing to those in need? Is it essential for your health and well-being to spend time alone, in meditation, contemplation, or prayer? Do you feel that you are connected to a loving higher power and presence? If so, your purpose may be to be a spiritual light to those who suffer.

The gift of the monk is a clear and centered awareness of self, their spirit, and the emanations of a higher loving presence. Satellites of divine energy, monks have an inner stillness that ripples outward into the world of chaos and despair as a balm of calm reassurance. Monks are anchors of light who emit a mysterious energetic signal. Most monks are emotionally, mentally, physically, and spiritually sensitive creatures who can become easily overwhelmed with too much outer activity, stimulation, and interpersonal interaction. It is for this reason that they retreat into themselves and seek out quiet places and harmonious environments.

From an early age, monks are aware of an invisible ray of purity and goodness. This reality is so tangible and real that they often set the bar high for their own behavior, thoughts, emotions, and intentions. With an acute sensitivity, they can also be painfully aware of their own perceived shortcomings and their propensity to be human. Their sense of spiritual perfectionism can be so extreme that even the smallest of infractions, such as becoming angry or being impatient with another, can affect their sense of self. While we all feel angry and upset and act in self-centered ways at times, the monk will be repelled by and work to transform and eradicate these human tendencies. Monks are on a quest to release their negativity, selfishness, pain, and desires and become pure receptacles for the presence of all that is good, loving, and forgiving. Although many monks feel as if they fall short of their aspirations, they remind us of the work that we all must do. Tending the inner garden allows for the full emergence of our spirit's light and love. The monk provides us with the encouragement and impulse to look within. Tremendous courage flows through their veins. Confronting our fears, pain, wounds, and the intentional and unintentional hurt that we have inflicted on ourselves and others may be the most daunting work we are asked to do. In usually unassuming and simple ways, the monk leads the way into the heart of the beast within. Yet for all their deep probing, the monk can swiftly ignite the light of compassion, kindness, love, and forgiveness and send it to those in need.

Although they often live quiet lives, most monks do not live in monasteries or in seclusion. Both male and female monks are often married or in a relationship and can be found in suburban homes raising children, working in all occupations, and participating in a variety of spiritual practices. Quite often monks have a regular meditation or prayer practice and spend time and money in pursuit of inner healing and wholeness. With the strong and undeniable instinct to attain higher levels of enlightenment and awareness, they may at times appear to be self-focused. Yet this is far from the truth. Their ability to transform and heal their own personal failings, pain, and judgments and discover inner harmony and goodness makes it easier for all of us to do the same. Their work, intent, and focus act as an energetic pattern that supports our own similar efforts.

The archetypal gift of the monk is an understated mystery. While monks rarely attract attention and ask for little, their spirits ascend into the realms of light and pure blessings. Putting aside their personal desires, fully realized monks intercede on behalf of those who are ill, lost, and lonely. Through their prayers, meditations, and intent, they petition the divine higher forces for blessings and healing. In this world of self-centeredness, pettiness, and conflict, they can be anchors for all that is holy.

If the archetypal gift of the monk flows through you, inner purification and spiritual focus are necessary to be able to fully actualize this mystical pattern. The more you release the trivial, vain, and self-serving, the more attuned you will become to your true self. It is in this awareness that you experience true happiness, love, and joy.

I care for my soul.

148. Channels

Through the archetypal gift of the channel, the sacred and divine makes its way into the physical realm. Angels, loved ones on the other side, spirit guides, divine love, and others' thoughts and feelings all flow in and out of the channel's consciousness. They are the vessel and the nest and are never truly alone. Spirit beings are ever ready to seize the opportunity to make contact with the human realm through the channel.

Many channels do not acknowledge their unique archetypal gift. They may feel uncomfortable with the idea that a love and presence outside of themselves has the ability to enter into their consciousness. The fear of not having control and being taken over by something or someone may cause some channels to deny and repress their ability. However, because archetypal gifts are innate and spring from the soul, they cannot be so easily dismissed. When this gift is repressed or not acknowledged, it does not simply go away. Instead, it is diverted into unconscious forms of expression. For instance, the channel who ignores their intuitive and psychic ability may dream of others or receive messages while sleeping. Many of my clients tell me of conversations and encounters they have had with loved ones while they sleep.

I have a client named Stella who told me that one night while sleeping, she was awakened by her boyfriend's grandmother who had died many years before. Exhausted from a busy work week, she finally gave in and said aloud to her half-awake boyfriend, "Your grandmother Weber says hello."

She then went back to sleep. The next morning, her boyfriend told her what she had said. Until he reminded her, Stella had forgotten the incident. Her boyfriend had not. He was quite happy to know that his grandmother was close and thinking of him.

Without knowing they are doing so, channels frequently express messages to others through simple conversation or by randomly contacting another in their time of need. They often underestimate the importance of the messages that they receive. I have a client who told me that her neighbor knocked on her door one afternoon with a loaf of freshly baked banana bread. The neighbor said that she was thinking of her and decided to bake an extra loaf. This act of kindness was especially surprising to my client, as it was the anniversary of her beloved grandmother's death. Unbeknownst to her neighbor, her grandmother had loved to bake and had frequently made banana bread for her.

These kind of incidents can be commonplace for the channel. It can be awkward when a channel receives a message for someone who does not necessarily believe that it is possible to communicate with the spirit realm or for those who do not believe in life after death.

Most channels work quietly and modestly and allow the love and wisdom of spiritual forces to flow through them wherever they are. With family, friends, and at times strangers, their words can be comforting, wise, loving, insightful, and exactly what another needs to hear at that time. Some channels use their natural gifts in a professional way and become mediums, psychics, tarot card readers, and intuitives. Surprisingly, many channels choose not to work directly with people. With their tendency to absorb the energy of those they are in close proximity to and to receive messages for others from the spirit realm, they prefer quiet environments where they can focus on the work at hand.

If you suspect that you are a channel, pay attention to your daily thoughts, feelings, sensations, and dreams. Tune in to the often subtle energy messages that may feel like mind chatter, inner restlessness, and fuzzy feelings. If you often feel overwhelmed but you are not necessarily in a chaotic or overly stressful situation, you may unknowingly be receiving too much intuitive energy. It is important for the channel to recognize their gift and create a positive outlet for its expression. You cannot shut off your archetypal gifts. They are an aspect of your authentic self that you are here to share with others. Set aside time on a daily basis to become quiet and just listen and feel.

As a channel, you are part of a network of celestial love and wisdom. Allow yourself to be guided. Take charge of your gift and integrate it into your life in a healthy and positive way. You have been given this gift to experience your interconnectedness with all living beings and be a blessing to the world.

I allow the spirit of love and wisdom to flow through me.

149. Alchemists

If you possess the archetypal gift of the alchemist, you have the vision and drive to change, alter, reform, improve, and transform yourself, others, and the world. You strive to actualize your dreams and do the difficult work of growing and changing from the inside out. As an alchemist, you give to others and to the world the inspiration and motivation to believe that with effort and focus, change and transformation are possible.

With a positive vision and belief in our innate goodness, alchemists are able to go through the step-by-step process to manifest and actualize this potential. They are not deterred or intimidated by the unknown or by obstacles. Instead, they are able to perceive the truth, as fuzzy as it often is, and use it as their compass. Alchemists are action-oriented. Rarely harsh and brazen, they can act with restrained artistry and skill. Alchemists tend to be courageous and determined to dispel darkness and be of service. They are the soil, rain, and sun that bring to blossom the seed of possibilities.

Many alchemists are drawn to work in which they can have a positive effect on others or on the environment. They are often psychotherapists, hypnotherapists, psychiatrists, social workers, or life coaches who assist others in the deep work of inner emotional, mental, or spiritual transformation. They may also be drawn to health professions such as physical therapy, medicine, or nutrition where they empower others to heal the physical body and become whole. Many scientists, chemists, and researchers are alchemists who seek to understand, convert, and alter core substances and materials. Some prefer transforming physical environments and may be builders or architects, interior decorators, or landscape architects. Many artists are also alchemists who transform environments and people through visual stimulation, music, or other creative pursuits. In any environment where there is the opportunity to create change and transformation, you will likely find an alchemist.

When alchemists are fully engaged in their archetypal energy, there is little that can stand in their way. You can see the element of fire at work in most alchemists. Look into their eyes and you will sense the flame of movement, change, and resolve. However, they are not always cognitively aware of what direction to take or exactly what they are doing. Their gifts often bypass understanding and surface through their passion and gut intuition. Alchemists are led by the invisible pull of unrealized potential and possibility. This is not a wispy fantasy, but a reality that goes deep into their bones. Their vision is always focused in the misty halo of what has not yet been realized. Where others see a barren field, the alchemist perceives a lush garden. As a counselor or life coach, the alchemist pushes their clients to work through their fears, take the next step, and trust the vision of happiness that they know is possible. Against all odds, it is the alchemist politician who tirelessly campaigns for improvement and reform, despite resistance from powerful forces.

Early in life, alchemists have a bit of restlessness and usually an excess of energy. Some become frustrated by the status quo and openly rebel against the conventional and established ways of doing things.

Alchemists often work hard at transforming themselves inwardly and outwardly. They want to be all they can be, body, mind, and spirit, and they may constantly seek improvement. This can drive some alchemists to be self-critical and unable to accept their perceived flaws. The challenge for the alchemist is to accept their individuality, trust their vision, and realize that not everyone has the courage and desire to change and transform. Patience, restraint, and being in step with what is possible at the moment often gets them further than expecting and rushing their own or another's change and transformation.

Being different is not always easy. Alchemists tend to be out of step with accepted norms. Even if by outer appearances they appear to live in the traditional way, they are attuned to a voice that few can hear, with their eyes focused on a vision that few can see. Like a seed waiting for the right moment to germinate and emerge, the gifts of the alchemist one day ignite with resolve and passion.

If you have the archetype of the alchemist as one of your gifts, remind yourself often that it is not only change that is important. It is the love and passion that moves through your heart to create a better way that makes a difference. Like most of the archetypal gifts, the alchemist contains paradoxes. While alchemists are driven to transform and create change, it is only in the present moment that their gifts are fully realized. In this way, the alchemist is a bit of a time traveler, spanning the past and the future to reveal and live fully in the truth of the moment.

I confidently accept change.

150. Identifying Your Archetypal Gifts

Your authentic self is fueled by the vibrant energy of your soul and spirit. You are more than your personality, your body, and your current conditions, beliefs, and thoughts. Your archetypal gifts are the bridge through which your soul energy passes into your everyday life. You can draw from the primal power of your gifts to guide you in expressing your purpose.

You have more than one archetypal gift. You have a predominant gift, and a few that you are developing, and some whose energy you are evolving out of. After reading over the descriptions of the different archetypal gifts, you may be confused as to what your gifts may be. You may identify with some aspects of several of them or you may closely identify with just one or two. Be patient. It may take time for you to fully recognize a gift's aspects and characteristics at work in your life. At times your gifts are obvious, but not always. If you are not sure if a feeling, tendency, or preference stems from an archetypal gift, allow yourself to be led by passion and intuition. Try on the energy of a gift by expressing certain characteristics of it and tune in to how it feels. If it is yours, you will experience an empowered sense of connectedness. Opportunities to further develop and express the gift will spontaneously surface.

Although you may or may not recognize your gifts, your soul sends you signs and signals when you are connecting with them. The following are a few telltale signs that you may have experienced when reading over the archetypal gift descriptions:

+ A feeling of tingling or shivering up your spine
+ The hair on your arms standing up
+ Warm feelings in your heart

- An inner surge of energy
- Feeling motivated and inspired to follow your passion
- Having a spontaneous inner vision of yourself engaged in a specific gift
- Recalling memories of feeling and acting in ways that are congruent with the gift
- Having an aha moment of recognition
- Feeling as if a missing piece of the puzzle of your life is falling into place
- Feeling understood and validated
- Feeling empowered and whole

Your gifts are innate and natural for you. Paradoxically, it is for this reason that we sometimes do not recognize them. By paying attention to your subtle feelings, tendencies, and actions, you can better identify which archetypes are deep at work within you. Contemplate these questions:

- *In what activities do you to feel most free and empowered?*
- *In what situations and circumstances do you feel goodness flow through you?*
- *What is easy and natural for you to give to others?*
- *What are you good at and what comes naturally to you?*
- *When you were young, what did you imagine yourself doing in the future?*
- *When do you feel that you are in the flow of a greater power and presence? What are you doing?*
- *What do others want from you? What is easy for you to give?*

- *What kinds of situations and circumstances do your find yourself involved in without any effort on your part?*
- *What are you drawn to? What comes easily to you?*

If you suspect that one of the archetypal gifts describes you, claim it. You will not know if it is your gift until you further develop and embody it. If its archetypal energy lies dormant within, your efforts to fully develop it will feel natural and proceed with ease. If it is not one of your predominant gifts, then there will be no passion and your attempts to further develop it will be met with obstacles and resistance.

One of the most powerful and meaningful actions that you can take in this world that is in need of so much love and positive energy and action is to allow the archetypal energy of your gift to flow through you and out into the world.

I embrace my archetypal gifts.

Final Thoughts

YOU ARE THE ONE

While writing this book, my life has changed. When I first started the manuscript, I moved into a new house. Now, as I put the finishing touches on the book, I am moving once again. In this house in the woods, near a lake, a new me has been emerging. Yet it is not so easy to pin down and fully identify who I am becoming. As the old me silently slips away without struggle, the new me has yet to fully make herself known.

Every book I write changes me, this one maybe more so than the others. The door to self, I have discovered, leads to a deep, open, and vast expanse, a step into nothingness that is cushioned with the odd comfort of freedom. We are always changing and evolving. Like the ocean tides during a full moon, new aspects of our authentic self surface and swiftly flow onto the banks of our awareness. As we embody and accept these new insights and revelations, what we thought ourselves to be recedes, pulled back into the immense sea of the unconscious. This cycle of evolution repeats itself over and over. The eternal tide of the authentic self is never static and is always evolving.

My wish is that you have the courage to accept this kind of fluid awareness of your authentic self. Flow with the moment-to-moment movement and light of your unencumbered soul. Lose all that you thought yourself to be. Without the burden of your emotional wounds, your pride, and your ego, you are transparent. Embrace your vulnerability with the full acceptance of what is and allow for the entrance of grace. Look deep within without judgment and fear. The fog will eventually clear and your goodness will shine through. Allow your gentle kindness and love to greet you each day. Look at yourself in the mirror in the morning with a smile of recognition. You are the one, brave and a beacon of light. Let your soul be seen. In this world of confusion and struggle, you are the lighthouse that shines bright in the darkness.

Bibliography

Andrews, Ted. *Animal-Speak: The Spiritual and Magical Powers of Creatures Great and Small.* 1993. Reprint, Woodbury, MN: Llewellyn, 2010.

Buxton, Richard. *The Complete World of Greek Mythology.* New York: Thames & Hudson, 2004.

Dillard, Sherrie. *Discover Your Psychic Type: Developing and Using Your Natural Intuition.* Woodbury, MN: Llewellyn, 2008.

Einstein, Albert. *The World As I See It.* New York: Citadel, 2006.

Emerson, Ralph Waldo. *The Essays of Ralph Waldo Emerson.* Cambridge, MA: Harvard University Press, 1987.

Hamilton, Edith. *Mythology: Timeless Tales of Gods and Heroes.* New York: Grand Central Publishing, 2011.

Keirsey, David, and Marilyn Bates. *Please Understand Me: Character and Temperament Types.* Del Mar, CA: Prometheus Nemesis Book Co., 1984.

Lennox, Dr. Michael. *Dream Sight: A Dictionary and Guide for Interpreting Any Dream.* Woodbury, MN: Llewellyn, 2011.

Myra, Jaya Jaya. *Vibrational Healing: Attain Balance and Wholeness.* Woodbury, MN: Llewellyn, 2014.

Myss, Caroline, PhD. *Anatomy of the Spirit: The Seven Stages of Power and Healing.* New York: Harmony Publishing, 2013.

Waite, Arthur Edward. *The Rider Tarot Deck.* Stamford, CT: US Games Systems, 1971.

Whitehurst, Tess. *Holistic Energy Magic: Charms and Techniques for Creating a Magical Life.* Woodbury, MN: Llewellyn, 2015.

Wilhelm, Richard, trans. *The I Ching, or Book of Changes.* Princeton, NJ: Princeton University Press, 1967.

To Write to the Author

If you wish to contact the author or would like more information about this book, please write to the author in care of Llewellyn Worldwide Ltd. and we will forward your request. Both the author and publisher appreciate hearing from you and learning of your enjoyment of this book and how it has helped you. Llewellyn Worldwide Ltd. cannot guarantee that every letter written to the author can be answered, but all will be forwarded. Please write to:

Sherrie Dillard
℅ Llewellyn Worldwide
2143 Wooddale Drive
Woodbury, MN 55125-2989

Please enclose a self-addressed stamped envelope for reply,
or $1.00 to cover costs. If outside the U.S.A., enclose
an international postal reply coupon.

Many of Llewellyn's authors have websites with additional information and resources. For more information, please visit our website at http://www.llewellyn.com.